ESOTERIC HEALING

Other books by Alan Hopking

The White Ring
The Christ's Reappearing
The Emergence of the Planetary Heart
Practical Guide to Esoteric Healing
The Esoteric Healing Handbook
Advancing in Esoteric Healing

Alan Hopking, M.A.
Founder of the Global Academy of Esoteric Healing
Faculty Member of the University of the Seven Rays, (Healing) USA
Faculty Fellow of the International Network of Esoteric Healing
Member of the National Institute of Medical Herbalists, UK
Member of the Register of Chinese Herbal Medicine, UK

Esoteric Healing

A Practical Guide
Based on the Teachings of the Tibetan
in the Works of Alice A. Bailey

ALAN HOPKING

Blue Dolphin Publishing

Published by Blue Dolphin Publishing, Inc.
P.O. Box 8, Nevada City, CA 95959
Orders: 1-800-643-0765
Web: www.bluedolphinpublishing.com

ISBN: 1-57733-110-9 paperback
ISBN: 1-57733-162-1 self-hardcover

Published originally as *Practical Guide to Esoteric Healing* in 1991 by
WhiteWays Publishing Co., 13 Cowper Road, Bournemouth, Dorset, U.K.

Permission to quote from the books by Alice A. Bailey has been granted by
Lucis Publishing Company, New York, and Lucis Press Ltd, London. The
extracts from the books by Alice A. Bailey may not be reproduced except by
permission from the Lucis Trust, which holds copyright.

If an ailment is severe or if symptoms persist, please consult a physician right
away. Especially consider one with a holistic approach. No part of this book
is intended to replace competent medical treatment.

Library of Congress Cataloging-in-Publication Data

Hopking, Alan N.
  Esoteric healing : a practical guide based on the teachings of the Tibetan
in the works of Alice A. Bailey / Alan N. Hopking.
    p. cm.
  Previous title: Practical guide to esoteric healing.
  Includes bibliographical references and index.
    ISBN 1-57733-110-9 (pbk. : alk. paper) — ISBN 1-57733-162-1
(self-hardcover : alk. paper)
    1. Medicine, Magic, mystic, and spagiric. 2. Seven rays (Occultism)
3. Bailey, Alice, 1880-1949. 4. Medicine, Tibetan. I. Bailey, Alice Anne,
1880-1949. II. Hopking, Alan N. Practical guide to esoteric healing. III. Title.

  RZ999.H665 2004
  615.8'51—dc22
                                                              2004020022

First printing, December, 2004
Second printing, July, 2005
Third printing, January, 2006
Fourth printing, August 2006
Fifth printing, March 2007
Sixth printing, August 2009

Printed in the United States of America
10   9   8   7   6

Dedicated to the true healer in everyone

"All that exists are aggregates of the finest energies." —Gautama Buddha

"The Science of Triangles governs the human frame in all its aspects, as well as the frame of a solar system." —DK

"Cause involves the idea of duality—that which initiates and that which is produced simultaneously by the initiation. The two ideas are inseparable. The effect involves a third idea ... thus effects are always produced by a juxtaposition of the pairs of opposites." —DK

"Only when the pupil or practitioner has an intelligent appreciation of the trouble affecting himself or his patient (when his objective is to equip himself or his patient for service); only when he has the ability to conscientiously follow the formulas and methods imparted (when he aims only at the acquirement of healthy vehicles for the better carrying out of the Plan); and only when the objective is unselfish (when he desires not to escape disease for his own personal benefit), will he be trusted to clear and enter the karma and so adjust rightly the form vehicles of the personality, only then will the formulas work in connection with the soul consciousness." —DK

"Any healing practice should be preceded by years of careful study about the nature of energy, of the ray types, of the centers; a minimum of at least three years should be given to this." —DK

"Healing, with its understanding of energy and forces ... will lead later to the rebirth of humanity." —DK (DNAI, p. 28)

CONTENTS

PREFACE

Purpose of this book

This book is a complete revision and enlargement of my first *Practical Guide* (publ. 1991). It is intended to open up the subject of spiritual healing as a science to a wider public. It is a text book for groups of healers as well as for the individual healer working within a subjective group. A subjective group is one whose members are linked by the common nature of their thoughts. There is already a small band of esoteric healers in the world working in conjunction with the Ageless Wisdom or Perennial Philosophy—a teaching about the spiritual way of life and an understanding of the spiritual dimension lying behind the happenings of the world and of humanity. This teaching arises in new form from age to age down through all of history. The author takes this esoteric teaching on healing and presents it in a form understandable to all. It is therefore useful to both the advanced and the neophyte.

The purpose of this book carries further my first book (Hopking, 1988), which was a compilation of all the references to the etheric body (the energy giving life to the physical body) found in what has become to most esoteric healers a text book of the subject, viz. *Esoteric Healing*, which is volume IV of a *Treatise on the Seven Rays*, by Alice A. Bailey (1951–70, v. 4). The present book greatly expands and deepens the understanding of esoteric healing as described in my book published in 1990 where I first laid out the practical steps for the use of esoteric healing as described by Master Djwhal Khul in Alice Bailey's books. As he says of himself, "He who is known as DK is planning to restore—

via his students—some of the old and occult methods of healing and to demonstrate:

- (a) the place of the etheric body,
- (b) the effect of pranic force and
- (c) the opening up of etheric vision" (Bailey, 1962, p. 759).

And elsewhere in another place he says, "There is a great need for you to collect and tabulate the scattered information (ancient initiation and the rays and the centers)[1] so you can register it as a whole" (Bailey, 1951–70, v. 5, p. 669). The word "register" is important in respect of our subject of healing. It is this attempt to facilitate this "registering" on behalf of all and more adequately which drives me onward with presenting this subject to sincere students of healing.

This book is for student healers of all levels who wish to learn about the etheric and the esoteric. With this in mind DK says, "Much good can be accomplished and a great deal learnt if those interested read, study, meditate, carefully experiment, and thus gradually build up this much needed science as a co-partner in the medical science of modern times" (Bailey, 1951–70, v. 4, p. 659). Hence, this book presents the principles and an approach to the practice of healing in the hope of clarifying to some extent the confusion which exists in some minds regarding esoteric healing. Confusion can arise because this form of healing is so new and very little has been written about it. Confusion also because esoteric healing constantly refers to the fact of the importance of the soul. Indeed, according to esoteric healing, healing is impossible unless it is the will of the soul.

Soul-centered healing

But it is of little use to talk about esoteric or soul healing unless one has some idea of what is denoted by the word "soul," as distinct from the mind. How does it differ from psyche or ego? In this book you will find much spoken about the soul. It is this you must distinguished from anything to do with either the personality, intellectual thoughts, emotions, psyche and psychic phenomena, or bodily feelings. On the soul and other points this book can offer clear information from the esoteric tradition, or the Perennial Philosophy.

Much of what is presented may not be scientific knowledge in the usual sense, but suggests avenues for future research or at least it will have suggested ideas. Furthermore, the subject of esoteric healing is presented with more clarity and definition than has hitherto been given in the past by others working in this field. As the Gautama Buddha reportedly once said, "Distinguish between those who understand and those who agree. He who understands will not tarry to apply it to life, he who agrees will extol the Teaching as remarkable Wisdom, but will not apply this wisdom to life. ... Those who understand are few, but like a sponge they absorb the precious knowledge and are ready to cleanse the horrors of the world with the precious liquid" (Roerich, 1971, pp. 143–44).

Fulfillment of law

It is important nowadays to be able to offer a reasoned explanation for the occurrence of healings and miracles, as well as for their failure to occur. For intelligent people can only see a miracle as a fulfillment of law, not as an abrogation of it. An intensification of nature rather than something unnatural. The perspective of this book suggests that there is no such thing as metaphysics, only physical laws yet to be discovered by the everyday investigator. This is not to say that everything is explained or completely explainable; that can never be, for if every mystery of nature were made plain, people would lose their particular prerogative, which is that of constant enquiry, and investigation of the world in which they live.

It is in the exercise of that prerogative that this book has been written, particularly with the practical side of healing in view. Such research, it is hoped, will be found helpful by all interested in this side of medicine, whether well acquainted with it or on the verge of entering the inner search and practice.

I hope that as you read through this book you will find it far simpler than others on the subject, which are usually more abstract and less practical. I know esoteric healing is not an easy subject to learn, as I find when I give courses on it, so it will not be as easy to teach through a book. However, this can be overcome if the student reads carefully and follows accurately the techniques described. A lot of practice is needed but the effort will bear fruit. This book can also be a useful reference for those who have already done a course in esoteric healing, or who are embarking on the university-level degree courses now available.[2] (Please see reference to these sponsoring organizations in Chapter 16).

ACKNOWLEDGMENTS

May I here thank all who have traveled with me along this path so far, both colleagues and students. I would like especially to mention: Susie Hopking (whose patience, support and enthusiasm have been for me a tower of strength during the long hours, months and years in my research and practice); Helen Frankland (whose quest has led to long and profound conversations, and with whom I have taught many courses in many countries, and who worked with me for the UK branch of the University of the Seven Rays, esoteric healing degree course for three years); Ann Higgins (whose interest and perception helped me at the start of this journey); and Janina Waloszek (whose esoteric insight never fails to astound). You have all been an invaluable source of inspiration and encouragement. Acknowledgments are also due to the many members of the WhiteWays Group of Bournemouth, U.K., from whom I have gained many important insights. Brenda Johnston (and her teacher Rex Riant), founder of the International Health Research Network (now known as the International Network of Esoteric Healing), who personally taught me the introductory elements of practical esoteric healing and in whose healing clinic I worked for two years with Ann and Helen; also Dinah Lawson and the other teachers of esoteric healing in different parts of the world. Thanks, too, to Nellie Grose, M.D., whom I discovered to be a close associate and dedicated colleague and who, with me, taught the first three-year degree course in esoteric healing with the University of the Seven Rays, in the United States. Thanks are also due to the Directors of the University of the Seven Rays and the Healing Faculty. Thank you, Anne Guest, Ph.D., and John Robinson, and especially Frances Harriman, for the time and constructive advice you gave during an early form of the manuscript. Also thanks to my good friends and fellow students. Dany Vecchio, M.D., and Daniel Krummenacher, Ph.D., who facilitated Frances' support.

I'd also like to thank the Prague Esoteric Healing Group who have, down the years of my teaching there, afforded me the many insights that have helped the shaping of this book. It is to them also that I owe the benefits of the many digital photographs contained here.

May I also here thank the publishers and printers, especially Paul Clemens of Blue Dolphin Publishing for his openness and readiness and belief in me as this greatly enlarged second edition began to take shape. I'd like to make special mention of Meredith, my son, who was a great help with the original computer graphics in the first edition. Lastly, salutation goes to my second son, Kingsley, who as a baby afforded me the profound insight into divine purpose now contained in the Appendix of this book.

Alan Hopking

1.

ESOTERIC HEALING—
A HIGHER DESIGN

Some factors in health and disease

Normal health may be said to be present when there is a harmonious inter-relationship between the individual and his or her[1] environment. Such a relationship, dynamic not static, involves an interlacing of outgoing and incoming forces at each level of consciousness and in each field of activity. It can never be considered as precisely determined, but rather is in constant movement and readjustment. When both the outwards and inwards flow is normal—normal, that is, for the particular individual concerned—the tendency is to feel well and happy. In other words, the person is for the time being well adjusted to the immediate circumstances whatever they may be and therefore is living in harmony with both the self and the world.

The three laws of health

There are three laws which control right living or which govern a person living in harmony of body:

1. The law controlling the will to live. This involves the First Aspect of Will and Power (Father, Siva, Life, Spirit). This law controls the respiratory system.
2. The law controlling the quality of rhythm. This involves the Second Aspect of Love and Wisdom (Son, Vishnu, Soul, Consciousness). It controls the cardiovascular and nervous systems.

1

3. The law controlling crystallization. This involves the Third Aspect of Active Intelligence (Holy Spirit, Brahma, Matter, Appearance). The law controls the metabolic system (the organs of assimilation and excretion) (Bailey, 1951–70, v. 4, p. 106).

"Happiness"

Happiness in this sense is neither simple contentment nor intense excitement, but rather consists in a harmonious or "right" relationship to life and experience. It is a basic condition in nature—one towards which the forces of nature tend. Never fixed or static, it is a constant flow of successive adjustment that results in growth: the assimilation of ever-expanding experience.

From this viewpoint, we can see how a conscious life can be maintained in constant health. But at the same time we can see how it could become subject to certain maladjustments if the laws of nature are not kept. The forces in the person's body can become confused, sometimes running amuck. A breakdown in the integrity of life occurs and illness results.

Disease

Disease is not an easy thing to define. *Taber's Medical Dictionary* (1977, p. D:47) says of disease: "Literally the lack of ease; a pathological condition of the body that presents a group of symptoms peculiar to it and which sets the condition apart as an abnormal entity differing from other normal or pathological body states." Such a definition simply describes disease as a state which is abnormal without undertaking to indicate from where it arises. In esoteric healing we seek to define disease in a way which includes some indication of cause. Thus we say: Disease is a result of an inhibited flow of soul[2] energy to the body. It is a process of liberation, for by taking on a disease, a person opens up to greater soul awareness—an aspect of consciousness not in expression at the time (Bailey, 1951–70, v. 4, cf. Law I & p. 32). So let us consider some causes of disease (see also p. 255).

A. Disease is something incomprehensible to all of us. Whatever it is, its cause lies way back in the lost past of our planet, something which esoterically we could vaguely term "cosmic evil," something that literally goes back to the "beginning" of life as we know it. But somewhere in us there is knowledge of its cause. This book tells us much of what we always intuitively felt was true but could not put into words!

B. Epochal causes. Human progress is made possible by the Law of Rebirth. It prompts the soul to reincarnate, that is, to periodically, "life after life for eons," choose and build suitable physical, emotional and mental vehicles through which to learn the needed next lessons. The history of humanity over the many thousands and tens of thousands (even millions) of years has led us to recognize three major and basic complications in the inherited force-fields of every person born:
   a. Misused application of the procreative energy;
   b. Misuse of the lower psychic powers for the acquisition of personal and selfish desires;
   c. Misuse of the application of thoughts and ideas for the purpose of personal power.
These have contravened the ideal of justice, brotherhood and freedom.

C. Lack of alignment and control by the soul, the true self. All disease is a result of the misuse of force in some earlier life or in this. This is what is called the "mismanagement of force," whether it relates to oneself or towards others (or to the environment). Under this major cause we find the many lesser causes, i.e., the etheric[3] causes leading to epidemics; the psychological causes leading to worry and irritation; obsessions, depressions and the problems linked with anger, hatred, grief, resentment, etc; the mental causes leading to fanaticism, frustrated idealism, etc.; and "discipleship causes" involving those who are more mystically inclined and those who are on a more mental (esoteric) path.

D. Excess or insufficient energy as it vitalizes and pours through the centers up the etheric spine and in the etheric head (Bailey, 1951–70,

v. 4, p. 270). This is the result of the misuse of force whether by individuals or by groups, and in some earlier life or in this (p. 112). In fact, disease is seldom of individual origin (p. 31).

E. Three major premises: First, subjective or inner conditions alone cannot cause disease. Second, the subjective is a causative factor[4] (p. 309) when in collaboration with the inherited tendencies of the physical body, since the soul chooses to incarnate in a specific physical body. Third, an outer condition alone cannot be a causative factor. Therefore, all ills are not purely subjective or psychological in origin as far as an individual is concerned, but rather are due to outer causes and to inner causes (p. 74).

F. Ninety per cent of the causes of disease are to be found in the astral body.[5] Wrong use of mental energy and misapplied desire are paramount factors. As the bulk of humanity is still in the Atlantean stages of consciousness, only five percent of the prevalent diseases are due to mental causes. Disease is therefore the working out into manifestation of undesirable vital, emotional and mental conditions. The remainder of illness is caused by external influences: bacteria, viruses, accidents and purely physical reasons.

G. Many diseases are of group origin, or are the result of infection, or are due to malnutrition, physically, subjectively and occultly understood.

H. Diseases for the masses, for the average citizen, for the intelligentsia and for disciples differ widely and have differing fields of expression. The Social (Lemurian) diseases, Cancer (Atlantean) and Tuberculosis (Aryan) affect the average person (who is not on the spiritual path) (see Chapter 8). Heart complaints and nervous diseases affect the intelligentsia and disciples.

I. Other causes of disease may be listed as: inherent in the soil; karmic[6]; national; racial; due to accidents; a conflict of forces; rampant or inhibited desire; dominating thoughtforms; friction of atomic substance; frustration of ideals; distortion of goodness, beauty and truth; separateness; lack of etheric coordination; personality focus; wrong spiritual practices; and so on. In sum, disease is due to "misaligned relationships," and this in turn could be defined as the blocking of the free life and the inpouring energy of the soul, the higher self.

Although disease is a fact in nature, it is also a result of the misuse of force. When this is accepted, we will begin to work with the Law of Liberation, with right thought, leading to right attitudes and orientation, and with the principle of non-resistance. We must remember too that the Law of Cause and Effect, or of Karma, governs all disease. Karma stretches deep into time and space.[7] From another angle disease has to do with "food" and "eating," for it involves assimilation of energies on all the planes of life and consciousness. Even "real" food (vegetables, fruit, milk, meat, etc.) is but the consolidation of higher energy for use by the physical body. Keeping to the purer foods (and not entangling the astral body with animal flesh) will help to open the consciousness to fuller expression, thus preventing or overcoming disease, especially at the earlier stages on the Path.

Finally, let us be aware of a further approach to the understanding of disease and its healing, one which is particularly relevant when we are healing a specific center (or chakra, as it is called in the East). DK says that any "cause" involves the idea of duality—that which initiates and that which is produced simultaneously by the initiation. The two ideas are inseparable. He goes on to say that the true effect actually involves a third idea ... thus effects are always produced by a juxtaposition of the pairs of opposites (Bailey, 1962, pp. 798–99). This must make us work back from the symptom or the effect being experienced in the patient as being the result of a juxtaposition of centers. Note also how it involves three forces and thus a triangle of energy. This movement of energies around the points of a triangle distinguishes esoteric healing in power and effectiveness from any other type of healing in the subtle bodies.

Setting the forces flowing

Disease, therefore, is a blockage: either an entity in itself (karma), or a lack of conscious expression. So the need arises to set the forces flowing through the body in order to incorporate wider aspects of the self. To do this, people usually seek aid from a specialist whom they believe can help. What therapy do they choose? Surgery (the first and lazy option, or last resort); orthodox methods using powerful synthetic chemical drugs (which the body having evolved over millions of years cannot recognize and reacts against, hence the side effects); the "natural"

therapies using herbs in various forms (very safe and based on knowledge gained over hundreds of years): herbalists (of whom the author
is one), homeopaths, aromatherapists, naturopaths; the diet therapies,
mostly involving vitamins; and Eastern methods. There are also the
manipulative therapies of chiropractic and osteopathy, which seek to
realign the body's bony system. Then there are the many therapies dealing with people's emotions—psychotherapy, psychiatry, hypnotherapy,
marriage counseling; and then one could choose from the many forms
of healing therapies—color therapies, crystal therapies, laying on of
hands, and spiritual healing. Each of these medical methods can be put
into one of three groups:
1. The ameliorative therapies
2. The psychological therapies
3. The spiritual therapies.

Each individual chooses a therapy according to his or her need and
belief. The first category deals primarily with the body; the second set
largely deals with the emotions and lower mind, which will affect the
body; and the third mostly deals with the person's soul, which will affect the personality and the body. It may be said, however, most of the
present "spiritual" therapies do not reach the soul.

True healing

From the esoteric standpoint, true healing, healing that will change
a person's life and inner motivation, can only happen when the soul of
the patient is involved. For this reason many so-called cures, where the
person throws away the crutches and walks, usually do not last. A return
to the former state is frequently worse than before, for the person feels
utterly demoralized, "let down by God." True healing is not like this. It
is seldom sudden, for it involves change and adjustment and reorientation from within. It calls upon the person to make decisions from within,
decisions which the soul wants, not what the little personality desires.
It usually involves mental and emotional change, by degrees through a
self-imposed discipline and training. But true healing will often entail
new habits of the body, nutritional change, and changes with regard to

the body's fitness, types of entertainment and relaxation. All these are influenced from within by esoteric healing, not imposed on the patient from without. We will learn later that few words are spoken during a consultation, neither by the healer to the patient, nor by the healers amongst themselves concerning the patient. It is a meditative, inner work, a subtle change of energies and forces by the patient in inner response to the healer's challenge.

Meditation

It is considered a prerequisite that one who wishes to practice esoteric healing should meditate regularly. One of the aphorisms I have stuck onto my computer monitor states that, "Meditation governs all expansions of consciousness." It is a constant reminder to me that to live life creatively and inclusively I am always to work at expanding my frontiers through meditation. It is a time of withdrawing within and exploring the realms of the soul.

There are many dangers that beset a path of meditation, due in large extent to having to live our lives in a busy world. Yet this activity in the world also works as a safeguard for us. Meditating too long and too often can lead to real problems psychologically and even physically, so early on the path of meditation we are to learn the virtue of discrimination. Meditation is a creative work with energy, our own energy, and right from the beginning we will be confronted by decisions and situations which require a deep and strong sensitivity and determination to discriminate what is helpful or harmful to us, and what is unnecessary or essential to us. It is important to go slowly in meditation to avoid the pitfalls and temptations that crop up. Always watch yourself and get to know how far you can go with safety. Never stretch yourself beyond those limits. Remember, eternity is long, and the good you build up slowly and consciously will last forever and will always be there for you to call on for assistance. Meditation is as important as your mealtimes, or brushing your teeth. Regularity keeps you nourished as well as unstained!

While this book is not about meditation, to practice healing in the way described here, meditation is not only recommended but essential.[8]

Thought power, a natural energy

When we get down to meditating in earnest, we are met with the ever awe-inspiring presence of thought. We feel it as a being, an entity which has a life and form. In fact, we recognize that, by producing a thought, effects inevitably follow. When I first confronted my thoughts and my thought-maker, I suddenly saw that I was in fact trapped by my own thought of myself. What I was in form, and soul, was nothing but a thought-expression of my present consciousness. This was a little frightening at first. I felt I was a prisoner of a process, that escape was literally impossible. It would be like moving from one cage to another. For a long time I worked with these ideas in meditation, sometimes thinking it was hopeless and pointless. But I came to a point when I had no alternative. I had to do something about it. I did the only thing that could be done—I accepted my predicament! I felt a great relief; I didn't feel I was giving in or becoming a mere plaything of my own thought. I realized that here was a potential for moving towards a concept of liberating thought itself, an activity which would or could actually leave me uncocooned—not reborn, just unraveled—as Being itself—who I really was—as created. So the search began, to explore all the ways to work with this energy of thought as the ultimate transformative power.

The use of thought in healing

In healing we also work in the realm of thought. We are manipulating energies of thought—the threads cocooning a patient in pain and suffering—and endeavoring through soul-to-soul contact to unravel some of the untidy or piled-up threads. Thought is substance and can bring about effects. Rightly directed, swathed in light and love, thought can heal. This has nothing to do with our mundane thoughts and desires, but is rather the reflective and responsive thought matching the energy emanating from the patient as a soul. We are often told that, to cure disease, we must draw health and strength from the great fount of universal life by our will and then pour it through the patient (Bailey, 1951–70, v. 1, p. 202). How do we do this? We can begin by allowing the centers of energy in etheric matter (the vital force) lead our thought back to the cause, which we can then balance or release, as explained later in this book. In this way we work intelligently with the forces and energies of a patient—not, let me reiterate, intellectually, but creatively, and based on "pure reason" from the soul, directing and focussing a source of energy which will bring about healing. The effects are inevitable, but usually entirely imperceptible and unexpected. Changes are a time of restructuring and reevaluating, sometimes bringing great joy and sometimes suffering and pain, but always resulting in release, and a greater sense of relief. Disease is a sign that purification is taking place. Our task is to assist the process. We try to unhook the chain from the wall itself. We do this only inasmuch as it is according to the will of the soul of the one being healed.

Spiritual healers do not work with the consciousness aspect of the patient. We work entirely with the life aspect (Bailey, 1951–70, v. 4, p. 628). The life force works through the heart center, utilizing the blood stream (love), while the consciousness aspect works through the brain, using the nervous system (will) (p. 337). The fine channels called "nadis," which make up the etheric body, represent the life aspect (pp. 197, 205). Love, which is related to the heart, is a substance as real as dense matter, and can be used to drive out diseased tissue and provide a healthy substitute in place of the diseased material that has been eliminated (p. 102). Of course, to love, one must think, and think creatively. In fact, love is the creative power of the Logos (Bailey, unpublished letters, p. 121). To heal, we have to create a healing thoughtform (Bailey, 1951–70, v. 4, p. 676). The function of every thoughtform is threefold:

a. To respond to vibration.
b. To provide a body for an idea.
c. To carry out a specific purpose (Bailey, 1962, p. 552).

Thought is the carrier, the engine, for love, which is the quality of the energy used in the healing thoughtform.

We are truly working with the law of Magnetic Impulse. With every healing done from soul level, we lift the whole of humanity (*see* Bailey, 1951–70, v. 2).

Healing as compared to cure

Cures are usually regarded as happening by themselves, requiring little or no inner work by the one being treated. For instance, we hear things like, "He cured me," or "It cured all my problems," or "I didn't have to do anything yet I'm cured!" Healing, however, calls for more thorough work. Even though healing from the spiritual level is to be regarded as the ultimate in medical therapy, cure is not inevitable. Life is not that simple. Healers are human like their patients. It is true, they endeavor to work closer to the source of life and creation for the benefit of their fellow men, but they do not claim to be that source. Their work is to reflect that source of life so that the patient can, from within their own individual spirit, which is usually a completely unconscious response, decide to change.

Healing helps people to release their attachments and expectations. This is real healing and cure. It also means transforming the face of disease. Disease emerges as a realization that that particular energy expressed by the illness is lacking or not being properly incorporated in the conscious life of the patient. When that element of consciousness is acknowledged and activated, the disease moves out; the patient is freed from disease because that consciousness is now part of his awareness and thought. This may mean putting off the physical body. We are not to shy away from death. Terminal illness can be a positive opportunity for rapid change of personality defects. After healing, a patient may come to accept their healing as involving leaving the physical earth and everyone on it.

Another point must be clarified which often worries both healers and patients. I refer to healers who are selfishly motivated. These are the so-called Black Lodge "healers" (who only work with the person-ality rays). They can, it is true, be more potent on the physical plane than White Lodge healers. Thus the spiritual healer, working with the energies of light, is seldom as effective on the physical body. But Black Lodge members are totally unable to work on a patient who is spiritu-ally oriented, neither can they work through a healer who is spiritually oriented (Bailey, 1951–70, v. 4, p. 705). This has to be noted. It is a great comfort to many.

Healing, and especially esoteric healing, contains many nuances leading towards wholeness, which is a better term than "cure." These may involve aspects of oneself which one was totally unaware of before. The bottom line of esoteric healing, and therefore all healing methods, concerns relationships. A person is confronted or faced by a number of possibilities. Each demands renewed effort towards improving one's relations whether it is to the environment, business or work, outside activities, associates and friends, family and home, or towards one's own inner self. In fact, disease and healing are both aspects of the great "relationship system" which governs all manifestation (Bailey, 1951–70, v. 4, p. 600). This is something to reflect on.

Failure of current healing methods

Much of the failure of healing methods employed at present is due to the inability of the healer to:

1. Establish the extent of the trouble, where it may be specifically located, and in what subtle body it principally arises and lies.
2. Know where the patient stands as a soul upon the ladder of spiritual development, and where, therefore, the healer must look for the source of the difficulty.
3. Differentiate between the diseases which are due to inner personal conditions, or to inherited tendencies, or to group distribution.
4. To know whether the disease should be handled by the local general practitioner, a natural therapist, a psychologist, or be treated esoterically with subtle healing methods (Bailey, 1951–70, v. 4, pp. 26–27).

THE RELATIONSHIP ASPECT

"Disease is energy which is not functioning as desired or according to plan. Inpouring energies are brought into relation with forces, and good health, strong and adequate forms and vital activity result; the same inpouring energies can, however, be brought into relation with the same forces and a point of friction be set up, producing a diseased area, pain, suffering and perhaps death. The energies and the forces remain of the same essentially divine nature, but the relationship established has produced the problem." —Djwhal Khul (Bailey, 1951–70, v. 4, p. 588).

2.

FUTURE HEALING TECHNIQUES

The past

There are many different kinds of healing whose arena is the field of energy surrounding a person. Many of these methods have come down to us from time immemorial. We instinctively put our hands on the area giving trouble. Everyone does it; for instance, when a mother puts her baby's sore hand in her mouth or holds her hand on the pain. Some of these ancient methods have been recast in modern form. Examples include the laying on of hands, spiritual healing, chakra healing, color healing, faith healing, magnetic healing and radiatory healing. Esoteric healing as described here is a new method of healing involving a combination of magnetic and radiatory healing.

Some great healers

It is beyond the scope of this book to do more than mention some great healers in the history of the world. A few have found their way into legends. For instance, in China healing was practiced as far back as 5,000 B.C. Shen Nong is regarded as the patron of Chinese medicine and reputedly wrote the *Shen Nong Ben Cao (Shen Nong's Materia Medica)*. His perception of the vital force (Qi or Chi) in the body has moulded both Chinese herbalism and China's unique system of acupuncture.

Another great healer was Imhotep. He was a court architect and court magician to King Zoser of the third Egyptian dynasty who lived about 2,700 B.C. Imhotep was thought to inhabit the body of a snake, a symbol which has since recurred frequently in relation to healing, not least in the winged staff and serpent of the caduceus of the Western medical profession today.

Then came Huang Di, the legendary and godlike Yellow Emperor, who is credited with the authorship of *The Yellow Emperor's Classic of Internal Medicine (Huang-di Nei Jing)*. His reign began around 2,697 B.C. It reportedly is the first book to describe the way energy moves around the body in particular paths, translated as "meridians" or "channels" *(jing-luo)*. *Jing* means "to go through" or "a thread in a fabric"; *luo* means "something that connects or attaches" or "a net." Meridians are the channels or pathways that carry Qi and blood through the body (though they are not blood vessels). These meridians comprise an invisible network of energy that links together all the fundamental substances and organs. To the Chinese these channels, though unseen, are thought to embody a physical reality (Kaptchuk, 1987).

Then came Buddha who gave directions for the healing of the sufferings of people by the enunciation of the Four Noble Truths: The student knows according to reality, this is suffering; he knows according to reality, this is the origin of suffering; he knows according to reality this is the cessation of suffering; he knows according to reality, this is the path leading to the cessation of suffering (Thera, 1983). This has been translated by Alice Bailey in her book, *Esoteric Psychology II,* as follows:

> Existence in the phenomenal universe is inseparable from suffering and sorrow. The cause of suffering is desire for existence in the phenomenal universe. The cessation of suffering is attained by eradicating desire for phenomenal existence. The Path to the cessation of suffering is the noble eightfold path.[1]

To this end the Buddha developed the Four Foundations of Mindfulness, which He declared to be the "Only way" *(ekayano maggo)*. This practice was to enable the pupil to realize the liberating truth of Anatta, the Not-self. Asserting the principle of energy, Buddha regarded all that exists as aggregates of the finest energies. Similarly, His affirmations about thought, acting at a distance, antedate our researches in the domain of thought-transmission and wireless communication and distance healing (Roerich, 1971).

Jesus the Christ was perhaps the greatest of all healers. His amazing influence continues unabated today. He is the "healer of the nations"; his healing sacrifice saved humans from the "sin" of the world (the reader may understand what this implies from an esoteric standpoint by the end of the book). His healing work for humanity enabled him to be a pioneer of the next phase of human existence in that he rose from the dead in a body not built by hands (or generative organs), a body entirely galvanized by the vital etheric forces. His resurrection body has been the source of inspiration and healing on all levels for two thousand years.[2] And there have been famous healers in all traditions since the life on earth of Jesus Christ.

The picture below is of the Annunciation by Nicolas Poussin, painted around 1650 A.D. I find it fascinating and truly inspired. It shows the Angel Gabriel with head forward, as though with His Ajna or brow center focussed on Mary's head center, which is radiantly alight with a white bird. His hands are extended, one holding her heart center and the other her ajna center, both hands far from the body and in her etheric field. To me this depicts an esoteric healer! If anyone has ever seen an esoteric healer at work, one would agree. By the way, this particular triangle pattern is called the Triangle of the Third Seed Group, which

The Annunciation
by Nicolas Poussin

*Reproduced with
permission from
Bayerischer
Staatsgemäldesammlungen,
München*

represents healers and medicine everywhere. Gabriel is performing a
miraculous operation in the etheric. How fruitful it would be to study this
painting from the esoteric angle, as it shows the conception of the coming Christ! Should you ever visit Munich, go and see the technique and
color of this masterpiece at the Bayerische Staatsgemäldesammlungen.
You'll be glad you did. Poussin himself has been acclaimed as "pictor
philosophus." Ethics, religion and a complex conception of the universe
are the keys to a full understanding of Poussin's genius.

Modern times

Throughout the modern era there have been many healers worldwide
who have stood out from the crowd by showing that there is a force,
subtle and intangible, which can be controlled by the healer's mind to
bring about healing. There have been books written by these healers and
biographies written about them, a collection of useful information.

Around these individuals who developed the healing powers latent in
everyone have grown many different healing organizations and groups in
the Hindu, Buddhist, Muslim, Christian and Jewish traditions, amongst
others all over the world. To be sure, there are healers in every land and
tradition and of all ages.

Clarifying the purpose of esoteric healing

THE VITAL FORCE IN THE BODY

In the past healing was done only on the physical body up to the
level of the "fourth ether" (the lowest level on which exists the etheric
body). But with the incoming of the seventh ray (the Aquarian Age) we
can now heal through the whole etheric body (without needing to touch
the physical components, since the etheric is the template of the dense
physical body). The seventh ray is gaining strength and impact. It is with
this understanding that we undertake to study and practice the science
and art of esoteric healing. Hence it is fundamental to become more
acquainted with the etheric body.

The "etheric body" is a great network of energy weaving through
and around the physical body. It is the vital force which maintains the
activity of every function of the body. It is the cause and the process of

the interacting cellular movements in the body. If there is a withdrawal of vitality, atrophy and flaccidity results. If, on the other hand, too much energy is pouring through to a limb, for instance, tetany or tension occurs. A balanced, rhythmical flow through and round the body is the goal of healing. To achieve the goal, however, may require techniques extremely complex and detailed and subtle. But the purpose is the same: to bring about homeostasis (balance) in the body tissues. In this way the etheric body is able to vitalize the physical body.

The etheric body is neutral in its relation to the rest of the subtle bodies, which include the energies of life, thought, abstract vision, and the intuition. Thus the etheric vehicle becomes a kind of crystal ball or mirror of the person. Onto it the whole of the person is reflected, from the subtler bodies "downwards" and "upwards" from the physical body. For this reason, the etheric body is frequently referred to as the "light body," in the sense that all is revealed in the light, nothing is hidden from the light. With etheric sight the healer is able to apply what is required by the patient. The etheric body is the reflection of the soul, formed by the soul of each cell in the body, merged as one. It is in this energy field that we work and gain vital information about the patient on the different levels of their being. More on the etheric body on p. 42.[3]

TEMPORARY CURES

Most healers, rather than using their higher mind, will unknowingly use an energy drawn readily from the planet, called "planetary prana," to effect a cure. It is only temporarily effective. It merely deals with the symptoms and effects rather than the causes. It is the task of the esoteric healer to work consciously in the etheric body, directing specific energies with clear thought from the soul to the patient, which will bring about a healing according to the will and purpose of the patient's soul. Such healing is permanent and will affect a person's future life. The methods employed are magnetic and radiatory healing, another name for esoteric healing.

MAGNETIC AND RADIATORY HEALING

As said earlier, esoteric healing primarily deals with the two activities controlling energy, namely, magnetism and radiation. What do these two mean?

Magnetism

A healer must be magnetic above everything else. He must attract:
1. The power of his own soul.
2. Those whom he can help.
3. Those energies, when need arises, which will stimulate the patient to the desired activity (Bailey, 1951–70, v. 4, p. 197).

Radiation

The healer must understand also how to radiate, for the radiation of the soul will do the following:
1. Stimulate to activity the soul of the one to be healed thus setting in motion the healing process.
2. The radiation of the healer's mind will illumine the other mind and polarize the will of the patient.
3. The radiation of the healer's emotional or astral body, controlled and selfless, will impose a rhythm upon the agitation of the patient's astral body, and so enable the patient to take right action, while the radiation of the healer's vital body, working through the spleen center, will aid in organizing the patient's force body or etheric body (Bailey, 1951–70, v. 4, p. 205).

We will be looking at these in detail in a later chapter. But it is interesting to see the difference and the similarity of these approaches. We use magnetic healing to attract to us our own soul, and the patients we can help. We are then able to radiate soul energy to activate the soul of the patient to illumine her mind and polarize her will, to control and balance the emotional body, and bring about greater organization of the etheric body, and hence the physical. In the esoteric healing as taught in this book we use both magnetic and radiatory healing, either concurrently or in alternation, according to the will of the healer and the demands of the patient's soul.

	Magnetic Healing	Radiatory Healing
Soul	Attracts own soul	Radiates to patient's soul
Mind	Attracts patients (for healing)	Illumines the mind and will
Emotional	Activates the emotional body	Causes right action on the emotional level
Etheric	Activates the etheric body	Has an organizing action on the etheric level
Objective	Patient's physical body	Patient's soul
Energy Wielded	Prana or vital planetary fluid	Soul Energy

Radiatory healing is brought about by linking the soul with the brain and the heart center (see Rule Five), then mingling the two auras on all three levels, both of them responsive to soul contact. The soul energy of the patient is then directed by the healer's soul towards that aspect of the patient's physical body needing healing. This process is said to occur consciously or unconsciously.

Radiatory healing uses the emanations from the soul. Magnetic healing involves emanations from the etheric vehicle. But where do these originate? It is suggested that the source of radiation, of which magnetism is a type, is in the domain of "beingness" or "consciousness," where the healer identifies with a greater life than what is generally accessible (see the Higher Triangle in the alignment stage of preparing to heal, Chapter 6). We can really *do* nothing to bring about the flow of radiation. No amount of visualization or mental movement or astral "pleading" or devotion will cause radiation. But there is a way of being which sets radiation into motion. A shift in identification produces the result; this shift is one of the mysterious results of meditation and the particular preparation healers undertake before a healing (McMillan, private paper). In comparing radiatory healing with magnetic healing the following quotes from various sources may be found helpful:

It is the admixture of love and will which produces radiation (Bailey, 1951–70, v. 5, p. 375).

Magnetic action is more closely allied to first-ray functioning (with the energy of will and power) than it is to the second ray (with the energy of love and wisdom), and is an aspect or quality of the Law of Synthesis (holding all as one) (p. 375).

Radiation is a tangible substance and potency, producing effects ... Joy is the most powerful impulse behind the right kind of radiation (Bailey, 1944, v. 1, p. 185).

Magnetic stimulation of the physical atom emanates from man on astral levels and later from buddhic levels, the levels of inclusive love (Bailey, 1962, p. 254).

Magnetism and the capacity to show love are occultly synonymous (p. 576).

He must demonstrate the laws of radioactivity in his own life on the physical plane. His life must begin to radiate, and to have a magnetic affect upon others. By this I mean he will begin to influence that which is imprisoned in others, for he will reach—through his own powerful vibrations—the hidden center in each one (p. 863).

When a healer works magnetically and radiates his soul force to the patient, that patient is enabled more easily to achieve the end desired—which may be complete healing, or it may be the establishing of a state of mind which will enable the patient to live with himself and with his complaint, unhandicapped by the karmic limitations of the body (Bailey, 1951–70, v. 4, p. 7ff).

In magnetic healing, the healer, or the healing group, does two things: 1) He attracts to the healing center that type of energy which will counteract the disease. 2) He attracts to himself and absorbs those forces which are producing disease, drawing it forth from the patient (see the Synchronizing Triangle, defined below) (p. 100).

In radiatory healing, the process is simpler and safer, for the healer simply gathers power into himself and then radiates it onto the patient in the form of energy. It should be directed to the center nearest to the location of the disease. In this work there is no risk to the healer, but if the element of will enters into his thought or the stream of energy projected is too strong, there may be danger to the patient. The impact of the force which is being radiated upon him may not only produce nervous tension, but may lead to an increase in the power of the disease and to its intensification by stimulating the atoms and cells involved in the activity of the force responsible for the trouble. Beginners must avoid any concentration upon the disease itself or the area in the physical body involved. They must carefully keep all thought in abeyance, once the preliminary work of visualizing the trouble and aligning with the soul has been done, for energy ever follows thought and goes where the thought is focussed (Bailey, 1951–70, v. 4, p. 101).

In magnetic healing the patient's physical body is the objective of the healing art, while in radiatory healing it is the patient's soul which feels the effect of the healing energy. In the first case the healer works with the prana or vital planetary fluid, and in radiatory healing with soul energy. We can therefore divide healers into two groups: one group wielding the vital etheric fluid which we call prana, and the second group working on a much higher level and employing an ability to draw down soul energy into the body (or rather, the personality) of the healer and—from the required center—to send it forth again into the appropriate center in the patient's etheric body, but this time through the stimulation of the patient's aura controlled by the patient's soul (Bailey, 1951–70, v. 4, cf. Rule 5).

The esoteric healer combines these healing methods, or uses one then the other, according to the needs of the patient.

Esoteric healing defined

Now we can turn to a specific definition of esoteric healing. It is not easy to define anything, let alone esoteric healing. There are always so many nuances left out of a definition. But to aid understanding, a simplified definition of esoteric healing follows:

Esoteric Healing is an art and a science calling for the use of the mind, but not the emotions, in the service of the intuition, for the purpose of transforming matter with life energies to bring about change that will benefit the whole.

For completeness I would like to add the following more esoteric definition: "Esoteric Healing is the release of the soul so that its life can flow through the aggregate of organisms which constitute any particular form" (Bailey, 1951–70, v. 4, see Law I).

Esoteric Healing is an exact science of contact, of impression, of invocation, which includes an understanding of the subtle apparatus of the etheric vehicle (p. 525). A healer is a transmitter of spiritual energy (p. 2).

Esoteric is a word that comes from the Greek, *eso* meaning "within," *esoteriko*, "from within." Thus, esoteric healing is to make sound from within. Sound can be variously understood, either as an inner vibration, or a radiation from within signifying wholeness.

An interpretation of the definition

How interesting that such a definition says nothing of humanity, disease, death, cure! Yet by understanding the meaning of definitions, these terms will emerge indirectly.

Let us attempt to elaborate.

"ESOTERIC HEALING IS AN ART"

This simply indicates that the use of this healing form is a practical skill, and yet it is not fixed or predetermined; it does not have limitations attached to it. Under its given principles, its methods can be employed to create new and better forms. In other words, esoteric healing can be developed into a personal creation rather like a painter and their painting. Each time a new picture is started, it is different. Art relates to intuition, and intuition to love.

"ESOTERIC HEALING IS A SCIENCE"

To take the simile of the painter one step further, each time a new picture is begun, there are rules to which the artist must conform. The easel must be at the right height; it must be placed in a position for the light to show the colors to be used. The paper, the paints, the brushes, the pallet, and so on, must first be available and ready. Then the artist must conform to the rules of painting a picture (and we know how broad these have become). But an artist wants to paint a picture, not write a book or give a lecture or do a scientific experiment. The end result will be a recognizable picture. This is the scientific part. The rules we are to conform to are the springboard into a new dimension. Esoteric healing, as a science, is objective; the healer does not intend to be involved in the result. The healer wants to do the work and then leave the impact to cause a response in the patient. To alter its progress new patterns are added to it (further consultations for treatment are arranged).

To be sure, esoteric healing, however objective, changes the healer as well, although not in the same way as it does the patient. Although there is an interchange of energies, both persons are changed in the way required by the circumstances during the healing. This is due to the specific patterns of both healer and patient. The changes are different and impersonal, and so they can be called objective. In this way we can see that esoteric healing is a science, since it relates to mind and to individually woven thinking patterns.

"ESOTERIC HEALING USES THE MIND BUT NOT THE EMOTIONS"

In esoteric healing we do not work from the desires and fears of the patient. We have no interest in psychic phenomena and regard it as an interference which the work of healing is better without. The esoteric healing practitioner believes the emotions and psychic states he might experience from contact with a patient to be illusions that are to be avoided. To work from the emotional or astral level actually encourages those illusions to be perpetuated and weakens the individual patient.

Like a scientist, the healer works from the level of the mind, making intelligent deductions and decisions based on thought and on soul impression. The healer works with energy wisely directed, deflected or retained. Intelligent intent lies behind all wise direction of energy. In this way the patient will not be bombarded with our desires and hopes. Instead, the patient will sense a clarity, a feeling of purpose and direction, either immediately or over time.

"ESOTERIC HEALING USES THE MIND IN THE SERVICE OF THE INTUITION"

This will take some explaining, but I will do this later and during the course of this book. Let me just say simply that the Intuition referred to here is not an instinctual feeling. It is more like being receptive to pure ideas, to thoughts which have their origin in the abstract realms where form has no place. By tapping into intuition, the esoteric healer believes he or she can work with the causes of the problem or illness which is being presented. The intuition is the diagnostic tool.

The healer is totally self-reliant. The soul is an initiate; the soul is a master. There is no need for intermediaries, guides, and inner teachers. There is no doubt that such guides exist on the subtle planes, but they are not reliable. Mostly they are promoters of glamor or personal aggrandizement in a disguised manner. Esoteric healing and the esoteric healer works from the soul plane or soul dimension. The healer as a soul is responsible for the work done, and knows that as long as work is from the soul and with the soul of another, the result will be sure. No matter what happens, it will be determined according to the will of the patient's soul. This is the assurance. Thus in healing, the healer aspires always to remain in touch with the soul.

"FOR THE PURPOSE OF TRANSFORMING MATTER WITH LIFE ENERGIES"

To be a healer means working with the subtle energies and forces which surround and permeate the patient from the level of the soul as reflected in the etheric body. These subtle energies flow "in" and "out" among the various bodies—physical, etheric, emotional, and mental. To bring about healing the healer, having discovered what is causing the trouble in the subtle anatomy, must be able to "manipulate" or transform that energy and so bring it into harmony with the person's life and purpose. Here "manipulate" refers to working with energy reflected from the patient to the healer using the hands and ajna center to benefit the person from whom the radiation arises. The esoteric method of healing is based on selflessness and harmlessness and thus it handles and transforms the rate and rhythm of the patient's energies (according to the will of the patient's soul), not for the healer's advantage but for the patient's. From a more esoteric angle, the whole of the fallen universe is invisible, yet embodied by the Fourth Creative Hierarchy. That is, the four kingdoms are aided by the higher kingdoms which have not manifested into matter, but have incarnated into the higher energies of this fallen Divinity or Cosmic Being. This Cosmic Being has been made manifest in matter for reasons of healing and must be returned to its high state of original consciousness and expression. This is only achieved when all beings achieve their own enlightenment—be it an atom, a stone, a plant, an animal, a human, a planet, a solar system, a galaxy. More about this in Appendix A (Chapter 8, p. 255).

"To Bring about Change which Will Benefit the Whole"

This stage, the last part of the treatment, brings about healing. The esoteric healing practitioner is not actually trying to cure or willing to cure. The patient and the patient alone, directed by the wisdom of the soul, permits the healing. The healer understands that this phase of the work may not actually involve a *physical* change or cure. The physical illness may be so advanced that organic reversal is impossible. But suddenly the patient may "accept" the illness, or "knows why," or "forgets the disease in a new wave of enthusiasm," among other mental or emotional changes. Healing always involves a widening or deepening of consciousness, inevitably benefiting humanity and the planet as a whole. The truth is that, whenever we give healing, be it on ourselves or on one who has asked for it, such service actually raises the consciousness of humanity, no matter how little.

With this preview of esoteric healing, let us take a little time to read the Laws and Rules of Esoteric Healing as laid out in the manuscript of the Ageless Wisdom and translated into English by Mrs. Alice Bailey with the help of an Abbot of a Tibetan Lamasery called Djwahl Khul (Bailey, 1951–70, v. 4, p. v). Try to commit to memory the first Law as it is foundational in all esoteric healing practice.

The laws and rules of esoteric healing[4]

Law I

All disease is the result of inhibited soul life. This is true of all forms in all kingdoms. The art of the healer consists in releasing the soul so that its life can flow through the aggregate of organisms which constitute any particular form.

Law II

Disease is the product of and subject to three influences: first, a person's past, wherein each pays the price of ancient error; second, inheritance, wherein each shares with all humankind those tainted streams of energy which are of group origin; third, each shares with all the natural forms that which the Lord of Life imposes on the body. These three influences are called the "Ancient Law of Evil Sharing." This must give place some day to that new "Law of Ancient Dominating Good" which lies behind all that God has made. This law must be brought into activity by the spiritual will.

RULE ONE

Let the healer train to know the inner stage of thought or of desire of the one who seeks help. The healer can thereby know the source from whence the trouble comes. Let the cause and the effect be related and know the exact point through which relief must come.

LAW III

Disease is an effect of the basic centralization of life energy. From the plane whereon those energies are focussed proceed those determining conditions which produce ill health. These therefore work out as disease or as freedom from disease.

LAW IV

Disease, both physical and psychological, has its roots in the good, the beautiful and the true. It is but a distorted reflection of divine possibilities. The thwarted soul, seeking full expression of some divine characteristic or inner spiritual reality, produces, within the substance of its sheaths, a point of friction. Upon this point the eyes of the personality are focussed and this leads to disease. The art of the healer is concerned with the lifting of the downward focussed eyes unto the soul, the true healer within the form. The spiritual or third eye then directs the healing force and all is well.

RULE TWO

The healer must achieve magnetic purity, through purity of life and attain that dispelling radiance which shows itself in every person when the centers in the head are linked. When this magnetic field is established, the radiation then goes forth.

LAW V

There is naught but energy, for God is Life. Two energies meet in the individual, but five others are present. For each is to be found a central point of contact. The conflict of these energies with forces, and of forces twixt themselves, produce the bodily ills of humans. The conflict of the first and second persists for ages until the mountain top is reached—the first great mountain top. The fight between the forces produces all disease, all ills and bodily pain which seek release in death. The two, the five and thus the seven, plus that which they produce, possess the secret. This is the fifth Law of Healing within the world of form.

RULE THREE

Let the healer concentrate the needed energy within the needed center. Let that center correspond to the center which has need. Let the two synchronize and together augment force. Thus shall the waiting form be balanced in its work. Thus shall the two and the one, under right direction, heal.

LAW VI

When the building energies of the soul are active in the body, then there is health, clean interplay and right activity. When the builders are the lunar lords and those who work under the control of the moon and at the behest of the lower personal self, then there is disease, ill health and death.

LAW VII

When life or energy flows unimpeded and through right direction to its precipitation (the related gland), then the form responds and ill health disappears.

RULE FOUR

A careful diagnosis of disease, based on the ascertained outer symptoms, will be simplified to this extent—that once the organ involved is known and thus isolated, the center in the etheric body which is in closest relation to it will be subjected to methods of occult healing, though the ordinary, ameliorative, medical or surgical methods will not be withheld.

LAW VIII

Disease and death are the results of two active forces. One is the will of the soul, which says to its instrument: I draw the essence back. The other is the magnetic power of the planetary life, which says to the life within the atomic structure: The hour of reabsorption has arrived. Return to me. Thus, under cyclic law, do all forms act.

RULE FIVE

The healer must seek to link the soul, the heart, the brain and hands. Thus can the vital healing force be poured upon the patient. This is magnetic work. It cures disease or increases the evil state, according to the knowledge of the healer.

The healer must seek to link the soul, the brain, the heart and auric emanation. Thus can the healer's presence feed the soul life of the patient. This is the work of radiation. The hands are needed not. The soul displays its power. The patient's soul responds through the response of the aura to the radiation of the healer's aura, flooded with soul energy.

LAW IX

Perfection calls imperfection to the surface. Good drives evil from the form in time and space. The method used by the Perfect One and that employed by Good is harmlessness. This is not negativity but perfect poise, a completed point of view and divine understanding.

RULE SIX

The healer or the healing group must keep the will in leash. It is not will that must be used, but love.

LAW X

Hearken, O Disciple, to the call which comes from the Son to the Mother, and then obey. The Word goes forth that form has served its purpose. The principle of mind then organizes itself and then repeats that Word. The waiting form responds and drops away. The soul stands free.

Respond, O Rising One, to the call which comes within the sphere of obligation; recognize the call emerging from the Ashram or from the Council Chamber where waits the Lord of Life. The Sound goes forth. Both soul and form together must renounce the principle of life and thus permit the Monad[5] to stand free. The soul responds. The form then shatters the connection. Life is now liberated, owning the quality of

conscious knowledge and the fruit of all experience. These are the gifts
of soul and form combined (Bailey, 1951–70, v. 4, pp. 532–36).

The basic laws governing the soul in healing

In trying to simplify these profound laws of healing I have distilled
the essential qualities of esoteric healing into seven statements.
1. All disease is the result of inhibited soul life.
2. Disease is the result of a person's past, inheritance, and the environment, both inner and outer.
3. The conflict of integrating the person's outer personality self and the
   inner spiritual self is a further cause of disease.
4. The soul is the healer of the form.
5. A person's imbalance is healed when the flow of life energy is directed, unimpeded, to the appropriate major energy center.
6. To release the imperfection in the patient the healer must use harmlessness.
7. The word of the soul governs both life and death.

These are the seven basic laws governing the attitude of the healer
to the patient. I have referred indirectly to these laws throughout this
book, so while I must introduce the student to them, I will not speak
at length about them here. They could best be used as meditation seed
thoughts to ponder.

1. All disease is the result of inhibited soul life.

Everything that exists in the world—from pebbles to people—is a
soul embodied. Everything in the world is subject to illness. For one
reason or other, the ensouling principle is not able to express itself
properly. Such inhibition makes for disharmony resulting in sickness
and dis-ease.

2. Disease is the result of a person's past, inheritance, and the en-
vironment both inner and outer.

The source of inhibition is explained in this law. What one sows, one
reaps. But what one sows is also dependent on other factors: where the
seed comes from, where it grows, under what conditions it grows, and

so on. Causes create effects, as is obvious to us in our everyday lives. The decisions one takes today will affect and change us tomorrow, but not in a deterministic way. To undo our misdirected actions, words, decisions, etc., may take a lot of guts and pain and brain. The "environment" refers to causes that exceed our capacity to comprehend. These causes belong to a distant past but which we have to work out in the present for the purposes of the future. This second statement is related to the much misunderstood and misused term, karma.

3. The conflict of integrating the person's outer personality self and the inner spiritual self is further cause of disease.

"The spirit is willing but the flesh is weak" is an old saying. A conflict between the desires and ambitions, hopes and fears, stresses and strains of the personality as opposed to the aspirations and spiritual ideals and purposes and vision of the soul can lead to a breakdown in the fabric of the body.

4. The soul is the healer of the form.

Only when the healer truly contacts the soul and works with it according to the soul's laws and purposes, and only when the soul convinces the personality to be submissive to the soul's plan, can healing be brought about and its effects made permanent. This statement can be understood as the Grand Design. To properly heal the form requires the person as soul-personality to really understand esoteric teleology, the cause and purpose of our existence, as described in this book.

5. A person's imbalance is healed when the flow of life energy is directed, unimpeded, to the appropriate major energy center.

This refers to the practical aspect of esoteric healing. All the many preparations and triangles which lead the life energy to its precipitational purpose must be understood and used for healing to be effected. The seven endocrine glands are the outer expression of the seven major etheric centers. All healing work is the full utilization of the subtle energies controlled by these major centers. The physical result will always be via the endocrine gland or glands of the center or centers involved. Most of the triangles used in esoteric healing include a major center that circulates the healing force through the physical body via the blood stream.

6. To release the imperfection, the healer must use harmlessness.

For effective healing that is safe and permanent, the will of the healer or any forcing process, spiritual, mental or physical, must never be used. Only that lofty quality of love may be used. What is love? In healing it is the energy of harmlessness. Stated in this way, using the word "harmlessness" ensures that the healer should at no time use force, or display methods, whether of thought or action, that would endanger the patient. Furthermore, we keep our hands off the patient at all times during the healing. The hands remain in the life-field surrounding the patient. Touching the patient during the process of esoteric healing short-circuits the love energy and renders it virtually inoperative. The hands are only laid on a person during specific ceremonial energy trans-feral. Examples of this are at baptism, or when one is made a priest or bishop or knighted, an energetic elevation of personal status. Soul and personality are more closely aligned. It must be emphasized that this is an inner conferral; outer titles count for very little in this work. Love is the governing attitude of the healer, and while the healer uses this great energy, no harm can be caused either to the patient or to the healer. Law IX, from which this statement is taken, is also a warning to those who would unscrupulously employ agents or potentizing forms that are not conducive to the free will of the patient's soul.

7. The word of the soul governs both life and death.

This statement from Law X refers to the free will under which all human beings live. The "word" of the soul is the real "name" of each individual on the soul plane, so this law clarifies the patient-healer relationship. The patient responds with free will to the healer's soul, determining how the healing should be used. Will it be to promote life in the world or to promote life out of the world, which we call "death"? Death in this respect would be regarded as a positive step for the patient. The esoteric healer knows that there is no death, that death does not exist, that death as seen by the ordinary world is really consciousness without the dense physical body, a new reality for the individual. Patients often do not have this attitude, so the healer must choose each word carefully and handle delicately the patient's confrontation with this form of birth. The patient is to be encouraged to look towards that inevitable time not with dread but with calmness, faith and expectation, helped a little if possible by some esoteric knowledge.

If I were asked to say what is the major task of all healing groups ... I would say it is to prepare human beings for what we should regard as the restorative aspect of death, and thus give to that hitherto dreaded enemy of mankind a new and happier significance. You will find that if you work along these indicated lines of thought, the entire theme of death will constantly recur, and that the result of this will be new attitudes to dying and the inculcation of a happy expectancy where that inevitable and most familiar event occurs. Healing groups must be prepared to deal with this basic condition of all living, and a major part of their work will be the elucidating of the principle of death. The healer, working from the level of the soul, always uses intuitively the right methods and triangles which are needed by the patient. When the healer is properly trained in esoteric healing, he or she can be completely confident about this (Two Students, 1985).

3.

OUR SEVEN ENERGY BODIES

Esoteric healers must understand the function and action of the subtle anatomy of the human being. The subtle anatomy refers to the energies and forces that underlie the physical body of organs and systems. This ethereal template gives rise to the cells and physiological interactions. Esoteric healing is carried out within this arena.

In esoteric healing we work with three subtle bodies in a patient because they are regarded as the "form bodies," the lowest expression of the soul; and all disease is the result of (the form) inhibiting the soul from expressing itself better through the personality (as Law I states). To reiterate, the three bodies or vehicles are:

1. The vital or etheric body, the force-body of our physical body, giving our physical organism life and movement.
2. The emotional or astral body, our feelings.
3. The mental body, our thoughts.

These are the so-called "auras" of man. They make up our personality. (Sometimes we see that a person has a radiant glow, a kind of "rude health." In that event we are actually detecting their "health aura," which lies closer to the physical body than the etheric.)

About the bodies

Before elaborating on the bodies or cloaks of the human, we should mention something concerning the bodies of the healer. Every healer needs to achieve purity or pure character. This attribute is something more than just being good. It deals with the matter aspect and has relation to the hold or control of the form nature over the man. Let's view this from the realm of the "occult," another word for the world of causes. If one or other of the three lower elementals (the physical, the astral or the mental) is the controlling factor in the life of a person, he or she is—by that very fact—put into a position of danger and should take steps to arrest that control prior to an attempt to enter into the formless realm. The reason for this will be apparent. Under the law governing matter, the Law of Economy, the elemental life will attract to itself similar lives, resulting in a dual danger. Esoterically, these dangers are:

1. Matter with a synchronous vibration collecting in the elemental form. This will tend to increase the magnitude of the task confronting the soul and sweep the lower self into increasing dominance. The "lunar lords" will become increasingly powerful, and the solar "Lord" or soul correspondingly less effective.
2. The healer will be surrounded in time by thoughtforms of a lower order (from the standpoint of the soul), and before penetration can be made into the Arcana of Wisdom and before the way into the Master's world can be found, the clouds of worthless and selfish thoughtforms that have gathered around the personality ego will have to be dispelled.

Unless the student of healing learns that aspiration and self-discipline must proceed side by side, it will be found that the spiritual energy contacted serves to stimulate the latent seeds of evil (fractors) in the personality, demonstrating what the great Lord taught when he pictured the man who swept his house, cast out seven devils and eventually was in a worse condition than ever (Bailey, 1951–70, v. 5, p. 8).

Every coherent system has its varying types of energy. Perfection, or the state of continuous enlightenment, is achieved when the dominating energy is the highest type of energy possible. If the lower energy of the aggregate of the form-atoms (the personality) becomes the controlling factor, three things will take place:

1. The physical form itself will grow by accretion and will become ever more potent, until the dominant voice of its "lunar lords" will stifle all other voices. The person could then be swept back into inertia, blindness and bondage.

2. The person may be under the control of one of their forms or, worse still, the captive of all three.

3. All subhuman forms in their aggregate will greatly hinder or even prevent the emancipation of the Real Man.

Who or what are these lunar lords? They are energies or lives that seek to control the lower threefold personality, and which fall into three categories:

a. The individual tiny lives, which we call the atoms or cells of the body. These exist in three groups and compose respectively the four types of bodies: dense physical, etheric, astral and mental.

b. The aggregate of these lives which constitute in themselves four types of elementals or separate, coherent, though not self-conscious, existences. These four lunar lords constitute what the Ageless Wisdom teaching calls "the four sides of the square." They are the "lower quaternary," "the imprisoning cubes," or the cross upon which the inner spiritual person is to be "crucified." These four elementals have an intelligence all their own, are upon an involutionary arc, are following the law of their own being when they tend to become powerful, and thereby fully express that which is in them. Involutionary lives have not reached the perfection of their lowest body, that is, material beings whose goal is self-consciousness. Man is self-conscious, thus on the evolutionary wave.

c. A dominant controlling lunar lord whom we term the "lower personality." He or she (if the personal pronoun can be used) is the sum-total of the physical, astral, and mental elementals. The "personality elemental" forces the "fiery energies" of the body to feed the lower three centers. The etheric body is simply the vehicle for prana or life, using the spleen center for that purpose. DK tells us that the etheric body has a unique and curious position, being simply the vehicle for prana or life, and the center which it uses exists in a category by itself—this center is the spleen minor.

The experienced healer or adept can, however, enter the world of form, contact it, work in it and remain unaffected by it, because there is nothing inside that responds to it. The healer sees through the illusion to the reality behind. Knowing where the self stands, nothing is found in the appeal and the demand of these lunar lords as attractive. The healer stands midway between the pairs of opposites. In the realization of the nature of this world of form, in a comprehension of the lives which compose it, and in an ability to hear the voice of the "formless One" above the strife of all the lower voices, comes the opportunity for the aspirant to escape from the dominance of matter.

The understanding of the sounds of all beings and the ability to speak the language of the soul is the clue to the work (Bailey, 1951–70, v. 5, pp. 8–10). The habit of purity relates the healer to Rule Two of esoteric healing, which states that the healer must attain that "dispelling radiance" which shows itself in every person when the centers in the head are linked.

One of the paradoxes of the spiritual life concerns the vehicles or bodies of the human. Let me just say a few general words about these three bodies before speaking more specifically about them.

We are not our physical body; we are not our emotions and feelings; we are not our thoughts. We have them and we use them; we observe them from a higher place within ourselves. The personality, composed of our body, emotions and thoughts, is not who we really are. Moreover, the personality as a whole or in its isolated parts can be violated, which can be very hurtful so long as we identify with these parts. But the soul is untouched. It remains pure. Its individuality cannot be violated; into the soul no one can enter. Here you are God. Remember this, for yourself, and for your patients.

These bodies are interrelated. They interpenetrate each other and the physical body. In constant movement, they surround the physical and go through it, approximating its shape or form.

When we feel peaceful, happy, angry, or exhibit other emotional states, we are experiencing aspects of the emotional body. But such feelings will also involve our thinking and our willing (the mental and vital bodies). Care is needed to distinguish just what we are experiencing.

EXERCISE

For an hour during your daily activities try to be aware of your whole subtle anatomy. Be aware of your postures (sitting, lying, standing, moving, etc.) and the emotional state you experience during this time. Do your emotions fluctuate reactively, alter slowly or remain fairly stable? See if you can also be aware of some of your thought patterns and ideas.

Learn to distinguish what your different bodies are "saying." You may want to keep a notebook in your pocket to record your observations.

* * * * *

Let us now begin our look at the subtle bodies with a broad overview. And, as is the general approach in esoteric studies, we start from above and move downwards to the lower bodies.

The constitution of man

THE THREE PRINCIPLES

To understand the nature of the soul, try to visualize humans as having subtle parts within: three energies consisting of three bodies in each.

The three energies are Spirit, Soul and Body. In each we see the qualities of will, love and activity (active intelligence). Other names for these are life, quality and appearance; or spiritual purpose, consciousness (love-wisdom) and formative expression.

Body

Desire for sentient existence and desire for service to humanity produce physical manifestation (Bailey, 1962, p. 760). Will-desire is the actual cause of incarnation (p. 799). In the Body are the three aspects which combine to make up the personality. We will count from the lowest or last-expressed body to the highest, making nine so-called "bodies":

9th. The physical and vital (etheric) body—(will) Personal Action. There are seven subplanes in this body: the three lowest are dense physical (solid), liquid, and gas. The upper four are the ethers which make up the etheric body.

8th. The emotional (or astral) body—(desire) Personal Love. Also consisting of seven subplanes.

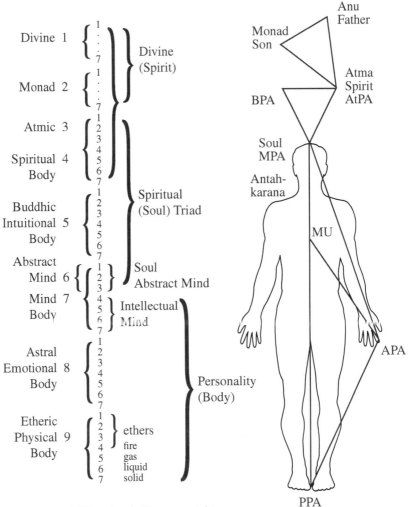

AtPA = Atmic Permanent Atom
BPA = Buddhic Permanent Atom
MPA = Mental Permanent Atom
MU = Mental Unit
APA = Astral Permanent Atom
PPA = Physical Permanent Atom

CHART I
THE CONSTITUTION OF MAN

7th. The intellectual (mind) body—(thinking) Personal Ideas. This consists of four subplanes; the upper three belong to the region of the soul.

The Body Principle or Personality therefore consists of eighteen subplanes, seven each for the physical and emotional bodies and four for the mental (concrete mind) body.

The distinction of consciousness (or individual self-awareness) is the cohering energy which joins or merges the above three (the Body) with the next three (the Soul)[1]:

Soul

In the Soul Principle, there are three aspects:

6th. The abstract mind (or pure ideas) body—Soul Activity. Here we find the three upper subplanes of the mental plane. On this level we find the Causal Body or Egoic Lotus or Soul in the usual sense.

5th. The intuition (buddhic) body—Soul Love. (Seven subplanes.)

4th. The soul will (atmic) body—Soul Will. (Seven subplanes.)

The Soul Principle (also known as the Spiritual Triad) has seventeen subplanes.

The distinction of higher initiation or spiritual consciousness, which remains only latent at this stage of our spiritual development, joins or merges the above three (the Soul) with the three spiritual dimensions:

Spirit

In the Spirit Principle, the Monad and the divine bodies, containing the three divine aspects of Will, Love, and Intelligence (Father, Son, and Holy Spirit) are seed qualities. With divine intention, we reach up to these when we align and attune ourselves before opening the Healing Triangle (see Chapter 6). These two levels consist of seven subplanes each, totalling fourteen. Therefore we find there are forty-nine levels of consciousness in our world. This dimension contains:

3rd. Divine intention—Active Intelligence. It is the Atmic Plane; the level of the Holy Spirit; the Lord of the Third Ray.

2nd. Divine compassion—Love-Wisdom. The Monadic Plane; the level of the Son; the Lord of the Second Ray.

1st. Divine purpose—Spiritual Will. This state of divine consciousness is where the different religions say we can meet "the Father" (or
the Father's House). Other names include Siva, Nirvana, Shambhala,
and the Lord of the World (Sanat Kumara); this is where the "Will of
God is known." The Divine Plane; the level of the Father; the Lord of
the First Ray.

The Seven Bodies of Man

Reorganized, the above information can also be listed as follows
in a form that is more commonly accepted. This is due to the "joining"
aspects as shown above:

1. The physical body (which includes the etheric body)
2. The emotional body
3. The mind body (linking the intellect of the personality and the abstract thoughts of the soul)
4. The intuitional body
5. The spiritual will body (linking the divine intelligence of the Spirit,
   and the spiritual will of the Soul)
6. The monadic body
7. The divine body (in Eastern philosophy called the Anu).

THE SPIRIT OR LIFE PRINCIPLE

The spirit expresses itself in the soul, and the soul expresses itself in
the personality. This is important to remember when healing. So you will
appreciate how the spiritual will of the soul expresses itself as physical
activity in the personality; and how intuitional love of the soul expresses
itself as feeling and desire in the personality. The mind stands central.
It expresses itself as concrete thinking in the personality, bound by that
distinctive note of consciousness and self-awareness. The soul may be
seen as the mediator between the spirit and the form of man. In man the
soul is like an immense searchlight, its beams turned in many directions
and focussed on many levels, making healing the body from the soul
level a real possibility. On its own level our self-conscious soul is beauti-
fully in rapport with the soul of all things. Our soul is an integral part of
the universal Soul, and because of this our soul can attempt awareness
of the conscious purpose of Deity. Our soul can intelligently cooperate
with the will of God, and thus work with the plan of evolution.

THE SOUL AND PERSONALITY PRINCIPLES

The existence of soul is, of course, still unproven, although it is re-garded by many scientists and philosophers as hypothetically possible. Scientific instruments are not yet sensitive enough to prove it as a fact. When proof is found, which may be in the near future (physicists are already discussing vibratory aspects of matter and energy, suggesting a higher dimension), the revelation will revolutionize our whole social structure and life. Medicine will pass into a new phase. All that the eso-teric and spiritual healers have been hinting at for years will be external-ized. One day, which is not all that far away, we will have a government body pouring funds into a research project to investigate the possibility of the soul as a reality in man.

To the extent you come under soul impression, and then soul control, and finally identification with the soul, you will move towards the cen-ter of fusion. As your love for humanity increases, and your interest in yourself decreases, so will you move towards that center of light and love where those who have achieved this union stand in spiritual being.

The soul is the mark of quality that each form expresses: it distin-guishes one mineral from another, one plant species from another, one species of animal from another, and makes one human different from another in appearance, nature or character.

An interesting esoteric link connects the vegetable kingdom and the human kingdom: "It is in the vegetable kingdom that we find one of the first and temporary approximations between the evolving human monad and the evolving deva monad. The two parallel kingdoms touch in that kingdom, contact again in the buddhic and merge in the second or monadic plane" (Bailey, 1962, p. 589) You will also note that in general the closer certain animals come to individualization (of soul and body) the fewer in their genus and the more independent they become (the herd becomes smaller).

The various qualities, vibrations, colors, and characteristics in all the kingdoms of nature, are soul qualities manifesting in form. And we must remember that it is the desire for sentient existence and desire for service to humanity which produces physical manifestation (p. 760). It is the quality of will-desire which is the cause of incarnation (p. 799).

Now let us look at each of these bodies in more detail.

The vital or etheric body

The etheric body, as indicated above, is the cause, the template of the dense physical. (For details of the physical body, consider consulting a good anatomy and physiology book.)

The etheric part of our anatomy is known by scientists as the L-force (life force) or bioplasmic body or the bioenergetic body. To the various philosophies or religions of the world it is known as the body of Prana (Hindu). To the Chinese we noted above that it is called Ch'i or Qi, to the Japanese Ki, to the Greeks Pneuma. In the Bible it is called the "golden bowl" or "chalice." This type of energy, like the physical body, is least conscious to us because it is below the realm of waking consciousness. The etheric body consists of previously acquired characteristics that have passed into the bodies of perfection called instinct or body nature or natural intelligence. Today, we far more readily live in our emotions and senses. We respond to the physical body from the emotional aspect. The vital body is completely identified with the physical. In fact, they cannot survive in this world without each other.

SOURCES OF ETHERIC ENERGY

Sources of energy for the etheric body include the following:

i. At conception our parents give us etheric qualities, our inherited vitality. From this energy our physical strengths and weaknesses derive.

ii. Another part of the etheric energy is acquired from the food we eat. Here we extract from whatever we eat the life quality that keeps us healthy. The most important source of this form of vital force comes of course from fresh vegetables and fruit. There are six types of food vitality which we use every time we have a meal:

   a. The bitter tasting foods have the energy function of draining and drying the physical body and thus preventing the body from becoming too wet and damp and emotionally liable;

   b. Acrid or pungent foods move and disperse the energies around the body;

   c. Sweet foods have the function of harmonizing all the etheric energies—we will find that this energy action originates in the spleen center;

d. Sour foods are astringent and have the function of holding the etheric energies in their proper courses and activities, a process controlled by the liver minor center;

e. Salty type foods sow the etheric energy of purification or detoxification through the organs, softening them, which is cleansing and therefore softening to the organs of the physical body. This is an important function and relates to the blood and base center of the etheric body, because it involves a certain determination and fixed purpose to undergo such a practice, properly speaking;

f. And, finally, we have the so-called bland foods, which leech out dampness and heaviness in the etheric, especially via the bladder.

iii. The third type of etheric energy enters the body along with the air we breathe.

iv. And the fourth type is given to us directly by the sun. This prana, is absorbed via the skin (we think of it these days as providing our daily vitamin D quota) and is especially affiliated with two etheric centers, namely: the spleen center and a center between the shoulder blades.

There are four distribution agents of life energy in the physical organism, namely, the etheric vehicle, the nervous system, the endocrine system and the blood stream. Of these the etheric body with its centers is primary.

These four distributary agents are directly related to the whole physical expression in that they are one system with a dualistic mode of radiation.

1st Ether (upper positive force). The first Ray energy, governed by Vulcan, causes the circulation of etheric energy and also has a connection with the lower receptive force of the fourth ether under the moon, the splenic system, and is therefore related to the fourth Ray.

2nd Ether (upper positive force). The second Ray energy governed by Venus rules the nervous system and links with the lower receptive force of the fifth subplane of gases, especially the respiratory system, and is connected to the fifth Ray.

3rd Ether (upper positive force). The third Ray energy governed by Saturn rules the endocrine system and is linked to the lower receptive force in the body via the sixth subplane of liquids, especially the kidney system, and is connected to the sixth Ray.

4th Ether (upper positive force). The fourth Ray energy is linked to the first ether by Neptune governing the circulatory or blood system, and related to the seventh subplane of solids in the bony system, and is connected to the seventh Ray.

Each of these links (upper and lower) can be related to soul and personality.

FREEING OURSELVES FROM INHERITED TAINTS

The inherited vitality, that which is given us by our parents and grandparents in a long line of succession (back to "Adam"), is the controlling influence behind all the etheric types of energy, all except one, that is, the energy related to the breath (the source of the respiratory system; fifth ray). DK says that it is through the breath that we can free ourselves from inherited taints. In esoteric healing the healer can use the breath to perform certain clearing functions in the patient, but we are to guard against employing this method lest we make the last condition worse than the first. Love must be the basis for the use of breath, which is a will faculty, hence the difficulty. My strong advice to you regarding the use of the breath is: learn, first, truly to love, for only then can you wield the breath in healing. They are one.

DEATH

The etheric is the cause of all motion and function in the physical body. All digestive processes, nervous impulses, breathing, and the beating of the heart are due to the action of the vital forces galvanizing our organs and cells. When we breathe our last, the etheric body withdraws from the physical (the lung minor centers are the last to let go of the physical body) and the latter falls limp and motionless. Then, as the separation is finalized and the life force of the vital body departs permanently, the physical casing becomes stiff and begins to decay.

THE FLOW OF LIFE-FORCE

When the etheric life-force flows round the body harmoniously, we enjoy health. The Chinese call this Chi or Qi, "balance." When this Qi gets "stuck" or is prevented from moving properly, ailments begin to appear. Likewise, when the vital forces do not "keep in their pathways" and so begin to zoom around the body too quickly and haphazardly, acute symptoms arise causing much pain or distress. A person whose etheric energy is congested might exhibit lethargy, cold hands and feet, aching back, and a lack of appetite. Conversely, the second type may show signs of hyperactivity, highly strung emotions, high blood pressure and insomnia. There are many interactions between these two extremes of contraction and relaxation, alertness and drowsiness, acute and chronic. The question is, what causes the etheric or Qi to flow in this way, too quickly or too slowly? The answer does not lie in the vital body itself, but rather in the emotional and mental bodies.

Five types of pranic energy, forming one closely knit unit, comprise the etheric sheath. They form a fivefold channel (*see* Hopking, 1994), energizing, galvanizing and controlling the entire human organism. There is no part of the physical body which this network of energies does not underlie or "substand." It is the true form or substance both of the human being and of all forms in existence. Where these lines of force cross and recross, as they repeat in the microcosm of man the involutionary and evolutionary arcs of the macrocosm of the universe, there are formed five areas up the spinal column and two in the head where the energies are more concentrated and potent than elsewhere. Thus you have the appearance of the major centers. Throughout the entire body, these crossings and recrossings occur, and so the equipment of energy centers is brought into being (Bailey, 1951–70, v. 2, p. 592). The etheric movement is difficult to chart because its movement is both out and in at the same time. For instance, energy flows out of the hands and fingers; in the same instant other energies are flowing in. This subtle movement of energy occurs throughout the organism; it is like the rhythm of inhalation and exhalation happening simultaneously, a most beautiful harmony to observe with the inner eyes.

THE CLOAK OF LIFE

The garment of life energy is secured to the physical by seven "buttons." The etheric body is like a coat penetrating and infusing the physical. It extends beyond the surface of the skin to a distance of about 2-6 inches (5-30 cm). Visualize a never-ending flow of forces. The "buttons" represent the endocrine glands, which are the transformers of etheric energy for the physical body. There are seven major endocrine glands in our bodies, condensations of the great vortices of the seven major centers.

The seven major centers are created where the fivefold channels cross twenty-one times. For example, the throat center is the etheric counterpart of the thyroid gland and parathyroid glands. This center controls, via the thyroid gland, all the physiological activities which have been discovered, from the metabolic rate to the creative aspects of mind and speech. We will look at each of the centers in depth in a later chapter, as they are an important part of esoteric healing.

The seven glands with their major centers are:

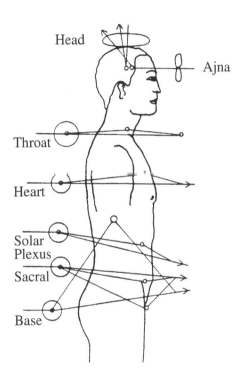

Pineal Gland—Head Center
(Crown Chakra, Thousand
Petalled Lotus Flower)

Pituitary Gland—
Ajna or Brow Center

Thyroid Gland—
Throat Center

Thymus Gland—
Heart Center

Pancreas Gland—
Solar Plexus Center

Sex Glands—Sacral Center

Adrenal Glands—
Base Center

THE LESSER CENTERS

There are many other lesser centers often appearing quite unrelated to any particular gland or organ. In the Chinese system of acupuncture, which uses needles inserted into the flow of Qi, there are points all over the body that "energize" the body and which can be used by the needler to effect certain changes in the body. Esoteric healers recognize various points or minute centers, but there is not yet agreement about how the

Chinese system compares to the system outlined in the Alice Bailey books. Nor do we use the points in the same way as an acupuncturist. According to DK, via Alice Bailey, seven streams of energy cross to make a minute point, just as the minor centers are composed of fourteen and the major centers twenty-one.

Here are some of the more important minor and minute centers as they are related to certain healing triangles and major centers. What follows is a snapshot of the most significant minor centers.

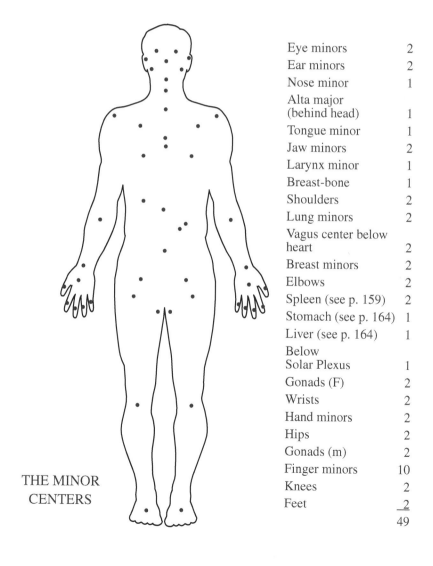

Eye minors	2
Ear minors	2
Nose minor	1
Alta major (behind head)	1
Tongue minor	1
Jaw minors	2
Larynx minor	1
Breast-bone	1
Shoulders	2
Lung minors	2
Vagus center below heart	2
Breast minors	2
Elbows	2
Spleen (see p. 159)	2
Stomach (see p. 164)	1
Liver (see p. 164)	1
Below Solar Plexus	1
Gonads (F)	2
Wrists	2
Hand minors	2
Hips	2
Gonads (m)	2
Finger minors	10
Knees	2
Feet	2
	49

THE MINOR
CENTERS

The two eye minors are usually controlled by the head center, although you can note how other centers dominate certain conditions (see *The Eyes Triangle,* #59, Chapter 7).

The two ear minors are controlled by the throat center for hearing, and the ajna center for conditions of balance.

The alta major center is under the control of the throat center; not a major center but more important than a minor center.

The throat center also controls the larynx minor, the jaw minors, the tongue minor, the shoulder minors, the two elbow minors (with the head center), the two hand minors, the breast bone minor, the two lung minors (the respiratory activity), and the diaphragm minute centers.

The heart center controls the vagus nerve center, the two breast minors (although the sacral is the main ruler of these two minors), the two lung minors (the blood-air exchange), a point below the heart, and the diaphragm minutes (with the throat center).

The solar plexus center controls the stomach minor and the liver minor. There is a vague connection between the solar plexus center and the spleen minor (actually a double-minor center) but the latter is at the present time somewhat of an independent center (cf. p. 87). The spleen minor has stronger links with the sacral center due to the third Ray, which rules them both, and the heart center (concerning prana).

The sacral center controls the two double gonad minors (linking the masculine and feminine attributes in each person and making the major center particularly powerful), the two breast minors, the two feet minors.

The base center controls the two hip minors, the two knee minors, a center below the solar plexus center, minute centers at the ileocaecal valve and the sigmoid flexure, and minute centers on and near the kidneys.

Thus, there are seven major vortices, forty-nine minor centers, and hundreds of lesser or minute centers in the etheric form.

In the case of a highly developed person, life energy flows unimpeded and in the right direction from these centers to the gland or organ in its jurisdiction. In an undeveloped human being this life energy flows impeded and imperfectly directed. In the same way, a person is either sick or well according to the state of the centers and their precipitation, the glands. The centers are the major agency upon the physical plane through which the soul works (according to the point reached under the evolutionary process), and the glandular system is simply an effect inevitable and unavoidable—of the centers through which the soul is working. Everyone's conduct and behavior upon the physical plane is conditioned, controlled and determined by the nature of their glands, and these are conditioned, controlled and determined by the nature, the quality and livingness of the centers. These in their turn are conditioned, controlled and determined by the soul, in increasing effectiveness as evolution proceeds. Of course, prior to soul control, they are conditioned, qualified and controlled by the astral body, and later by the mind. Obviously, our goal in this present cycle is to bring about this control, this conditioning, and this determining process by the soul (Bailey, 1951–70, v. 4, pp. 623–24). Thus, the healer deals with one of the seven expressions of prana, called the life principle, ignores the gland (the effect), instead working directly with the center (the cause) which controls the area under its influence.

In all this the healer has to think clearly before the desired results can be brought about.

How, technically, does the life force flow into the human body? From the etheric body, as an emanation of the person, it flows to the seven centers. It then divides into two streams, one stream (of consciousness) flows into the nadis, the tiny threads of force which underlie the nerves, and into the nerves themselves, and from there into the endocrine system. The other stream (of life) flows from the centers into the endocrine system directly and into the blood stream, via the hormones. These two streams affect consciousness and life in the human being (Bailey, 1951–70, v. 4, p. 628). Esoteric healers always work from or with the life stream (the central jewel of each center), which then radiates out to the consciousness aspect (symbolically, the petals of the lotus).

The esoteric healer need not acquire the detail of the other physical systems nor engage in intricacies of lesser interior anatomical and physiological relationships. All we need to remember is that the primary effect of the glands and of their secretions is psychological, while also having a powerful physical influence (p. 625).

THE ETHERIC ESOTERICALLY UNDERSTOOD

Readers who are new to this subject can skip this section for now. Come back to it later. It can wait.

If we accept that every cell in our body (all sixty billion of them) is a life in itself, then we must also accept that there are many more atoms in the body, each embodying a life and a purpose in themselves, each a life in its own right, just as humans are lives, individual and weaving their own destiny. They each have purpose; they each have an elementary personality and soul. The human etheric body is the combined souls of all the billions and billions of atoms or cells in our body (Bailey, 1951–70, v. 1, p. 54). These individual tiny lives exist in three groups and compose respectively the four types of bodies: dense physical, etheric, astral and mental. The aggregate of these lives constitute in themselves four types of elementals or separate, coherent, though not self-conscious, existences. These are what the Ancient Wisdom calls the four Lunar Lords, known esoterically as the Imprisoning Cubes. Here is to be found the cross upon which the inner spiritual Man is to be crucified. These four elementals have an intelligence all their own, are upon the involutionary arc, and are following the law of their own being when they tend to become powerful, and thereby fully express that which is in them. It is interesting to note that the dominant and controlling Lunar Lord which is the sum-total of the physical, astral, and mental elementals, and is called by us "the Personality" feeds the lower centers with fiery forces, and has nothing to do with the etheric elemental. The Etheric Lord has an unique and curious position, being simply the vehicle for prana or life, and the center which it uses (the Spleen Center) exists in a category by itself (Bailey, 1951–70, v. 5, pp. 9–10).

From another angle we have to recognize that the lower mind element is the basic factor in the production of the etheric body. Whereas kama (desire) is the prime factor in calling the dense physical vehicle into being (Bailey, 1950a, pp. 144–45). But as we learn to understand the sounds of all these elementals and to hear the voice of the formless one (the Soul), and speak its language, which leads to the final liberation and which will in due time lead these lives themselves into the realm of self-consciousness (Bailey, 1951–70, v. 5, p. 10), so we will accept the intricate integration and interdependence of all these entities during their evolutionary development.

At this point I would like to offer you (from the Master DK) the suggested key phrases concerning these four elementary Lords whom we are responsible for. Which belongs to which, you ask? The Master replies, "Knowing that you will apprehend the implications and will seriously consider the purport" of these hints.

1. In the ordered regulation of the life comes eventual synthesis and the right control of time with all that eventuates therefrom.
2. In the right elimination of that which is secondary, and in a sense of rightly adjusted proportion comes that accuracy and one-pointedness which is the hallmark of the occultist.
3. In the right aspiration at the appointed time comes the necessary contact and the inspiration for the work that has to be done.
4. In the steady adherence to self-appointed rules comes the gradual refining of the instrument and the perfecting of the vehicles that will be—to the Master—the medium of help among many little ones (Bailey, 1951–70, v. 5, p. 11).

The etheric is the reflection of the soul, hence its purity. (Note that disorders of the etheric reception and distribution of prana, and of the web itself, originate from outside our etheric itself, cf. p. 187; also see Cosmic Fire, 1962, pp. 104–09.) It is thus the energy through which we as healers work. One of the other reasons for working through the etheric is that there is no such thing as consciousness upon these levels (p. 178). These four levels simply constitute the lowest correspondence to the four planes whereon the Monad and the Spiritual Triad are active, and upon those levels there is no such thing as consciousness as we understand it. There is only a state of being and of activity for which we have no adequate or illustrative words. The four higher planes of our solar system are the four cosmic etheric planes, and one of the lines of development is to function adequately in response to the life of the planetary Logos upon those planes. This constitutes the main field of unfoldment and of acquired wisdom for all initiates above the third degree.

Let us end this little esoteric section with a chart which encapsulates a lot of words and to which the trainee healer can return time after time:

Ether	Plane	Initiation	Karma	Center	Finger	Center	Energy	Note/Sound
1	Divine	4th	Personal	Head	Index	Point	Monad	D, F
2	Monadic	3rd	Mental	Heart	Middle	Triangle	Rays	G, E
3	Atmic	2nd	Astral	Throat	Ring	Petals	Soul	A, B
4	Buddhic	1st	Physical	Base, Sacral and Solar Plexus	Small	Circle	Personality	C

The emotional body

The emotional body, also called the astral or desire body, we know all too well. Through the astral body the soul is able to contact sensation (Bailey, 1973, p. 141). Dualistic in its activity, the emotional body is the see-saw of our sensations and feelings. On the scales we can be weighed down by sadness, grief, sorrow and depression, and on another occasion the pan can be tipped in the direction of joy, happiness, excitement, elation. But what are scales if not for balancing? The healing treatment endeavors to bring about a state of peace and equilibrium in this complex system of attraction and repulsion. The needle of the scales must be brought to the vertical point, and the pans on either side must remain poised and still. We hear echoes of ancient texts: "Remain in the world but not of it," "Be still and know," "He knows peace who has forgotten desire" *(Bhagavad Gita),* "There is no joy but calm" (Tennyson, 1842, p. 2)—all recommending detachment, non-attachment, and tranquillity as the basis of true happiness. Balance makes for contentment.

A Sea of Trouble

The astral body can be viewed as the source of all our troubles. It is symbolized by water, the ebb and flow of the tides, and by the waves of emotion. The majority of illnesses have their root in unbalanced emotions. Worry and stress, ambition and greed, hatred and selfishness, resentment and envy are the modern deadly "sins." All of them derive from an ignorance which thinks of nothing but itself. We are surrounded by the offsprings of ignorance every day of our lives. They are part of our existence. What happens in our homes and what happens in the world is the result of the emotional struggle of the pairs of opposites. These energies stream around us and around the world, at one moment fiery, angry, jagged, sharp and destructive. A moment later they are replaced by generosity, love, gentleness, compassion and support. A proverb says, "After the storm is calm." As Goethe once wrote, "On all the peaks lies peace" (Goethe, 1780).

Our emotional body is strongest—most whole—at the central point of balance between the two extremes. Balance gives it beauty and radiance and magnetism. The center is the transcendent point, the apex of the triangle, the bridge into a new dimension.

Upon the stream,
between the two extremes,
there floats the eye of vision.

A COAT OF MANY COLORS

How can healing help? Just as the etheric body's energy centers are connected to the etheric spine via the different endocrine glands, so the astral body is connected to the etheric body by swirling "buttons" (the size of saucers). The body of desire is colorful, like Joseph's many-colored coat. Energies of varying wavelengths are caught in the whirlpools, to which they are attracted magnetically. These centers act as transformers of emotional energy, conveying it to the relevant etheric center to be stepped down to the physical layer for the physiological functioning of the body. Thus the emotion of anger, say, towards one's spouse can cause sacral center problems such as inflammation of the uterus or prostate. If the anger is due to unexpressed personal fears and inhibitions we may find ulcers in the stomach or duodenum. These symptoms suggest what is going on in the emotional body of the patient. Symptoms, you might recall, express inhibited aspects of consciousness. Of course, the emotional energies are subtle and may take many years to manifest. Esoteric healing displays its power by treating the astral body as a whole to bring it into balance so that it may service higher or more purposeful energies. In other words, esoteric healing can aid the expression of negative aspects of consciousness before they damage the physical body. Put simply, esoteric healing is preventive medicine.

ASTRAL CENTERS

So let's outline the centers of the emotional body and their relation to specific emotional polarities.

Center	Balanced expression	Astral Extremes
HEAD	Desire for a spiritual purpose	Pernickety – Fantasy
AJNA	Directs the energy of desire	Over-vigilant – Delusory
THROAT	Desire to serve others	Vanity – Servitude
HEART	Unconditional and impersonal love	Self-absorption – Over-distanced
SOLAR PLEXUS	Desire for pleasure	Addiction – Glamorization
SACRAL	Desire to regenerate and protect	Perversion – Married to God
BASE	Will to have	Acquisitiveness – Unearthly

The mental body

The outermost envelope of human energies is the mental sheath or body. This is the body where thinking takes form. Here the intellect governs, and abstract ideas can become working ideals. Many terms describe the mental body: rational, intellectual, deductive, analytical, logical, knowledgeable and even philosophical. By these terms it is clear that we are talking about a mind which thinks and concludes. Compared to the warmth and embrace and closeness that the astral body can exude, the mind can seem cold and distant.

Like the etheric and astral bodies, the mental vehicle has its main centers of force as well as its secondary or minor centers. To reiterate, these centers in the several bodies are connected and are within each other. The only separation, differentiated energy, or vibration that distinguishes, say, the astral heart center from the mental or etheric heart centers is the fact of the energy itself.

In the world today there are comparatively few persons who actually "live in their head," whereas the percentage of those who "think with their emotions" is upwards of ninety percent. This might account for the vast populations in India, Africa, China and South America where education is limited and mental stimulation practically nonexistent. Even in the West we could say that the majority of people, even though literate and numerate, are more inclined to emotional living than to intellectual pursuits.

The Mental Centers

The mental centers and their major focus of energy express themselves in the following way:

Head Center	philosophical thinking
Ajna Center	thoughts of personality, will, and ambition
Throat Center	creative thought or deductive reasoning
Heart Center	thoughts of compassion
Solar Plexus Center	mental desires
Sacral Center	thoughts about family affairs, personal education
Base Center	mental drives leading to intellectual achievements

Let us review our brief introduction to the anatomy of the personality, looking at it as a whole.

The personality

The personality comprises the mental, emotional and physical bodies. People assert themselves through their personality. Depending on where their consciousness is focused, they will be either emotionally expressive, mentally expressive, or both. One person may have as the basic drive in life the emotional path, where desires are expressed, along with fears, wants and hopes, passions and pleasures, while engaging in very little intellectual activity. Another person might be more polarized in the mind, appearing "cold" and over-rational. Such a person is probably a scientist or an intellectual while having very little time for feelings and desires. The person can think things through clearly, and does not easily get trapped in fears and phobias. But the person might not communicate love well.

BALANCE

Balanced people are somewhere between these two extremes. They have an intellectual bent and a general knowledge of the world while also having the ability to express themselves emotionally in pleasures and through family bonds. They regard extreme behavior as harmful and damaging to individuals and to the overall health of the wider community and planet. An emotional extremist, however, gets caught up in psychic practices or embroiled in phobias. Some people have been forced into situations of emotional instability due to circumstances and conditioning. I am not condemning or judging them. In healing this is never done; we try simply to listen, to look, and to love. Every person is different. Everyone has particular gifts and problems. Everyone is trying to find something more meaningful, more fulfilling and sustaining, whether it be in personal relationships, in work, in the home, in the environment, or in the inner life.

Now, we have had a brief tour of the several bodies of the personality, noticing in a general way how each expresses itself. You will find the word "expressing" cropping up. What is expressing, or rather *who* is being expressed through the mind, the emotions, the vital and physical bodies? The soul. The soul also has modes of expressing itself. These are called the soul bodies.

The soul bodies

The other component of concrete thinking—the wellspring of intellectual concepts, percepts and deductions—is the abstract thinking faculty, the realm of ideas and formless thoughts. This "upper" part of the mental body is called abstract mind, or, more usually, the soul. The soul is beyond personality influence. Thought ceases. There are no desires. The emotional loves and hates have been left behind. In the realm of the soul there is a sense of tranquillity and composure, a tranquillity which is not passive and inert, but poised and ready to act. What is this state and how can we get into it? The soul is immersed in a sea of illusion, hence it is necessary to interact with physical reality, which means suffering resulting in wisdom (Bailey, 1973). (The esoteric reason for this is explained later, in Chapter 4.) In soul consciousness, the essence of everything is available; there is no longer concern with details; the world is a world of realities, where deception is not only impossible, but also unthinkable. As souls we no longer deal with emotions, ideas, or conceptions, but with the thing in itself (Leadbeater [1925] quoted in Powell, 1978).

WHERE IS THE SOUL?

Personality problems and actions, joys and sorrows, wishes, hopes, and ideals do not exist in this "place." The soul dimension is different altogether, a place where there is no space/time, and no polar opposites. The trouble is that since it is so totally different, not many people know what this place is, let alone how to get there! Popular deluders and spiritual hoaxers are quick to sell phony admission tickets. What we have to remember, however, is that consciousness houses all states from the lowest to the highest. We have the capacity to witness them, to identify with them and to develop them. Everything from the lowest to the highest is moving, growing, evolving in consciousness.

Through the processes of life and living, growth is achieved. It is as though we have a flowering plant within us representing the states of consciousness we have won. Some people's "plant" is a tender shoot with only a few leaves on it. Primitive people, they might be struggling to survive, thinking mostly about finding food and shelter. Other people's "plant" might be much larger, having branches growing in many directions. These people have found the ability to work and influence others, and to be of service to their fellows, while getting their daily bread and protecting their family. Then there is a person's "plant" which has become a strong, beautiful, flowering tree with fruits sweet and abundant. These are people who have developed a still wider consciousness and who are working in more profound dimensions. They can help humanity to make changes that will be beneficial to its future. These are the "saviours" of our planet. Of course, there are many stages between these different grades, but it illustrates how people grow in consciousness. And the purpose of evolution is to develop consciousness. In the human stage of evolution the purpose is to evolve the causal body, that is, to gain wisdom from experience (Lansdowne, 1987). Again, this is not a condemnation or judgment of the lower stages or of any stage. It is simply an observation, a recognition of the essential and necessary steps that must take place on the road to heaven.

Heaven is the same as the soul. "The kingdom of heaven is within you," said Jesus. "Seek ye the kingdom of heaven and all will be given unto you," he said also. Some people "take heaven by storm," meaning that by strict training, anyone can gain higher consciousness. The soul is a state of mind but not of thought.

The healer in esoteric healing is called to enter the consciousness of the soul and from there to do the work. This might at first seem to be an impossible task. Thankfully it is not! Luckily, we are in the position to enter the soul because the soul is only one step further than we are at present. It is the next state of achievement for humanity. What's more, the healer works in the patient's soul as it expresses itself via the etheric body. From there we have easy access to the higher consciousness of the patient. While the next step for the mind (intellect) is the soul, the next goal of science (and of the physical body) is the etheric body.

Another important way to view the soul is as the principle of sentiency. Underlying all outer manifestation, pervading all forms, and constituting the consciousness of God is the principle of sentiency. The stages of sensitivity through this soul principle mark the stages and king-doms of the world and of heaven. Simply owning sentiency produces space, the environment. As soon as this "ground" becomes qualitative, reactive to another, the other, the not-self, we find matter (the mineral kingdom). Later, as this develops (in time and space), plants emerge in all their diversity; from them evolve the animals; then come humans who then advance into higher realms of experience, known as aspirants, dis-ciples, initiates, masters, *nirmanakayas,* and gods. Esoterically, you will understand, the most advanced began these life-processes first, whereas the least advanced, which we see today as stones and metals, atoms and elements, began their evolutionary development latest or most recently. They are our younger brethren. This, of course, gives a new perspective to Darwinism and neo-Darwinism.

THE SOUL IN THE WORLD

The human, the soul, has struggled through the centuries, master-ing life in a most remarkable way. Now many of us no longer need to go out with our spears or guns, spades and tractors to get our food. A few do it for us. And we do other things for them. We no longer have to cut down trees and build fires to keep warm. A few do it for us. We no longer have to build houses and make clothing. A few do it for us. We no longer have to be on the lookout all the time for bandits and thieves. A few do it for us. And so on. When these groups of "few" interact, we get a community, a nation, a world—a world of human beings locked in interdependence with the world around us. There's still a lot to do for our world. Improvements are needed, greater understanding is needed, more cooperation is needed, greater sharing is necessary—before the goal can be achieved for which we entered this sphere of suffering. We have a way to go before these ideals are tangible. We are struggling to mount the slopes of mind. At times they are steep. But, more and more, man is moving into these greater heights with a wider, more inclusive view. And some are already mounting higher. They are the pioneers. Some of these pioneers are the esoteric healers.

A SOUL'S LADDER

The soul's "garments" are the personality. They are threefold: un-derclothes, a suit, and a coat (physical-etheric body, emotional body, and mental body). The soul works through these. The physical is divided into visible form and the invisible (to most people), vitality being the power which enables the dense form to function. The soul body is beyond personality consciousness, yet the personality is the threefold expression of the soul. So let's look at the soul more closely.

The soul is also threefold. Each of the soul's bodies directly influences the personality bodies. This is wonderful to know, for the personality is like a ladder which comes down from heaven for us to ascend!

The Soul's Ladder (the Cosmic Egg)

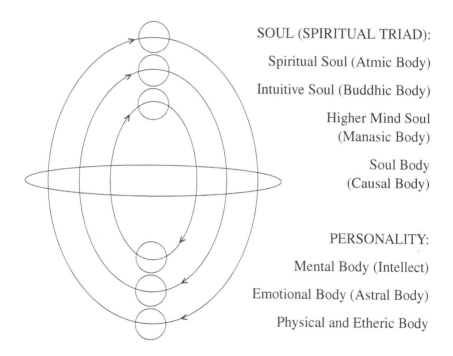

SOUL (SPIRITUAL TRIAD):

Spiritual Soul (Atmic Body)

Intuitive Soul (Buddhic Body)

Higher Mind Soul
(Manasic Body)

Soul Body
(Causal Body)

PERSONALITY:

Mental Body (Intellect)

Emotional Body (Astral Body)

Physical and Etheric Body

You see these interactive steps? We will start from the higher mind.

The higher mind

The higher mind incorporates: the Soul, the Causal Body and the Mental Permanent Atom. All these terms must be explained and then experienced by the esoteric healer.

AWAKENING THE SOUL

The higher mind links with the mental body via the soul or what is called the *antahkarana,* the bridge. These two aspects of the soul, its two basic qualities, bring into being the human kingdom and enable man to contact both the lower kingdoms in nature and the higher spiritual realities. The first, the quality of mind in its lower manifestation, is owned potentially by every atom in every form in every kingdom in nature. Such intelligence is a part of the body's nature, inherent and potential, and is the real basis of brotherhood, of absolute unity, of universal synthesis, and of divine coherence in manifestation. The other, the higher aspect, is the principle of self-awareness, and when combined with the lower aspect produces the self-consciousness of the human being (Bailey, 1951–70, v. 1, p. 55).

There is a real and established connection with the higher mind by the personality, but it is unconscious at first. That is, we can live perfectly reasonably without any "higher awareness." But as the consciousness unfolds and the personality gains wider and profounder experience, both through suffering and pain as well as through the wonder of achievement and human interconnections, there starts the process of questioning and "wakening up to the spirit." This opens up the person to a whole new world of beauty and of causes. What was before simply accepted and worked with, now is questioned and subjected to rigorous tests and trials. If physicists, for example, hadn't questioned and tested the boundaries of perception, we would never have realized the theory of relativity or quantum theory. The veil is being pierced which separates the subtler levels of insight and realization from the more "earthbound" emotions and thoughts. At first these insights are few and far between, but they come regularly enough to keep the person searching, like the donkey after the carrot. Sometimes this insight is so strong and so totally different from one's normal way of thinking that the person can change completely from being one kind of person to being, for example, very religious, or rigidly vegetarian, or ambitiously political. The ray of vision may, of course, work the other way, making the person depressed, insecure, and motiveless. Esoteric healing can help much to alleviate these symptoms.

THE CAUSAL BODY AND SOUL BODY

The causal body, found in the higher mind, is the part of the soul that absorbs all the good, the pure, the true, the beautiful that is done in the personality life. In so doing it leaves behind all the dross, the unclean, the lies and unkindnesses, and everything that goes against the law of love and brotherliness and progress. Hence, when a baby is born, it is innocent, pure, and untainted, for it is the direct result of the causal body's expression of the last life.

The so-called permanent atoms are found within the causal body. Each permanent atom is a kind of policeman or guardian angel for each of the temporary bodies. Thus we have a guardian angel of the physical body—looking after (watching over and keeping records of) all the good, true and beautiful done in the physical life. There is a guardian of the emotional body—watching and recording the same in the emotional life. And there is a permanent atom of the mental body, a being who guards and files all the good, true and beautiful done via the mind and intellect. These are all held in the causal body for safekeeping and are used during the formation of the new bodies each time we come down to a new birth. So with every new incarnation we can become more advanced (or rather, more like our true self, the soul) than the last life. This is the law of evolution, which is the law leading to perfection and enlightenment. It is clear that there will be deficiencies in each permanent atom. Since we are not perfect and have not developed each body perfectly (as shown in our actions, words and thoughts), called the Path of Initiation, the deficiencies in each permanent atom (physical actions, emotional control, and mental understanding) will come out as imperfections or diseases, to make us aware of the area needing development and incorporation into our consciousness. Such is the thoughtfulness of life!

Notice the law of polarity at work governing the work of the causal body. Our real design is to pass beyond the controls of the opposites and realize a world of non-distinction, a vision of oneness, wholeness; a realization that all is in the one and the one is in the all: Unity. This is the mark of a high initiate, a mark leading away from the world of effects and into the world of causes, a mark which eventually brings about the destruction of the causal body itself and signals the entry into a new world of service not requiring any further births on earth. However, until that time, we are under the rule of causal polarity. This means that whatever we do will be attracted to one or other of the polarities, sometimes referred to as "good karma" and "bad karma." Whatever we sow, we will reap.

Good karma is everything that is helpful, beneficial, loving, selfless, up-building, or what we say is good. Bad karma results from actions that are counterproductive, selfish, destroying, damaging, hurtful, malevolent, or what we term "evil." The "good" is gathered by the causal body's permanent atoms (according to whichever body carried out the action, and usually a combination of all of them); the bad or evil is gathered in the opposite pole to the causal, waiting until we have cleared the debt necessary to be accepted into the higher register. Such debt is termed "samsara" in Buddhism, meaning it is the transient and ever-changing trap which binds us to ever-repeated rebirths. These energies are then used by the soul, working through the causal body, to build another body for further refining in the world. (Said in a more esoteric way, these energies are then used by the soul, working through the causal body, to build another body from the planetary substance for further refining in this world, leading eventually to restoration or resurrection of the planetary life and the liberation of the life called "human being.") They act as nuclei to attract the relevant "particles" of matter (mental, astral or physical) from the highest aspect of these bodies (governed by the permanent atom of that body) to the lowest vibration (governed by the polarity). (There is an occult hint here which I do not wish to expand on, but it relates to the whole question of eventual abandonment of the need to incarnate.)

This helps us to know who we are, and why we are the way we are in our different personality bodies. The liberating principle, if we could but put it into practice, is to balance and accept ourselves as we are, to see ourselves as whole (through our imperfection into which we were born) and walk on, keeping to the fulcrum point, the middle way, the present moment. Toward this awareness the esoteric healer works. It is this that resolves the causal polarity and obliterates disease, each disease relating to a specific causal polarity.... If you can't understand any of this, don't worry, move on and read it again some other time.

Here are just a few of the marvelous qualities to be found in the soul: love, inclusiveness, joy, sharing, loneliness (or spiritual aloneness), impersonality, detachment, freedom, serenity, tranquillity, responsibility, wisdom, intuition, a sense of the unfolding Plan for human evolution.

The intuitive soul

The intuitive part of the soul incorporates the intuition, and the intuitional permanent atom. Please refer to Chart I earlier in Chapter 3. The intuition concerns unity and is the capacity of the Self to contact other Selves. We no longer identify with the former not-self (Bailey, 1962, p. 201). On the intuitional plane we find our planetary Logos's centers or chakras, connected to the fourth ether of man. The whole of the intuitive soul, being the middle aspect of this upper or higher or spiritual triad, is related via the soul in the higher mind to the middle principle of the personality, which is the emotional body. The spiritual triad consists of the abstract mind, the intuition and the spiritual will, called in this book the soul. Viewed from the personality these phases of consciousness are indeed spiritual, hence esoteric healing incorporates spiritual healing while also involving the monadic levels of being.

The spiritual soul

Little can be said of this level, for it lies ahead on the Path for most of us. The spiritual soul incorporates: the highest aspect of the spiritual triad, the true purpose and will of the soul, and the spiritual or atmic permanent atom. This exalted part of man, an area of our consciousness which is very different from the personality part, is related via the soul-in-the-higher-mind to the lowest aspect of the personality, the physical body. Only in our highest ideals can we conceive of consciousness in the spiritual triad. Healers who have triadal consciousness and who can, via the spiritual triad, exercise the potency of the will and monadic life, will always be successful healers (Bailey, 1951–70, v. 4, p. 547).

THE BRIDGE

Notice that all the communications between the higher mind, intuition and spirit and the personality are done via the soul aspect in the higher mind. Thus the soul acts as a bridge between the spiritual world and the world of the personality. Once the bridge has been crossed, or can be crossed backwards and forwards without fear of falling off, so to say, then the specific dimensions of the intuitional soul and spiritual soul open up to experience. Until such time, those higher dimensions are stepped down so that the soul in the higher mind can experience them. In this respect the soul acts like a transformer. (Refer to Chart I and the diagram earlier in Chapter 3.)

The permanent atoms in the three soul bodies are virtually unused and remain like unfertilized seeds, pure and angelic, until such time as the bodies of the spiritual triad begin to be used. Then they will act exactly like the permanent atoms of the personality bodies. It requires building yet another bridge, which will be built only when the first bridge between the personality and the soul is no longer needed. How this bridge is built and how we have to dig away the dirt, impediments and debris is described in certain of the healing triangles and elsewhere.

The monad

The subtle anatomy of the human being has now been outlined. The life of the human being first expresses itself via a spiritual triad that is focussed in the soul, that is, in the consciousness of the higher mind. This threefold body manifests on earth as a personality in the form of a mind, emotions, and a physical-and-vital body. The monad is the source of light, not only to the human family, but also to the planet acting as the receiver of light from the threefold Sun. It is the lens through which the light of the Solar Logos can flow to the planetary Logos, preserving and holding steady in that light the vision, the purpose, the will, and the creative intention of the planetary Logos (Bailey, 1944, v. 2, p. 400). The monad is the real, immortal part of man. The head is analogous to the spirit aspect, which on the physical plane corresponds to the two eyes (Bailey, 1951–70, v. 4, p. 165). In the soul the monad manifests as the "Jewel in the Lotus," and the life thread or the *sutratma,* which is embodied in the heart center. Further, the monad is the real individual identity who is struggling to get to know herself so that she can be of service to her fellows and to the planet on which she has been assigned a specified task—a task which is unique to each one of us, but one that is compatible and ultimately cooperative with those of all the others. This is the grand purpose and plan for humanity (sixty billion human monads, of whom only some eight percent are in incarnation at any one time)—a purpose and plan we are only just beginning to understand and comprehend. (For more on this theme, see Appendix A at the end of Chapter 8.) In time we will really know, and then we will even more wholeheartedly throw ourselves into the work. At present it is but dimly visioned and we move on practically in the dark, led and encouraged by a few who have traveled a little further on the way and who know the terrain. But at times we are misled by some who misunderstood the indications, or who deliberately misinform the gullible, or mistakenly acted on a false notion of the ancient teaching.[2] We will know about the Plan, as understood by those Masters who have learned the lessons and transmuted certain qualities, when we have related the monad to the personality, a way called "the Sushumna Path" (Bailey, 1951–70, v. 4, p. 183). All we know about this Plan at the present stage of our evolutionary development is that we are to develop and establish good will and right human relations.

4.

THE PURPOSE OF DISEASE

The whole question of healing, whether it involves taking a medicine, or having a manipulation or receiving some form of counseling, or in some other way, inevitably requires someone to be the receiver, the patient, the client, the case—the one who is "ill" and needs help. On the other side is the therapist, or healer—the doctor who tries to get the patient well. Between the two sides there is an exchange of energy. The transaction begins as soon as the patient asks for help. Something further occurs when medication is given. Some patients get well, some do not, some respond quickly, others slowly, some develop secondary problems, some change their habits permanently, others do not or feel they cannot, and so on. These are some of the many aspects of any form of medication or therapy. Again, we are dealing with energy: energy absorption—energy rejection, energy referral—energy deferral, energy reflection—energy deflection, energy invocation—energy evocation. A tablet or a mixture of herbs is but a mental pattern, picture or symbol, a specific energy combination formulated to suit a particular patient with a particular set of symptoms. If this is imperfectly conceived, the remedy won't work properly. Should there be a good resonance between the two, however, the person will get better. A healer is working in the same way, but the "tablet" we offer is unpackaged, acting directly in some subtle body or sub-plane of the personality consciousness on the cause that is blocking or hindering higher (soul) energy from expressing itself. Acting on this causative level is the ideal "time-release," for the healing energy then has to filter down to the physical body. The effectiveness of the healing depends on the readiness of the patient to express more of who the real self is. And since this readiness is frequently inadequate or weak, the symptoms usually persist and the patient (forced by the symptoms to face this weakness) returns week after week for further treatments.

Results in the present

In medicine of whatever form, from surgery to esoteric healing, we are dealing with the patient's past. Put simply, all illness and disease is the result of the individual's past. Confronting this reality is like gazing up at the stars at night. Every twinkling light that is reaching your eyes is at least four years old, and in the case of some stars, thousands of years old. The light you are seeing left its source thousands of years ago; the reality is not there! Similarly, the patient we greet is not the real person, not the source of their expressed light. But in healing we go up to meet the star itself, the source, the soul, the patient's true self.

From the simple physical level, there is a cause and an effect. For instance, when a person does not eat a balanced diet, the result will be digestive disturbances. Any form of abuse will lead eventually to illness. But some diseases defy people's understanding. "He was such an outstanding athlete, ate properly, worked hard, cared. You couldn't have met a nicer person and one in better health. Why then did he suddenly have kidney failure?" In esoteric healing we are permitted in some measure to know the meaning, to get the answers.

Causes of illness

The esoteric healer recognizes that there is to be found in one or more of his bodies—physical, emotional and mental—the cause of an illness. Generally speaking, physical diseases are of ancient origin, whereas mental illnesses are the most recent. The idea is that illness "descends" from subtle levels down into the physical, like silt in a stream. By the time it reaches the physical, the "point of friction" is usually old, rather well established, and the person's consciousness has been conditioned to believe it is unable to express the higher counterpart of this kind of energy in the present life. Normally, the energy is inherited at least from a past incarnation. This idea is not new. It is well known that stress or anxiety, for example, is a precursor of irritable bowel syndrome, colitis, gastric ulcer, headaches, stiff neck and shoulders. Illness from a certain angle is nothing but an imbalance of energy flow from one body to the next due to the misuse of force by individuals or by groups in some earlier life or in this (Bailey, 1951–70, v. 4, p. 112). Such imbalance can result in physiological changes, psychological disturbances or mental imbalance. Simply put, these are the areas where balance or harmony must be restored for healing or cure to be effected. This is what every therapist or doctor recognizes, whether consciously or unconsciously. So our first task is to understand the source of disease.

We can blame no one for the illness we have

We cannot even blame ourselves (that is, the self of this incarnation). This is not easy to accept, especially when it is recollected how parents may have fed their children, abused them, or injured them emotionally by restriction or anger, or mentally tormented them through subtle means. The best that can be done is to acknowledge the injustice and realize that it was due to the individual who is meant to learn something from it for the future. As you sow, so you reap.

This principle (as hard and as cruel as it sounds) includes all illnesses met with, whether they come to us from outside, as it were, by bacterial or viral invasion of our bodies (which then causes the body to erupt and react and which can then become chronic and go on for years), or come from within, lodged in one or other of the subtle bodies and seemingly impossible to grasp or extract or extinguish. In whatever circumstance the illness shows itself to you, the illness belongs to you. It is yours. You have caused it to come to you. After all, the symptoms of disease are those aspects of your consciousness not being expressed by you. They are qualities being inhibited and repressed.

We may not understand the set of circumstances which led you to this outcome but knowledge of the reason is not necessary to acknowledge a reality. For some reason, you chose your parents, you chose the country and place of your birth, you chose the environment in which you grew up, you chose the influences that steered you into different activities, and finally you chose the illness that you have. And are we not all ill in one form or another? Through these various circumstances we are learning to gather experiences for a fuller expression of our soul life. We choose these things so that we can learn something about ourselves which we could not have learned in any other way.

More than this, and this is the Ancient Wisdom's wonderful explanation of the problem of disease, the illnesses we experience have nothing to do with us in reality; we are actually permitting the faults of the planetary life to be transformed through our conscious handling of the symptoms. We are doing it as an act of love for the healing of the planet. Let me try to explain.

Every one of the human family (sixty billion of us, including souls not incarnated in a physical body) is handling an aspect of this Being's tragic betrayal. When this great Life went astray in a cosmic sense, which is beyond our present spiritual comprehension, its whole organism collapsed in a kind of coma-like paralysis (more fully explained in Appendix at the end of Chapter 8). Understanding this should help us deal with disease and illness with greater acceptance and intelligence. As a hierarchy or collective, before time began, we chose together to sacrifice our monadic consciousness, our oneness and harmony with the Divine for the purposes of Another, an Unknown Brother who had in some way misconstrued the Plan. Like a brother, we went over to offer our assistance. To cross this cosmic barrier meant a complete forsaking of everything we had and were. For this reason, humanity as a whole is esoterically called both the Lords of Sacrifice and the Lords of Love. To save this planetary Initiate, the human hierarchy (including and involving all kingdoms) had to enter and identify with the body, the atomic structure, of this dis-eased Being. We can see by this that it is only by taking matter into ourselves (and we do this by "getting into earthly bodies"), matter which has been "both tainted by origin and tainted by alienation" (as explained in an ancient text) that we are actually able to spiritualize it. Such a sacrifice takes pain and suffering, endured in love and knowledge of the truth. In this way we will "restore the Plan on Earth, and seal the door where evil dwells." The pain and suffering which we experience by having waking consciousness in the body of flesh (let alone in a diseased state mentally, emotionally or physically) is traumatic and distressing to the spirit or monadic self. Indeed, most people can only endure it for sixteen hours a day before our higher self must be returned to itself (in unconsciousness), for that is its sacrifice, which we call sleep. Pain in itself is the guardian of the form and the protector of substance; it warns of danger; it indicates certain definite stages in the evolutionary process; it is related to the principle whereby the soul identifies itself with substance. When the identification ceases, pain and disease and also death lose their hold and the man stands free, because disease and death are qualities inherent in form, as it has become for this poor, lost, deranged Lord.

Esoteric views of the nature of disease and its cure are not widely known, even by long-standing esoteric students. They need not be regarded as true, but hypothetically possible; and until we know, let us simply acknowledge that it may be so.

The sacrifice of the solar angels brought the fourth or human kingdom into being. The "returning nirvanis" (as they are called in esoteric literature), with deliberation and full understanding, took human bodies in order to raise those lower forms of life nearer to the goal. These were and are ourselves. The "Lords of Knowledge and Compassion and of Ceaseless Persevering Devotion" (another name for us as a group) chose to die in order that lesser lives might live, and this sacrifice has made possible the evolution of the indwelling consciousness of Deity. This consciousness, having worked its way through the subhuman kingdoms in nature, needed the activity of the solar angels to make further progress possible. Herein lies

a. Our service to the Being of Life, through sacrifice and death;
b. Our service to other souls, through deliberate self-sacrificing purpose;
c. Our service to other forms of life in other kingdoms.

Taking a body is occultly considered to be death. But we are the angels who "chose to die, and in dying, lived." Through this sacrifice, matter is lifted up into a higher state. This is the mystery hinted at in the world Scriptures, the secret of the ages. It fills the pages of *The Secret Doctrine* by H. B. Blavatsky and the books by Alice Bailey. We cannot arrive at the realization of that supreme sacrifice that we made with deliberation in the early dawn of time (cf. Bailey, 1951–70, v. 2, p. 92).

Disease or illness is an opportunity

The pure Monad, the true Self, has taken fallen substance as his/her body. This substance is matter practically devoid of light. The Monad tries to express its pure light through this substance, however it is fractured, ruptured, distorted, disturbed. These dis-eased symptoms of substance are called FRACTORS. Everything, be it in thought, feeling or action, that does not sparkle with the pure gentle light of love, happiness and the simplicity of goodness is a fractor of the real you. Throughout life we work to remove or transform these fractors. In esoteric healing such fractoral removal means life transformation and a greater expression of health on all levels.

We have chosen everything that has happened to us up till now, the present, and if we are ill, we accept this as a fractor self-induced. We now can turn and face the future. "This is what I am now, but what am I to be in the time to come?" The future is fashioned by how we deal with our present state (we are predestined eventually to work with spiritual law). All healing methods are about working with energy and about trying to alter the vibratory rate of the flow of energies in the body. We can respond positively to the disease and gain a greater awareness. Or we can be passive and unconscious of the presented opportunity.

Our Life can feel threatened, tested by stress, illness or disease. How will we handle the challenge? Will we give in to the disease's transforming powers and opportunity, which have arisen as a result of the pure inner monadic light having been "fractored" by the planetary substance we have taken on as a body, and die (and this stage is frequently necessary—some people will resist this with all their might, prolonging the fight, and holding the door closed despite the inevitability of the illness to end in death, but again this is necessary for them to experience). If, however, the disease is shaken off, the person is transformed and returns to life a different person. We go through something of our own past, fight it by means of our present consciousness, and overcome it. A door is opened and we meet a new set of possibilities. That which was resisted and feared is restored to self-consciousness and the person becomes a little more whole. (See Appendix A at the end of Chapter 8 for a full disclosure of our origin and our esoteric purpose.)

The immune system

Disease usually appears to come from "out there" and less so from within. But recently there has been much talk of the breakdown of the immune system being the cause of all illness. Of course, in our understanding of the subtler causes of disease, that is not really quite accurate. The immune system breakdown is itself the result of some other cause. Looking at it from an energy level, we can say that the immune system, as the first line of defense, resists change. From the angle of energy descending through the subtle vehicles, the system acts as the last gateway, while also contributing positively to change. Simply put, when disease approaches, there is within us a barrier and a buffer which will:

a. Resist and defeat.
b. Resist and be changed.
c. Resist and be defeated.

In the first instance (resist and defeat), the immune system is well equipped. It probably has met the invader before and quickly routs it. In healthy people this happens all the time. It means we can do the changing and developing of consciousness on a deeper level. But when there is a need to develop the kind of consciousness which cannot be done by the mind alone, then the immune system breaks down, and with the aid of outside help (medications of whatever sort), the defenses (immunoglobulins) are strengthened and the illness is defeated (resist and be changed). With its defeat comes added strength to the immune system, which can be summoned again if needed. In the third case (resist and be defeated), the body says, "This time I cannot move on in life without the process of dying and death." This is a difficult decision for some people to take, especially younger ones, and sometimes it will be drawn out, often very painfully, over a number of years.

Resist and be changed

Let us proceed to the second category, "to resist and be changed." How esoteric healing affects disease actually includes all three forms of change, but appears to be more applicable to the second insofar as it involves the flow of daily life. The first change is not noticed, the last change ends life. Disease is the result of the past. Now we have to move one step closer to understanding it: disease *is* the past. When we get ill, we are meeting with some aspect of our past that we cannot accept, and which now is confronting us. This is what is called a "fractor"—an aspect within the substance of ourselves with which we are now better equipped to deal. You often hear ill people calling out, "Why me?" and "Why now?" Part of the answer is, any part of the past which was not resolved is held in the body (mental, emotional or physical) to be worked out later.

Let's explain further. Earlier we noted that when humans express the good, the true, and the beautiful, we are exhibiting the only aspects of our lives that have any lasting effect. Whatever else transpires during our little lives is of no real consequence. Yet nothing is really lost. What we are is only an expression of a whole host of memories. When we are born, we are innocent—that is the revelation of our causal body and its permanent atoms. As we grow, things that were faced in the past, but were not turned into good, have to be faced again. But because they belong to the past and should have been overcome then, their return is often much more urgent. They demand resolution and change *now*. This is disease. We face the past, we face our past, we face ourselves. Moreover, disease is not simply a fight with past failures, it is actually a release. Until we have faced disease (and even death), we will be bound or held by the ropes of earlier opportunities that have turned into present restriction. These ties have to be cut, or be unraveled and thrown off. So, from disease we gain greater freedom, which will result in greater achievement and fulfillment. Through this process of transmuting the past, we help the purification and restoration of the life of the planet earth.

5.

OUR MAJOR LIFE CENTERS

Dealing with the phantoms, apparitions, chimeras or illusions of the past in the form of present illness alters energies in our other bodies and centers. Healers must be aware of the qualities and influences of the major etheric centers. Balancing the energies in a center is one thing, but working with the centers of energy as vortices in a finely tuned circuit is quite another process. Esoteric healing entails (i) pouring energy into the center that governs the troubled area of the physical body, stimulating the center higher than the one controlling the particular area and, (ii) by intensification of the higher center, reducing the vitality of the lower. These two ways of using energy and thought are the two fundamental methods of directing energy to diseased areas (Bailey, 1951–70, v. 2, p. 284). These in turn are related to the two major predisposing causes of physical trouble arising within the physical organism, namely, the understimulation or the overstimulation of the centers (p. 283).

The incoming energy is transmuted within the center into forces, that is, the primary energy is differentiated into secondary energies. The rate of transmutation, the strength of the resultant aggregation of forces, and the subsequent radiatory activity (causing the dense physical body to be conditioned) are dependent upon the extent of the unfoldment of the particular center involved and upon its awakened or unawakened state. The outgoing forces from a center play upon the "nadis," which are the etheric counterpart of the entire intricate network of nerves constituting the nervous system. This network of nadis affects people according to its life pattern, which is governed by the personality ray (Bailey, 1951–70, v. 4, pp. 195–96).

Although a deeper description of the rays and the centers must await a later book, let's take a brief look here. (For more about the rays, see Chapter 10.) I need to say something briefly about the rays and the centers although I do not want it to sound too technical or complicated, but it is something to be aware of in your future work as esoteric healing practitioners. What I want to say is this: One ray rules one center at any particular period in a person's life. However, the center will differ depending upon which stage we are on the evolutionary ladder. For example, in an average person (a person not on the Path), Ray Three rules the sacral center, but it rules the throat center of the disciple and the ajna center of the initiate (after the third initiation) (p. 121). For simplicity, according to the science of esoteric healing, the following is the general standard:

Ray One rules the head center.
Ray Two rules the heart center.
Ray Three rules the sacral center.
Ray Four rules the base center.
Ray Five rules the throat center.
Ray Six rules the solar plexus center.
Ray Seven rules the ajna center.

Ray Three also rules the spleen center as well as the alta major center, and Ray Six rules the vagus nerve center. For those who would go on to utilize the details of this information as practitioners of Esoteric Healing, I will tabulate the rulerships according to the three stages of evolutionary development: average person, disciple, and initiate.

	Average Person	**Disciple**	**Initiate**
Ray I	Heart	Base	Head
Ray II	Solar Plexus	Head	Heart
Ray III	Sacral	Throat	Ajna
Ray IV	Throat	Sacral	Base
Ray V	Ajna	Solar Plexus	Throat
Ray VI	Head	Heart	Solar Plexus
Ray VII	Base	Ajna	Sacral

These each form powerful triangles that could be used to heal and would be especially useful in the individual where any one center has a problem, providing the healer is able to discern the patient's place on the Path. Remember the esoteric principle of empowering the higher and reducing the vitality of the lower.

Now, for the sake of clarity, let us see how this looks from the angle of the centers, working from average person, disciple, initiate:

	Average Person	**Disciple**	**Initiate**
Head Center—Rays	VI Neptune	II Uranus (Heart of Sun)	I Pluto
Ajna Center—Rays	V Venus	VII Uranus	III Saturn
Throat Center—Rays	IV Mercury	III Saturn	V Venus
Heart Center—Rays	I Vulcan	VI Neptune	II Jupiter
Solar Plexus Center—Rays	II Sun	V Venus	VI Mars/Neptune
Sacral Center—Rays	III Earth	IV Moon (Saturn)	VII Uranus
Base Center—Rays	VII Pluto	I Pluto	IV Pluto

Let's also look at the details of the stages on the Path in the sequence of the rays to the centers:

Rays	**Average Person Centers**	**Disciple Centers**	**Initiate Centers**
I	Heart	Base	Head
II	Solar Plexus	Head	Heart
III	Sacral	Throat	Ajna
IV	Throat	Sacral	Base
V	Ajna	Solar Plexus	Throat
VI	Head	Heart	Solar Plexus
VII	Base	Ajna	Sacral

EXERCISE

1. If you are gaining sensitivity and you are unsure which ray governs each center, align, attune with your higher self, and then connect with each of the seven rays as you hold each center—a response will be forthcoming. You must remain completely objective and detached

as to the result. Get your results confirmed by another esoteric healer if necessary.

2. You can also use this method to find out your Ray Chart (the ray of your soul, personality, mental body, emotional body and physical body) saving you much time and effort in reading and being confused by the intricacy of the subject. After proper preparation (alignment and attunement with your soul) esoterically place one hand into your soul energy and scan each ray from one through seven to get a response. You will *know* which has the greatest response. You can also use this method to find out your sub-rays. But mind, you always keep objective and detached; work on yourself as if on a stranger.

It is the condition of the centers which produces, basically, all the difficulties, permitting entrance to infections and germs which might not otherwise cause trouble (Bailey, 1951–70, v. 4, p. 207). These rays and centers are related to the two major psychological types, for according to the temperament so will be the types of disease, and the temperament is dependent upon the ray quality; these types are the extroverts and the introverts (p. 66). The problem today is that more and more people are working with the spiritual, aspiring to be seers, and too little with practical down-to-earth living offering a service to the community in which they live. Such aspiration tends to stimulate the subtle organization of energies, which may cause mental derangement, delusions, hallucinations, and sometimes insanity. Certain nervous complaints—affecting at times the muscular equipment, causing twitches and jerking—can be traced back to overstimulation of one center or other. To help such aspiring patients, teach them methods of divorcing themselves temporarily from the source of this mystical or spiritual potency. Or show them how to deflect the forces pouring into and through the various centers to those centers which can more safely handle them, thus producing a more even distribution of energy. We should also teach them how to use such forces effectively in outer service.

The whole problem of how to respond to energy is not an easy one, due to two events happening in the world today. First, the coming in of the Aquarian, Seventh Ray energies, and the passing out of the Piscean, Sixth Ray influence. Second, the movement towards the extroversion or externalization of the great energies to which the mass consciousness responds; and the movement towards the introversion or the "turning inwards" of the intelligent consciousness of those who are awakening (entering the Path, or being accepted into initiation). So when dealing with the centers we are to be aware that the problem of the average person is connected with the solar plexus center; and the problem of the disciple, the advanced aspirant, and the initiate of the lower degrees is connected with the creative center, the throat (Bailey, 1951–70, v. 2, pp. 513–22).

What is an etheric center?

Etheric centers or chakras, as noted above, are points where the lines of force composing the etheric body cross each other, thus forming vortices of energy. Where many lines of force cross (symbolically twenty-one), a major center is to be found. Where fewer lines of force cross (symbolically fourteen and seven), we find minor and minute centers respectively. There are seven major centers with three other centers regarded as of major importance (making ten centers), forty-nine minor centers (twenty-one of which are more important) and hundreds of lesser or minute centers.

A center is fourfold in structure. Symbolically, it is seen as a point, a triangle, petals and a circle. The point is the so-called jewel of the center, the life expression, where the monad can touch the personality. The triangle indicates the link with the spiritual triad, the achievement gained in the soul, the rays of monad/soul/personality, that is, the true spiritual achievement in the integrative development between the higher self and lower self. The petals are the expression of consciousness. And the circle indicates the aura and personality achievement in the particular center. One half of the center, the outer half (therefore one half of the lotus petals), is brought into increased activity upon the probationary path; the other half begins its intensified vibratory activity upon the path of discipleship. But the intensification of the center of the lotus (though the One Life controls both soul and body) only takes place when the two later techniques (of transference of energy, see later on in this chapter) of fusion and duality are carried successfully forward (Bailey, 1951–70, v. 2, p. 385; cf. p. 106).

The understanding of force, of force transmission, and of the effects of liberated force upon the higher planes is the secret of occult knowledge. Force or energy flows in from the soul. It works through the etheric centers and produces results on the physical, emotional, and mental planes, varying according to the age of the soul. As yet, through lack of alignment, this egoic force does not reach the physical brain as fully as it later will, but it does reach the centers in astral vehicles, accounting for much of that lack of emotional control so common in the world today.

Eventually, after many, many lives of learning through the equipment of the personality to serve as a soul, and after we have fulfilled the training requirements on the Path, the centers will become globes of radiant fire with the spokes of the wheel merging and blending into a "fire that burneth up the whole." As an ancient text states:

> The secret of the Fire lies hid in the second letter of the Sacred Word (AUM). The mystery of life is concealed within the heart. When the lower point vibrates, when the Sacred Triangle glows, when the point, the middle center, and the apex likewise burn, then the two triangles—the greater and the lesser—merge with one flame which burneth up the whole.
>
> The fire within the lesser fire findeth its progress much impelled when the circle of the moving and the unmoving, of the lesser wheel within the greater wheel that moveth not in Time, findeth a twofold outlet; it then shineth with the glory of the twofold One and of His sixfold brother. Fohat rusheth through space. He searcheth for his complement. The breath of the unmoving one, and the fire of the One Who seeth the whole from the beginning rush to meet each other, and the unmoving becomes the sphere of activity (Bailey, 1962, pp. 172–73).

The healer has to think clearly before bringing about the desired results, but the energy poured into the patient's vehicle is not mental energy, but one of the seven[1] forms of pranic or life energy.

This travels along the line of force or the channel which relates and links all the centers and connects those centers with the glands (Bailey, 1951–70, v. 4, p. 627). Therefore, we see energy flowing from the centers into the denser channels called nadis which underlie the nervous system as a whole (the consciousness stream), and via the endocrine glands into the blood stream via hormones (the life stream). But remember the healer only works with the life aspect (not the consciousness aspect), endeavoring to work through the very heart of the center where the point of life is to be found. From this point, life rays out into the petals of the center (the consciousness stream), which thus adjusts and aligns the patient towards greater receptivity to their solar angel, the higher self, the soul. Clearly, therefore, and this is worth repeating, disease is to be found in the activity or the non-activity of the centers (since the centers govern the correct functioning of the entire organism), producing both physiological and psychological effects. The importance of the endocrine glands cannot be overestimated. They are a miniature replica of the septenary constitution of the universe and are the medium of expression and the instrument of contact for the seven ray forces. The Master DK confirms that the medicine and the healing methods of the future civilization will be built around this still unrecognized truth (p. 140).

In all our work as esoteric healers and as servers in the world of causes for the betterment of humanity, we must remember that we are working with the science of energies (called the science of occultism) and that this will eventually lead us to what is called the science of laya yoga or the esoteric science of the force centers (Bailey, 1951–70, v. 3, p. 515). This book is an outgrowth of the science of energies. With this understanding we are not to take lightly what we therapeutically discover in these areas when we are working with these energies. This chakra sensitivity to threefold balancing is far more advanced than what is popularly termed "energy work." So we are called on to respect the human energy fields we enter: they are intricate, delicate and intimate, deeply personal and karmically sensitive.

We will now briefly review each center, starting from the lowest and rising to the highest. Unless otherwise indicated, all of the major centers are in the etheric vehicle outside the dense physical body.

Base center

Average person—Ray VII; Disciple—Ray I; Initiate—Ray IV. Pluto is the planet whose influence governs all the stages of this center's development.

Its Sanskrit name is Muladhara. The fires of the animal plane are centralized in the base center. These fires are saturated at a spot that stands in relation to the physical body as the physical sun to the solar system (Bailey, 1962, p. 55). The base center is found near the coccyx of the spine, about two to six inches outside of the dense physical body in

CHART OF THE CENTERS
(From *Cosmic Fire,* Bailey, 1962, p. 817,
"The Egoic Lotus and the Centers")

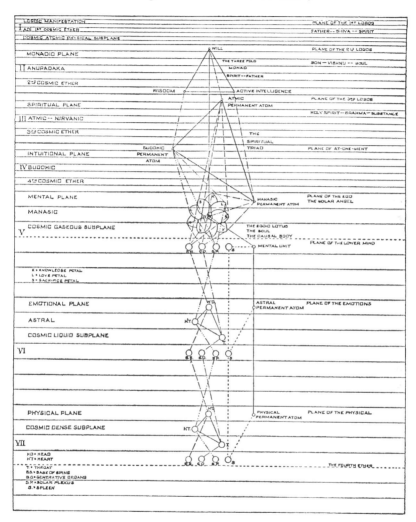

the etheric spine. It is found on the fourth ether of every plane (p. 817). This center attracts the energy of personality-will into activity when purpose is focussed through the head center. The base chakra is strongly influenced by the law of attraction, or rather the law of acquisition on the different levels.

Just as we can acquire possessions in the physical world, we can do the same in our subtle bodies. Where there's attraction, there's repulsion. The base governs elimination, emotional, mental, and spiritual. This center drives the adrenal glands, found like hats on top of the kidneys. The base center, by controlling the adrenals, causes the hormone adrenaline to be injected directly into the blood stream. Adrenaline fuels the basic drive to human activity, most noticeable whenever there is an emergency wherein the "fight or flight" mechanism is set in motion. The ancient instinct of fear and self-preservation anchors the personality in the current incarnation. Look at a simple physiology textbook to find out the way adrenaline is utilized in the body, and also the problems it causes when there is too little or too much being passed into the blood. In esoteric healing it is not particularly necessary to know this physiology, although it may be a help to understanding the physical mechanism of the base center. The base center governs the legs (e.g., specifically the knees to flee with), as well as the spine, for through the base center we depend on our uprightness, the way we carry ourselves, the way we walk and stand and sit. In your client's postures you can be guided as to how their base center is functioning. Spinal problems always have a base center involvement; in fact, the base center governs the whole skeletal system. Wherever bones are diseased or a problem, the base center will be implicated. The base center controls the kidneys as well, and rules the bones, the muscles, the skin, the hair, sinews—the scaffolding of the body.

Biologically, the adrenal glands are double in origin: the medulla, of nervous tissue origin; and the cortex, from primitive kidney origin. The adrenal function reflects this double origin. The medulla is in charge of helping the activity of the sympathetic nervous system, while the cortex is involved in the regulation of the metabolism, mainly through the glucose and sodium balance. The base center has a special relation to the spleen center (see below, in the Spleen Triangle of Force) (Bailey, 1962, p. 55). The smell sense is controlled by the base center. The base center also is the harbor of our unconscious fears and instincts for survival as well as for success and achievement (ambition). Over-activation of the base center can cause stress changes in the body, which may include high blood pressure and have related kidney involvement. The elemental being of the physical body (one of the three lunar Lords)—that is, the essential materiality of the dense body—is in the base center (Bailey, 1951–70, v. 2, p. 304).

The base center is a four-petalled lotus, a powerful symbol linked to the Mother of the World, the Earth, the Cross, the Square, and the fourth (human) kingdom of nature. The "kundalini" energy sleeps in the base center. This chakra comes into its true functioning activity when two major fusions have been effected: that of the fusions of the three bodies into one coordinated personality, and when soul and body are at-oned (p. 435). At the first initiation or expansion of consciousness, man consciously connects with the will of his intelligence and he discovers the light of his true nature (Bailey, 1979, p. 106). Ray I, the fifth initiation of Revelation, and the base center are all connected (Bailey, 1951–70, v. 5, p. 340).

The purpose of the base center is to give order to the person, to arrange the person's life so that there is a reason for living and a right to life. Neatness, tidiness, punctuality, clarity of purpose and direction are some of its positive and balanced qualities. But this neatness can also become over-disciplined. Unbalanced energy flow through the base center can result in inability to change, insecurity, in a driving ambition without thought of others, aggression, and manipulative activities. Or the exact opposite of these can occur when the energy flow is not getting through, demonstrating as inertia (spinelessness, no will to think or do), lack of ambition or motivation, carelessness, coldness, laziness.

Sacral center

Average person—Ray III; Disciple—Ray IV; Initiate—Ray VII. Uranus is the governing influence assigned by the Master DK, but esoterically this center is governed by the Moon (linked to Saturn); it is also strongly governed by Earth in the early stages.

The sacral center is found a little further up the spine, outside the juncture of the lumbar and sacral vertebrae. The eight-petalled sacral center controls the gonad glands (testes and ovaries, with their hormones testosterone, estrogen and progesterone) and the whole reproductive system, including the breasts. Any physical problem in these areas implies sacral involvement. Sacral energies govern also all the fluids of the body, including blood, lymph, semen, amniotic fluid, mucus, and urine, which relates the center to the kidneys as well. This center, along with the base, governs the legs (specifically the hips and feet). It is the center of birth, on all levels and from many angles (e.g., it has a strong influence over rebirth, new birth, new beginnings, the first initiation, and death—the birth into a new dimension, and so on). Neoplasm (cancer) is the result of rapid rebirth of tissue cells—all cancers are due to misappropriated sex energy. The sacral energy is mainly to do with self-perpetuation, so it has a powerful attractive or magnetic quality towards its complementary opposite. Simply stated, it is the sacral center which sends out bleeps to the opposite sex. And since this is the center which, as it were, brings two people together for regenerative purposes, we can see how it has a particular relation to the vital etheric body. Sacral energy gives a person vitality and attractiveness.

This center also concerns everything to do with family connections, inheritance, ancestors, that is, protectiveness, the sexual lusts and instincts (really the urge towards unity and the innate desire for the mystical marriage), fears, resentments, bonds, loves, hates, and all familial difficulties. The sacral center is the origin also of the sense of superiority or inferiority.

This center also governs personal education and family responsibility, a greater sense of impersonality leading to the sense of group life. Once the sacral is correctly led up to the throat center, the creative process is transformed into sound thoughts and pure speech.

Clearly, the sacral is a creative center. Anyone having attended a human birth stands agog at the magic and miracle of its technique, conflict and complexity, organization and sheer marvel. This may well reflect the nature of the mental body's elemental being which is related to the sacral center (later to be transferred to the throat center) (Bailey, 1951–70, v. 2, p. 304). Its relation to the throat center connects it to the "True." The failure of the personality to respond, and its inability to express the True (Bailey, 1951–70, v. 4, p. 569), is to be seen as the failed alignment between these two centers. Be true to yourself, using the fulcrum of harmlessness.

The esoteric nature of this center involves two important foundations. The first, which goes back into the night of time, involves separatism, symbolized in the story of Eve being born from the "rib" of Adam—the separation of the sexes (the sacral was the dominant center in old Lemuria, eighteen million years ago). Lemuria was a land mass now covered by the Indian Ocean. All separation, division, polarity and opposition is said to have underlying sacral influences. The lack of confidence found in many people who are not able to express themselves as who they truly are is due to this center's lack of creative harmony with the throat center. The second attribute of the sacral center is its capacity to regenerate or "build." These building energies are etheric, controlled by beings called the lunar lords.

This center, therefore, can be brought into healing circuits when, for instance, vertebral discs have collapsed, or when joint capsules have been worn, resulting in osteoarthritis. One of the key esoteric methods for bringing the etheric building energy in is to employ the patient's mental body's sacral center, for it is here that the patient will learn how to integrate the sacral and throat centers with due personal responsibility and a greater sense of self-education regarding the patient's relationship between family, friends, food, and the environment.

The sacral center has a particular relation to the etheric body as a whole. The etheric (its four subplanes) are the lowest correspondence to the four planes whereon the monad and the Spiritual Triad are active, and just as on those levels there is no such thing as consciousness as we know it, in the etheric we do not have "consciousness," but rather a state of being and of activity. In this sphere we are called upon to function adequately in response to the life of the soul (on higher levels, to the life of the planetary Logos) (Bailey, 1951–70, v. 5, p. 178). This throws new light on the strength and use of the sacral center. A hint as to how we can respond is given us by the expressions of the plant kingdom in relation to the deva kingdom.

Spleen center

This is a third ray center peculiarly influenced by Sun and Earth energies.

The spleen center is not one of the seven major centers, but its importance warrants some description. Its central force field is at the back of the etheric body, close to and connected to the physical spleen itself, to the left of the navel. The etheric spleen center is not controlled in any way from the etheric spinal column as are the other major centers. The spleen center is a double minor center, i.e., one center superimposed on the other. These two vortices have six petals each, making it a twelve-petalled lotus, linking it to the other twelve-petalled lotuses (heart, heart-in-the head, egoic or soul lotus, planetary heart, etc.) but giving it a massive twenty-eightfold energy structure (more powerful even than the major centers), as opposed to the usual fourteenfold energy structure of other minor centers. (Recall that minor centers are formed by fourteen energy crossings over one point.) It is via the spleen that the negative or receptive life of matter and the living energy of the positive etheric body are brought together, and then a "spark," as it is called, is made between the physical plane and the inner living bodies of man (through the medium of the etheric body) (Bailey, 1951–70, v. 4, p. 335). It is a center of the third ray of matter, which was particularly dominant during the ancient civilization of Lemuria. This is the center most involved when there is too much or too little energy in the personality life, when the person feels depleted or highly strung. The spleen center assimilates the energy or nervous force often referred to as planetary prana, which is distinctive from the individualized life force. The incoming prana rises to the heart center and connects with the individualized life stream. There is a very important energy circuit that comes off this center called the Spleen Triangle of Force, and that has a powerful reflection in the head called the Immortality Triangle. The spleen center which governs the working of the body, i.e., the amount of life-force available in the body, just as the liver center, a minor center close to the liver, governs how the body works, i.e., how smoothly or erratically the organs function.

Prana varies in vibration and quality according to the receiving entity. You can begin to see how different centers are related to others and how the whole begins to be revealed as a system of coordinates. The spleen center is frequently called upon in esoteric healing to help replenish deficient energy in an area which is dis-eased. Probably over 90% of patients at this time suffer from depletion of this energy, so one can appreciate that getting this center functioning and its energy circulating is primary in a healing treatment. The spleen center is connected to many electrical circuits within the body. From a higher angle, the astral spleen vitalizes the emotions, and the mental aspect of the spleen vitalizes thoughtforms by means of will (Bailey, 1950a, p. 72).

Esoterically, the spleen center is directly connected with the *antah-karana* (a bridge from the personality consciousness to the soul). This connection goes from the spleen center to the physical permanent atom (first ether) to the astral permanent atom (on the first subplane of the astral plane), to the mental unit (upper limit of the personality, the fourth subplane of the mental body), to the jewel of the lotus or Soul, through the manasic permanent atom (first subplane of the mind), to the Spiritual Triad itself. This makes the spleen very special, a center which stands apart, a center highly advanced to the extent that its physical expression is virtually transmuted already into its etheric counterpart.

Certain natural healers who have no specific spiritual or esoteric training and who often don't even have a particular spiritual orientation are able to heal using the energy flowing from this center. They usually have no knowledge of how or why they have this healing ability. The healing force is a strong current of vitality from the planet being transformed by the splenic center and moving out to the patient. Such healers are working only with the spleen center and not with any of the major centers. However, their results can be as effective as an esoteric healing treatment, though the results are usually temporary. Such healers, and all healers working with faith or without knowledge, are, as my colleague Janina Waloszek once said, like lay people turning on the light compared to an electrician turning it on—the result is the same but the latter knows how it happened! The days of the former type of healers, I believe, are numbered. The point is, disease is a defective circuit and, without inner knowledge of the esoteric anatomy and the esoteric techniques of healing, the former types of healing will have very limited value, or none at all.

The spleen center is also linked with the pituitary gland (see the Immortality Triangle), a clue as to its place in the head centers. Its energy is not transferred to any particular center (as for instance the solar plexus energies go to the heart center and the sacral energies go to the throat). The splenic energy is consciously diffused to all the centers. When its correspondence in the head center is activated, it becomes an agent of occult healing; through it, the healer, by an act of will, absorbs the prana and vitality from the ethers and then breathes it out again upon the patient to be healed by an act of compassionate healing (cf. Bailey, 1962,

p. 859). This is exactly what the esoteric healer does after performing the various vitality triangles, described later.

To keep the spleen center in good condition (since few people have the faculty of stimulating it through the esoteric use of the word OM), absorb pranic energy from the sun (through sunlight, sun-ripened foods, fruit, nuts and cereals, fresh air from forests and coasts, and sleeping with a window open at night), as well as move the emotional body by high aspiration, keep open to the downflow of force from the causal and intuitional levels, and keep the mental life intense, vibrant, and animated by a powerful will. In this way, the spleen will progress and be in a healthy condition (Bailey, 1950a, p. 71). Where this is not the case, the person will experience devitalization, a feeling of congestion, depression, physical heaviness, inertia, fuzzy thoughts, and the paradoxical tiredness with sleeplessness. This may be the result of congested, burnt or punctured webs (cf. Bailey, 1962, p. 104; 1951–70, v. 4, pp. 74–75). One way of helping this condition is the use of the Two Triangles of Force (#25, p. 186).

Solar plexus center

Average person—Ray II; Disciple—Ray V; Initiate—Ray VI. The Sun is the first influence over the solar plexus; later it changes to Venus and Mars/Neptune.

The solar plexus center, located a little above the sacral center, directs energy moving inwards from the back through the spine (at the junction of the thoracic and lumbar vertebrae) to activate the endocrine part of the pancreas, the islets of Langerhans, producing insulin. It is primarily a center for transferring energies upwards to the higher centers. As it does this, certain elements with it can lock onto certain ideas, thoughtforms and processes, resulting in the problem of glamor. Some of the problems associated with the transfer include moodiness, worry, tension, agitated excitement, stress, temper, irritation, selfishness, fervor, obsession, lower psychism, hallucinations, nervous disorders, violence, fanaticism, and insanity. All of these can be said to be psychological cleavages, both deep-seated and superficial. In their effort to control the astral body, aspirants often resort to a process of direct inhibition and suppression, resulting in the solar plexus becoming a "great reservoir of drastically retained energy" (Bailey, 1951–70, v. 4, p. 239). This causes many problems, even cancer, in the pancreas, stomach, liver, gall bladder, or intestines. What is required, rather, is the transmutation of the emotions into aspiration, altruistic devotion, as well as love and directed control.

The solar plexus center dominates the whole of the digestive system, so any problems or illnesses located in the stomach or intestines (including the pancreas, liver and gall bladder) will implicate the solar plexus center. We all know that "crunch" in the solar plexus region when we feel angry or upset; solar plexus energy governs the emotional body. It gives us animal instincts and rules personal desires. It can often easily be augmented by other people's emotionalism so that we feel engulfed and driven forward on a wave of mindless sentiment, noticeable, for example, in groups of people demonstrating for a "cause." The center quickly reacts without thought. This can be good (it can save a child in danger, for instance) or bad, so that the person in a blind fury does things they later regret.

Solar plexus energy can be overwhelming. It requires strength, control, and the development of rationality to bring this powerful center into permanent balance. For many this is not easy. For others it feels as if the very basis of their life is pulled from under them; they live *on* and live *for* their emotions. Their feelings result in deep personal fears, antipathies, and the "seven deadly sins" (pride, envy, gluttony, lust, anger, greed/covetousness, sloth). When the heart center is in balance and in control, the nature of the solar plexus center is revealed. This kind of person is fun-loving, genuinely concerned about others, easy to talk to without fear of offending, seldom gets too embroiled in other people's affairs, and so on.

The solar plexus center is a great receiving center in preparation for transferring energy from below the diaphragm to the centers above where the effects of personality are not so important. The elemental being of the astral body expresses its life through the solar plexus center, whose energies are later transferred to the heart center. The words "to dare" give the clue to the subordination and reorientation of the personality via the solar plexus, the main center for this transmutative work

(Bailey, 1979, p. 278). Such a person is developing the seven virtues (humility, kindness, abstinence/temperance, chastity, patience, liberality, diligence).

Heart center

Average person—Ray I; Disciple—Ray VI; Initiate—Ray II. Vulcan is the initial influence over the heart, with Neptune and Jupiter coming in later.

The feeling consciousness of the soul is focussed through the heart center. This center anchors the life stream from the monad. Esoterically, the heart of the foetus thrills with life between the third and fourth month after conception (Bailey, 1962, p. 684). This center is located just below and between the etheric shoulder blades, passing into the body between the fourth and fifth thoracic vertebrae. Its energy flows from the second subplane of each plane and from the love petals of the causal lotus (p. 817), to that somewhat inactive (or misunderstood) gland, above the heart, called the thymus gland, producing the hormone thymosin. (Thymosin alpha-1 is a synthetic hormone used for hepatitis B, cancer and AIDS.) The thymus is particularly active during childhood, indicating two things: first, that the heart center is open during babyhood (to eighteen months it breaks down mother's milk) and throughout the stages of growing up (from two to twelve years it helps develop the sex glands, working with the sacral center)—open to instruction about compassion and true love; second, so that the parents can gently train the child into the ways of decency, politeness, respect and love; this is the heart's need for right discipline.

During puberty the thymus determines the height of the individual, while the ajna's growth hormone is via the pituitary gland. The heart center is open because at this stage the solar plexus center is virtually closed (it starts to open at around seven years old), and the heart center influences on the solar plexus will determine how it might react in adult life. Otherwise, controlling the solar plexus will be that much more difficult to attain. The reversal of openness between these two centers takes place at puberty. From that time the thymus gland begins to atrophy rapidly. It then takes spiritual effort, and, if instinctual compassion has not been built in by the parents, intellectual understanding to reactivate the heart center. Loneliness and depression are closely associated with the loss of this gland.

The heart center, whose twelve petals link it with the heart center of the planet, which is the planetary hierarchy or fifth kingdom, governs the heart and the circulatory system. It is also closely connected to the lungs and respiration as well as to the spleen. The heart center also governs the immune system and the lymphatic glands of the body, for where there is love, no harm can come. Love is the coherent force which makes all things whole (Bailey, 1951–70, v. 4, p. 356). Hate, which is opposite to love, results in self-destruction, hence the autoimmune diseases. The heart center is the controller of spiritual work, group activity and interaction. It is the organ of fusion and inclusiveness (while the head center is the organ of synthesis). Stress can unbalance the heart center, causing blood pressure imbalances, insomnia, and problems like petit mal or grande mal. Also, greed and overconcern or protection of one's so-called "rights" can unbalance the heart center. Immunodeficiency and autoimmune diseases can be helped via the heart center. Impersonal relationships and the sense of inclusiveness affect this center's activity (Bailey, 1951–70, v. 4, p. 159). The heart starts functioning after the second initiation, where one ceases to think solely as an individual and in addition becomes attuned to group consciousness. It then acts as a distribution center of hierarchical energy via the soul. In this connection the heart is the exit at death for aspirants and for men and women of goodwill (p. 472). This center is linked closely with the ajna or brow center, and, as the heart center becomes fully alive, so the ajna's gland—the pituitary body—enters into activity.

The vitality which comes from the etheric body works through the blood. This wavelike rhythm throbs through the body using the heart as an external "valve" and "conducer"; the pumping action does not actually exist; the heart appears to pump but actually it is simply the result of the rhythmical action of the vital force on the blood stream as a whole. For it is the interaction of the heart, the blood stream and the nervous system that controls the assimilation of prana, or life energy, into the spleen from the etheric body. In fact the cardiovascular system is so closely connected to the etheric or vital body that it is practically impossible to distinguish them. Those who are more mentally polarized in their lives and those who are on a spiritual path that involves intelligence and reason (without emotion and devotional feelings) are often prone to heart complaints (not chronic cardiac failure, however), neural illnesses and autonomic nerve difficulties (Bailey, 1951–70, v. 2, p. 536). People who are governed by laws and rituals and repetition in their lives have problems and diseases of the blood stream. It is interesting to note that the heart center and heart organ are governed by the ray of love (the second ray), and that the circulatory system is governed by the ray of ritual and magic (the seventh ray), the two primary rays of healing among the seven (Bailey, 1951–70, v. 2, p. 622; also, Bailey, 1944, v. 1, p. 641). (More on this center, see p. 194ff.)

Vagus nerve center

The ray influences over this center are: Average person—Ray III; Disciple—Ray VI; Initiate—Ray II. Planetary rulers are Earth, Mars and the Sun (the pranic aspect).

The vagus nerve center, while not one of the seven major centers, is in some systems considered to be among the most important. This center can be said to be the most advanced of the minor centers, not so much in its vibratory status (for in this case the alta major center in the head is greater, nor yet in its highest development, for here the spleen center is greater), but in the sense of its purpose, action and usefulness. It has fourteen petals. Do you see its connection with the spleen center? The vagus nerve center reigns supreme for those who are entering the path of the spirit, those people who have determined that they want to develop along the lines that evolution has laid down or predetermined. For the aspiring disciple, one still lacking in complete soul control and monadic direction (Bailey, 1951–70, v. 4, p. 122), this center begins to have a major influence on life. It is a call, finally, to group service (heart). This center is not found in the etheric spine, like the major centers, but is further inside the etheric body, near the thymus gland (p. 73). The healer can locate it between the shoulder blades, with its precipitation just above the heart and thymus gland, and on the vagus nerve, the tenth cranial nerve. There is a plexus of nerves above the heart and below the aorta; this is the externalized vagus nerve center. The physical nerve travels down from the brain to the heart and lungs, then to the digestive organs.

The vagus nerve, having its origin in the medulla, is also connected with the alta major center. It is largely autonomic in its functioning, though it does transmit back some sensory information from the mouth and pharynx. Almost all of the information from the medulla concerning essential body functioning is sent along this nerve. For the disciple not under direct monadic control, it is the major pathway for information filtering down through the head centers. The spine takes up this function after the third initiation. The branches of the vagus nerve terminate in the heart, lungs, stomach, liver, mouth, tongue, larynx, pharynx, pancreas and pass down through the splenic flexure in the large intestine. It seems plausible that the alta major center uses the vagus nerve to regulate immune response, since the latter is connected with the heart center and is subservient to it (being related to its pranic function).

Like the spleen, the vagus nerve center is currently the main center for the reception of prana, and forms a radiant etheric triangle (see, below, the Pranic Triangle), which is the originating impulse for pranic circulation in the body (Bailey, 1962, p. 98). There is an important triangle connected with this center, with growth and expanding consciousness, called the Kundalini Triangle, discussed later. The energy points of this triangle do not actually involve the vagus nerve center, but the triangle as a whole affects the vagus nerve center, activating it and helping the person to aspire towards soul control. The energy points are: the head center, the heart center and the base center (Bailey, 1951–70, v. 4, p. 335).

There are three interconnecting regulators which control or fail to control the physical body:

i) the etheric body through the seven major centers and the minor centers;

ii) the endocrine system through the seven major glands;

iii) the nervous system, and particularly the vagus nerve with its effect on the heart and the blood stream.

Here we are specifically interested in the third of these regulators, remembering its connections with the etheric or vital body and with the endocrine or hormonal system. When this center rhythmically flows, bringing about harmony and balance, the nervous system will work efficiently and effectively for the person. But as soon as this center becomes overstimulated, or defective in its handling of the energy arriving at its crossroads, all kinds of illnesses and deficiencies associated with the nerves begin to show symptoms in the physical body, for instance, in the muscles. Such illnesses are particularly linked with those who have begun the spiritual journey of life. Frequently a person "new born" or "reborn" becomes fanatical or obsessed, but if this trend is redressed so that they become more reasonable and less blinded, the tide can be turned. Otherwise, there is a likelihood of physical nervous problems in the future.

Throat center

Average person—Ray IV; Disciple—Ray III; Initiate—Ray V. Mercury has the initial influence, then the planet Saturn has a long hold over the throat center; the advanced influence is by Venus.

This center is the highest in the etheric spine. It is silvery blue and inverted in the early stages, with its sixteen petals reaching over the shoulders and down to the two lungs. As the life of discipleship proceeds, certain of the petals rise to sound in the two ears, in the medulla and in the carotid of the alta major center (Bailey, 1951–70, v. 4, p. 155). The energy attracted to this center flows in from the back through the spinal column between the seventh cervical and the first thoracic vertebrae, and vitalizes the physical body via the thyroid gland and parathyroid glands in the neck. Apart from having a direct influence over the whole respiratory tract, this center governs the entire digestive system from mouth to anus (p. 44). The creative consciousness of the indwelling soul is focussed in the throat center (Bailey, 1951–70, v. 2, p. 304). Hyperthyroidism (producing an overactive metabolism) occurs when the throat center is prematurely awakened (p. 536) or due to high stress. Overstress is the cause of the "burn-out" of the thyroid—resulting in hypothyroidism, and dependency on thyroxin or herbal medicine.

When working with the digestive system, we usually hold the throat center when working on any areas down to the stomach (to the cardiac sphincter) but not including it; after this point the solar plexus center is usually held simultaneously. In an act of criticism, or if someone has real hatred for another, this negative energy is absorbed by the throat center and flows like a river of nails into the solar plexus center where the first symptoms of gastrointestinal disease will manifest (Bailey, 1951–70,

v. 4, p. 39). Criticism is a virulent poison, especially when voiced—it actually hurts, even damages, the one criticized (even more than the one who is criticizing, hence the danger, karmically). However, for the one who is detached and full of love, the attack can be nullified. But DK says, "Where there is any physical weakness or limitation, *there* will be found the localization of the projected poison" (his italics) (Bailey, 1951–70, v. 2, p. 617). Voiced or silent, criticism can seriously distort the throat center and affect other centers in its insidious contagiousness. It must be rooted out before group work is to be undertaken. Gall stones are a definite indication of criticism.

The greatest influence of the throat center is over the lungs and respiratory system along with the ears and the vocal apparatus. The creative or destructive weaving of sound is controlled by the throat center. In this act, it is closely connected with the heart center, for the throat center governs the actual air intake, the act of respiration; and the heart center controls the point of absorption of oxygen into the blood and release of carbon dioxide to the lungs, the so-called blood-air exchange. Asthma, bronchitis, respiratory diseases—all are related to throat center malfunctions. To correct the problem, the afflicted person needs to be honest in their thinking, speaking and actions. And since the throat will become the clearing house for transferring energy of the lower centers into the head center as we advance in spiritual life, we need to take extra care of our thoughts and words (Bailey, 1951–70, v. 2, pp. 515, 553).

The throat center has some connection with another important body system, the lymphatic system, even though the latter is governed by the heart center. The throat center influences the shoulders, arms and hands. Just as the sacral center functions to create physical life through regeneration, so the throat center, the sacral's higher correspondence, is activated by higher creativity and controls the adaptability of thought and ideas. When our thoughts and desires become rigid and unclear, causing congestion in the throat center, arthritis can build up. Rheumatism comes about due to one's inability to live up to the highest goal and the inability of the soul to produce an expression of "the true"; such a person is always conscious of the unattainable and of the urge to betterment (Bailey, 1951–70, v. 4, pp. 567–68). Faulty calcium levels in the parathyroids cause arthritis. This gives us a connection between menopause and osteoporosis, and the need for HRT (hormone replacement therapy). In your healing work see if you can make a link among the thyroid, the parathyroids, the pineal, and the pituitary (or the triangle of throat center, head center, and ajna).

Astral instability, another problem of the throat center, occurs when higher creativity is not properly channeled from the sacral center, leading to perversion of the sex function, what DK describes as "ancient evil predisposing habits" (Bailey, 1951–70, v. 4, p. 63). Here we find the condition, homosexuality, and its connection to Lemuria. Such persons may well have been mystics in a past life who had learned sexual control and had touched the heights of spiritual contact, but the throat center was not developed sufficiently to arrest the energy, whereupon it passed straight down to the sacral center becoming recoiled (retrovibrational) sexual activity (cf. Bailey, 1951–70, v. 2, p. 538). Hence the real need for right thought and right speech. The throat center is the genuine guardian of our health, the sentry on the bridge between the head and body.

The throat center promotes self-awareness by directing our lives towards the helping and lifting of our fellow humans, via understanding, cooperation and constructiveness. These processes are initiated by communication; the right use of the voice can lead to momentous changes, which will benefit the whole. Politicians and educators are both strongly influenced by this center, and, interestingly, the throat center governs the whole field of science (Bailey, 1951–70, v. 1, p. 208). But whether directly or indirectly, we all have this center playing a major role in our lives, for sound is the throat center's expressive sense.

Alta major center

Ray III is this important head center's influence, linked to the karmic aspect of Saturn.

The alta major center, unlike the vagus nerve center, functions as a major center, but it is one of the 49 minor centers for the average person. The throat center connects with it at the moment when the antahkarana is begun to be built. You will find this center at the back of the head, the knob at the very top of the back of the neck, indicating its place of entry into the head. The physical gland it creates is the carotid body, found on either side of the upper part of the neck; it monitors oxygen content in the blood, and controls respiration. In anatomy books you will find it pictured where the common carotid arteries divide as they enter the brain. The carotid body, and hence the alta major center, are obviously under the influence of one of the seven major centers, in this case, the throat center (Bailey, 1951–70, v. 4, pp. 155–56). In fact, DK describes the alta major center as the physical center whose higher center is the throat. The alta major center is also described as a nerve center at the top of the spine where the cranium and the spine make approximate contact. When this congery of nerves is fully developed, it forms a center of communication between the vital energy of the spinal column (the kundalini fire) and the energy of the two head centers, namely, the center at the top of the head and the brow or ajna center. It is the physical correspondence to the antahkarana,[2] which is found on higher levels (Bailey, 1962, pp. 961–62).

The alta major center has a unique position: first, because of its position in the head triangle and, second, due to its powerful link with the cerebellum, the medulla oblongata and the spine. The cerebellum in the hind-brain controls the voluntary muscles and movement (linking it to the base center). The medulla oblongata contains the critical regions that govern breathing, heart rate and blood pressure (connections with the throat and heart center). This center's development leads to an acquired and conscious control of one's dharma or soul work on earth, a realization of what one is to do in life as opposed to being tossed about like a leaf in the wind (a reference to the creative thread of pingala). It therefore has powerful connections with ancient memory (the "chit" of satchitananda, which occurs when the three head centers function together to give this enlightening experience) in many forms, and also has a major influence over the memories held in the cortex. When functioning, the alta major center has the power to bring down intuitive vision into consciousness. This center can be said to be the healer's conscious link with the higher mind, for through the alta major center our higher intelligence is activated through thought. And energy follows thought. Through the alta major center the spiritual will of the head center is balanced, well symbolized by the horizontal poise found between the left and right eyes. (In fact, from the esoteric angle the eyes actually distribute these energies.)

To hold this center, you will find that it has a dual input (due to the two carotid bodies at the bifurcation of the common carotid arteries on either side of the neck) and a single outlet. With thumb and forefinger of one hand enter the ingoing stream at the back of the head, and with the other hand's index finger placed about eight inches (20 cms) from the front of the head (near the hairline of the mid-forehead), meet the outstreaming force. In this way you can bring this center into a balanced rhythm.

The alta major is the center particularly related to sleep and to the working out of past experiences in sleep. Dreams are derived from this center. There is a special exercise done at night to help develop this aspect of the alta. It is called the Ruckshau, or backward look over the day. Just before you go to sleep at night, sit for a while and review the day you have just had, backwards. In sequence, you are witnessing the results or effects of the causes first, then the originating influence second. Observe, see how it was dealt with, and be aware that you are in the harness. How you respond determines the result. By learning from these experiences we can actually shorten our time in the astral world (kamaloca) after death. Another aid to rapid evolution is to go to sleep with our consciousness gently focussed in the ajna center.

Ajna center

Average person—Ray V; Disciple—Ray VII; Initiate—Ray III. To begin with, Venus directs the ways of ajna; then Uranus organizes her; finally Saturn is met. Mercury (with its positive directional activity) and Moon (with its link to astrality and illusory visions) can also be found as potent influences of the Ajna Center.

Located outside the area between the eyebrows, the ajna center is often referred to as the third eye, but the third eye only opens when the alta major center, head center and the ajna are in synchronous vibration. The energy of the ajna is twofold, flowing in at the front (it is the only major center that has its inflow from the front of the body) and out at the top of the head on the midline just behind the crown center. Its twofoldness is due to its integrative function. The gland this center precipitates into is the pituitary body in the brain, an organ having two lobes (anterior and posterior) held together by a stalk. Called the master gland or the conducting gland, the pituitary controls all the others in the body, like the conductor of an orchestra. It is the seat of personality power (Bailey, 1951–70, v. 2, p. 553). In this connection would it seem remarkable to you that the pituitary gland commands a total of nine hormones? The ajna also has strong links with the hypothalamus, which governs the autonomic system. It is closely related to the two eyes and to all frontal areas of the head, including the nose (although not the sense of smell, which is ruled by the base center).

Ajna is ruled by the monadic plane (Bailey, 1950b, p. 167). It is an organ of idealism, which in a strange way characterizes the fifth ray. Ajna at once controls the expression of the personality and "grounds" and distributes the spiritual energy of the soul. The ajna only begins to function usefully when a person has begun to grow spiritually and has built a certain amount of love and selfless service into his or her life. When the ajna is active, it has a twofold flow, inwards and outwards. The outward flow enables a healer to have inner vision and perception concerning the patient's underlying condition and then to creatively work to correct it. Remember, the healer seeks by the power of the soul, working on the higher levels of the mental plane and through the etheric head center, to stimulate the point of soul life in the etheric body of the patient, which is attracted, if possible, to a fuller inflow of soul energy of the patient into the head center, in order that the life thread may carry a fuller supply of life to the patient's heart (Bailey, 1951–70, v. 4, p. 541). Generally this correction will involve motivating the spiritual side of the patient towards practical expression. The inward flow of the ajna is utilized when the healer is balancing the centers (see Chapter 6).

Linked to the alta major center, the ajna center controls the cerebellum (which controls muscular action, coordination of movement and balance) and the central nervous system. DK says there is a close physiological relation between the parathyroid glands and the pituitary body (p. 155), which is yet to be discovered by physiologists. Just as the gland consists of two lobes and a "stalk" joining them, so the ajna center has three sections:

  i) The upper ajna (relating to the anterior pituitary gland with its seven hormones) governing all the centers in the body, their endocrine glands and the expression of these through the circulatory system and heart. With this part we express imagination and have the power to visualize (Bailey, 1930, p. 141).

ii) The middle ajna (analogous to the pituitary's stalk), which has five points related to the five major centers up the spine. We are told that the ajna blends and fuses five types of energy (Bailey, 1951–70, v. 1, p. 290). In diagnosis we make a particular connection to the middle ajna (see Chapter 7, p. 155).

iii) The lower ajna (the posterior pituitary gland with its two hormones), governing the whole of the central nervous system with a special relation to the alta major center and throat center. Through the posterior pituitary the reasoning mind has its seat (Bailey, 1930, p. 141), and through it we express desire in its highest form (Bailey, 1951–70, v. 4, p. 149).

To effect certain results in healing, we can direct our attention via the hand held at the front of the head to one or other of these three parts. When the ajna is out of balance, problems may occur in the ears (cochlea, not ear drum; in other words, balance not hearing), eyes, sinuses (a secondary problem to throat center problems), or lower brain area. Or difficulties can ensue in areas in the body governed by other centers, for instance, gynecological problems. Wrong control of ajna energy leads to serious eye trouble, aural difficulties, neuritis, headache, migraine, nerve difficulties in the body, pituitary body difficulties, psychological trouble and physical trouble (Bailey, 1951–70, v. 2, p. 535). Overstimulation of the ajna, by focussing the lower energies into it, may result in the egomaniac, a monster (in the extreme, like Hitler), epilepsy, eyesight problems or even blindness (Bailey, 1951–70, v. 4, p. 176). The ajna is the most important center in magnetic healing. Its powerful energy is always transferred to the etheric body of the patient via the hand minor centers of the healer.

There are many subtle correspondences relating to the ajna. For example, the ajna registers and focuses the intention to create. It embodies the idea lying behind the act of creativity. The organ of creativity itself, however, is the throat center. The two lobes of the pituitary gland (the "wings" of the ajna center) correspond to imagination and desire in their two highest forms. It is the organ of idealism, therefore closely related both to the heart and to the solar plexus (here you may notice a hint regarding the Lower Clearing Triangle, described later). Ajna fuses the creative energies of the throat and the sublimated energies of desire or true love of the heart. In the work of the higher healer, working out the divine purpose according to the Inner Plan, the ajna center becomes the directing agent or the distributor of the blended energies of the Divine Man (Bailey, 1951–70, v. 4, p. 581).

Head center

Average person—Ray VI; Disciple—Ray II; Initiate—Ray I. Neptune is the first influence, followed by the Heart of the Sun (linked to a strong Uranian impression); Vulcan is the last planetary governor (supported earlier by Pluto).

Above the top of the head, a fiery display makes all the other centers pale by comparison. From the heart of this many petalled lotus issues a flame of fire having the basic hue of a person's soul ray. This flame mounts upward and attracts downward a sheet of electric light, which is the downflow from the spirit on the highest plane (Bailey, 1962, p. 170). The head center, often referred to as the crown center, was regarded as the "seat of the soul" by the ancients. The mental consciousness of the indwelling soul is focussed in the head center (Bailey, 1951–70, v. 2, p. 304), which itself is controlled by the logoic plane (Bailey, 1950b, p. 167). The crown center controls the will and destiny of the soul in incarnation, directs all the other centers and links one to one's higher self. It is developed chiefly through meditation. Its outflow at the top of the head emanates in two streams, due to the two aspects of the etheric center (the outer circle of hundreds of "petals," plus the heart of the head center consisting of twelve petals or energy outflow). This center is also known symbolically as the thousand-petalled lotus flower. The energy of this center flows in from the top of the head via the fontanel and precipitates in the pineal gland in the brain, producing melatonin.

Not much is known about the pineal gland's function. It appears to be almost nonfunctional in humans (although very active in some animals, for instance, in one class of ancient lizard still surviving in New Zealand, the Tuatara, which is said to live to an age of over 300 years). Through the hormone melatonin, however, it has an influence over the diurnal rhythm (or circadian biorhythms) of our lives. Melatonin is now available for insomnia, as an anti-depression supplement and a counteractive to jet lag. The fact that melatonin is available (like the other centers' hormones) suggests humanity's development and influence on the head center has begun. The gland is affected by light, possibly because it has a pigment similar to that in the retina of the eye. Like the thymus gland above the heart, the pineal gland is more active in childhood, becoming atrophied in the adult. So it is considered to have a connection with the earth as an energy being and with the will to remain alive, the will to be.

The usefulness of the head center only becomes apparent when the person has had wide experience and has developed a certain degree of wisdom, discrimination and spiritual integrity. The head center anchors the consciousness stream from the causal lotus on the soul level. There are, under or within the range of the highest head center, seven head centers, which are synthesized after the fourth initiation. I believe the sites of the seven head centers (not including the three major centers which we know to be pineal, pituitary, and carotid) are as follows: head center = upper brain (cortex); ajna = lower brain; throat center = medulla; heart center = third ventricle; solar plexus = hypothalamus; sacral center = thalamus; base center = cerebellum.

The head center governs the cerebrum (the main part of the thinking brain matter) and the right eye (although this is not always the case, see later). Awakened prematurely, the head center can cause (in advanced humanity) inflammation of the brain, brain tumors, and insanity (also schizophrenia—caused by an over-active alta major center whereby it impinges and interferes with the normal consciousness with the past or illusory states [hearing voices]; or due to the web in the head being partly punctured). In the average person energy can pour through the head center to one of the five centers in the body where the consciousness is focused and there cause problems. If this center should be overstimulated, epilepsy, headaches, migraines and growths in the brain tissue could form, or certain neuroses become apparent. Underactivity of the crown center will be seen as diminished consciousness, poor memory, and fuzzy thinking.

Some students want to work with the centers in the head or with the crown's petal energies. While this is possible, it is usually useless due to the head center's undeveloped state. The head center only comes into conscious function when the kundalini fires have risen significantly, and the person is highly developed spiritually, morally and philosophically. The head center represented in the seven planes of consciousness is literally mere buds in the majority. Students often confuse working with the soul with working with the head center. Our work with the soul is our work with all the seven centers and their relevant triangles for that person—a much more beneficial service.

Upward pointing triangle:
HdC = soul focuses its mental consciousness
HtC = soul focuses its feeling consciousness
ThC = soul focuses its creativity

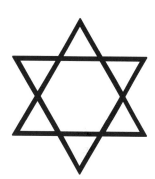

Downward pointing triangle:
BC = Elemental of physical body
SPC = Elemental of astral
SC = Elemental of mind

Summary

The major vital centers in the body control and influence the entire body of systems and organs:

The Base Center—the bony system especially the spine, as well as the kidney system; also the musculature; locomotor system.

The Sacral Center—the reproductive system and organs.

The Solar Plexus Center—the intestinal system including the liver, gall bladder, stomach, pancreas, and the nervous system; digestive system.

The Heart Center—the cardiovascular system and circulation, the immune system, the lymphatic system and spleen, and the vagus nerve.

The Throat Center—the respiratory system, the alimentary canal, and the metabolic system.

The Ajna Center—the endocrine system, integrating all the systems; and also the nervous system.

The Head Center—the central nervous system, and brain and mentality.

SHARING

"Only through a sane and worldwide grasp of the New Age principle of sharing will human ills be cured; only by the right distribution of energy will the ills of the physical body of individual man also be cured. This is a fundamental (I would say the fundamental principle) of all spiritual healing. In the last analysis also this presupposes an eventual and scientific recognition of the etheric body of the planet, and consequently of man." —Djwhal Khul

6.

THE ART OF ADMINISTERING ESOTERIC HEALING

Why should we opt to use esoteric healing rather than say flower remedies, homeopathy, psychotherapy, naturopathy, orthodox medicine or any other form of treatment? Esoteric healing can bring healing to all seven of our bodies of consciousness. It can be used alongside all other therapies, orthodox and complimentary. Now let us see what esoteric healing is, what it claims to do, and how we are to dispense it therapeutically.

So far we have been laying down some ground rules so that we can begin to work with this form of medical treatment. Now we need to review its pharmacology (or pneumapharmacology)—how it works in the body.

How does esoteric healing work?

From a scientific point of view, when a drug is taken (and this includes all kinds of medication taken into the body), there are constituents that reorganize the working of the body. The body's response to illness is increased so that the illness can be "thrown off." (Of course, we know how most chemical drugs suppress the symptoms of illness rather than bring about wellness.) Everything that is imposed on the body changes it according to the laws of the body, to good or bad effect. Esoteric healing is no different. Drugs or herbs or homeopathic potencies, acupuncture, manipulations or massage—all these work on the physical body, reverberating upwards towards the subtle bodies of the etheric, astral and mental. These methods start their action in the realm of effects and cure by reorganizing cellular function first, or calming the emotional body. Other therapies, such as psychotherapy, counseling, hypnosis, and so on, which work more on the emotional body, effect change by showing the patient how to relax and think differently and more widely. Esoteric healing also imposes a different rhythm on the body, but, and this may distinguish it from all other therapies (even other forms of spiritual healing methods), not from the personality levels at all. Its new rhythm comes from the vibratory status of the soul. Soul to soul. The healer's soul influences the patient's, then the patient imposes on her own body the soul purposes for her body and life. This is how esoteric healing achieves its healing. For healers to help, of course, requires training and technique.

There are kinds of spiritual healing in which the healer simply tunes into the client or into God or Christ, and allows the reorganizing energies to flow down, called "channeling." In esoteric healing, we also make our alignment with God, the Source of Life, and Christ, the Second Aspect, Love (the state of cosmic consciousness, that sees the oneness and loves all beings without distinction), but then we train our own conscious, active intelligence and employ it in the work of healing. We do this in line with the teachings of the Ageless Wisdom. In other words, our work with the Christ is not denominational; esoteric healers do not need to belong to a church. The Ageless Wisdom includes all the great Masters who have founded religions and notes the relevance of these systems for the purposes of emergence—the emergence of the soul and the emergence of the next Master, the coming Christ or Messiah or Maitreya or Imam or Bodhisattva (see Hopking, 1994). Humanity as a whole, with all its religions and departments of life in our wonderful civilization, is working together (however inscrutably) for the same divine Plan.

As stated above, healers work with the life principle, not with some vague energy which is set in motion by the power of thought or by the potency of love. The energy poured into the patient's vehicle is not mental energy, but one of the seven forms of pranic or life energies. The perfect healer works through the closed and sealed point within the center or chakra (the very heart of the center, cf. p. 78) which then affects the petals (the consciousness aspect) (Bailey, 1951-70, v. 4, pp. 627-28). The patient is, as a whole, a center! The healer heals from the center of this

center, which is the patient's heart center—the life principle. Out of this
center radiates consciousness. In this way change is wrought. Shall we
see how this is brought about esoterically, using a flow chart?

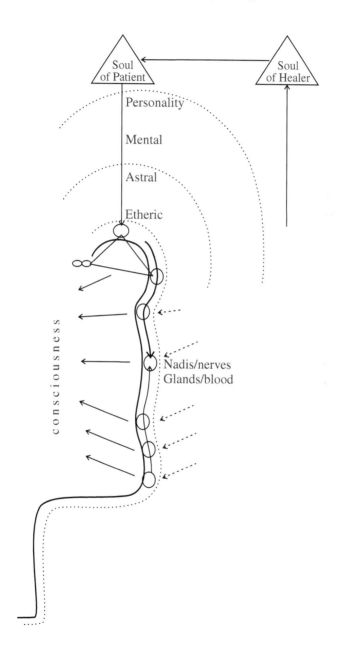

Alignment

The first task, then, is for the healer to align the soul with that of the patient and with a high spiritual source.

A little more must be said about the alignment, as seen in a wider context. A spiritual person is recognized as both a successful worker in the world and an occult student. Such a person reaches the conclusion that behind all the many causes with which one has been engaged is a CAUSE. This causal unity then becomes the goal of the search, which is eventually demonstrated in life as continuity of consciousness. To attain this awareness such a person must gain access to the nature of the soul, the medium through which the spirit ever works. And to do that, we must learn to function as the soul, detached from the world. When this is mastered, that person becomes "a conscious part of that soul that permeates and pervades all that is in manifestation." We must try to link ourselves in consciousness with the soul as it expresses itself in the etheric body. There is a very magnetic mantram that can be of assistance in linking with the soul, called the Soul Mantram, from the book *The Rainbow Bridge*, by two students of the blue books" by Alice Dailey with Djwhal Khul, published by Rainbow Bridge Productions. The *Rainbow Bridge* book recommends that "*no work should be undertaken until this mantram has been said*" and "after the invocation has been said, the Soul Star will obey thought and move within the vehicles and the electromagnetic field.... It is a most powerful, versatile, and useful instrument of White Magic. *It will not respond to anything else.*" Accordingly, without prejudice, I recommend that this mantram may be said during the phase of alignment before an esoteric healing treatment:

The Soul Mantram
I am the Soul.
I am the Light Divine.
I am Love.
I am Will.
I am Fixed Design.

This mantram is adapted from that given by DK which he says was "taken from a very ancient disciples' manual." The full version is as follows: "I am the Soul. And also love I am. Above all else I am both will and fixed design. My will is now to lift the lower self into the light divine. This light I am. Therefore, I must descend to where the lower self awaits my coming. That which desires to lift and that which cries aloud for lifting are now at-one. Such is my will" (Bailey, 1944, v. 2, p. 123).

Why so much emphasis on the etheric? And why does esoteric healing put such emphasis on this relationship of the soul to the etheric body? Let us build on what we have said above about the soul and about the etheric.

The etheric body in the human being:

a. Is the symbol of the soul in that it has within it seven focal points of energy. The soul is influenced by seven ray energies. Each one influences one etheric center.

b. Is the physical correspondence to the inner light body, which we call the soul body or causal body. It is called the "golden bowl" in the Bible.

c. Is a body of light.

d. Has a rate of vibration that always synchronizes with the development of the soul.

e. Is a coherent force, linking and connecting every part of the body structure.

f. Is the microcosmic "web of life," for it underlies every part of the physical structure.

g. Carries the life principle throughout the body.

h. Enables the soul to be en rapport with the environment.

i. Produces eventually, through life and consciousness, a radiant activity so that each human being can distribute light and attractive energy to others in the human kingdom.

j. Is indivisible, coherent and unified, symbolizing the unity and homogeneity of Life or Energy. There are no separated organisms in the etheric vehicle. It is simply a body of freely flowing force.

k. Links the purely physical with the purely subtle, just as the soul links the three worlds of the personality—that is, the physical, emotional and mental—to the higher planes in the solar system.

l. Symbolized by a five-pointed star.[1]

Knowing that the soul expresses itself through the etheric body should give us hope and encouragement when we start to align with the soul. Alignment produces a downflow of life from the life within, which results in sound vehicles. It is only as the personality becomes merged in the soul, and when the polarization shifts from the lower to the higher, that the work of the soul healing the form becomes possible. The more the consciousness is stabilized in the soul, the less will disease affect one, for such polarization will act like an instant transmuter. Karma will quickly and safely be worked out.

Disease appears where there is a lack of alignment between the factor of life (the soul) and the factor of form (the personality). There is a definite need to exert the will when we begin the work of alignment, for, says the Tibetan Master DK, "the real work of the soul is accomplished only when there is alignment of the threefold personality with the soul and its stabilization there. This is done by an effort of the will." One result is an unimpeded funnel to the brain. Put another way, the lower self is in chordal tune with the soul. This does not, however, make the soul any more aware of or interested in the personality's disposition and little ideas. But the soul is conscious of the limitations within the personality nature and of the barriers opposed to the inflow of soul energy. The details of the person's life and thought and feelings are of no interest to the soul. The soul is occupied with recognizing hierarchical planning, with registering world need, and with responding (very faintly at first) to monadic flow. The soul always works in terms of the group and of the whole.

Such "attitudes" of the soul, when brought into alignment with the personality of the patient, can produce changes in their vocation. Soul guidance is a result of meditation, discipline and service, and when a direct channel of communication is set up from soul to brain via the mind, the condition is true divine guidance. But caution is needed. Such guidance can be distorted and misinterpreted if the mind is not developed, the character not purified, and the person not free from personality control. How easily can unimportant people and beginners interpret calls and messages they hear or receive as coming from some high and elevated source (devas, angels, Masters, high disciples, initiates), but they are in all probability hearing that which emanates from their own subconscious or from their own souls (Bailey, 1944; 1950a; 1957; 1962; 1951–70, V. 2 & V. 4).

How to start healing esoterically

You can well imagine that, in view of the complexities of people, their diverse personalities, their arrangement of etheric centers, their problems in the past, their relationships toward themselves, toward others and the world, and so on, that esoteric healers can and do enter intricate and sensitive etheric webs. To gain this entry usually requires a long training and personal guidance (a minimum of three years is recommended by DK). Longer might be needed for those who have not meditated or who have difficulty relating to the subtle anatomy of energies and forces. As in any other of the healing professions, students learn scientific facts and theories regarding health and disease. This is followed by training in the techniques involved in their healing method (use of drugs, manipulations, etc.) and in what happens to the body of the patient when the different therapeutic agents are used. How to approach patients, how to diagnose, how to prescribe, what therapeutics to avoid when certain conditions present themselves, what to do in emergencies, in acute cases, in chronic cases, what to do if there are adverse reactions to the treatment given, treatment for the dying, and so on—all these are also addressed in training one in the science and art of esoteric healing. But as in any other therapy, no one needs to go to the doctor for everything. We change our diet for a time, we take an aspirin, we make an herb tea, we ask our partners to massage us, we seek the advice of a friend, and so on. So there are simple home techniques that can be used and applied by anyone, either to oneself or to another.

Esoteric healing as presented here can be used for this simple home use. This book is a simple, practical handbook for anyone, while also indicating the deeper aspects, the more specialized applications. These latter techniques may seem difficult at first and will more than likely necessitate attending classes and a practicing clinic.

Radiatory healing technique

The first thing a beginner might prefer to learn, therefore, is radiatory healing by itself. It is an advanced form of healing because one of its prerequisites is that you be in touch with your soul, but it is simpler to learn and far more easily mastered than magnetic healing. This means that you may be a beginner in the healing art but proficient in meditation and soul contact. Then, later, you may want to progress to the more advanced methods of magnetic healing that this book teaches. For those of you who want experience of esoteric healing using radiatory healing first, here is an outline of the form.

1. Having made your alignment with your soul, by an act of will link up as a soul with the souls of your group members.

2. Now permit this contact with the soul to descend so that you also link with their minds and their emotional nature. Remember that energy follows thought, and the linking process is inevitable when you use your imagination with intention. Having done this, you can function as a group. There is no further need to be conscious of the group—it has been established. You now work as a group.

3. Now build or open the triangle of healing: send a line of white light from your soul, to your brain, to your heart center. Focus all these energies in the head, radiating out to the aura (yours and the patient's), picturing yourself as a radiant center of energy or a point of vivid light. It is this light that will be projected upon the patient through your ajna center.

4. Now say the Group Mantram: "With purity of motive, inspired by a loving heart, we offer ourselves for this work of healing. This offer we make as a group and to the one we seek to heal." As you sound this mantram, visualize the linking process going on, linking you to your group, and the group to the patient. This activity is done through your ajna center.

5. Now direct your thought to the one who has come to you for healing. Link up with the patient, so that the patient becomes a reality in your consciousness and close to you.

6. Now recall the difficulty, ailment, or inharmony, about which the patient has come to you; bring it to mind, then dismiss it. Now simply concentrate upon the love force you are going to work with.

7. Feel a deep love pouring into you. Know that this is light substance which you can and will manipulate.

8. Now send it out as a stream of radiant light from the ajna through your hands which are held about six inches (15 cm) in front of your eyes, palms turned outward. The stream of radiant light is thus directed onto the patient. As you visualize it pouring out and sense the

patient receiving it, say the Radiatory Mantram aloud, slowly and deliberately, in a low voice, seeing only a concentrated radiating love pour to the patient: "May the love of the One Soul, focussed in this group, radiate upon you, my brother/sister, and permeate every part of your body—healing, soothing, strengthening, and dissipating all that hinders service and good health."

9. Now withdraw your energies from the aura of the patient, leaving the person free, without dependence on you, and walking the way of their own plan and purpose. Silently give thanks for this opportunity to serve.

10. After a little time, ground the patient into the physical vehicle and restore their ordinary consciousness, by gently placing your hands on their shoulders to indicate the healing is over.

11. After the healing, the Master DK emphasizes "the urgent necessity for *complete silence and reticence* (his italics) in relation to all healing work. Never let it be known by anyone that you are working in this manner, and never mention to anyone the names of those you are seeking to aid. Do not discuss the patient under treatment even among yourselves." He goes on to say, "if this basic rule of silence is not kept, it will indicate that you are not yet ready for this work and should discontinue it." He further explains, "This injunction is far more important than you can realize; for speech and discussion not only tend to deflect and dissipate force, but violate a fundamental rule which all healers are trained to keep."

More about the advanced use of radiatory healing can be found in Alice Bailey's *Esoteric Healing* (1951–70, v. 4, pp. 103 ff. and 653–58). The true healer who is experienced in these methods employs both forms, radiatory and magnetic healing, with equal facility and interchangeably as required (see pp. 143, 153).

Training in a clinic

It is the purpose of this book to offer preliminary training so that readers who have no esoteric knowledge can gain entry into the fascinating and rewarding world of esoteric healing. Much depends on the reader studying and following up all this information, on experimenting and on linking up with other esoteric healing practitioners. When you have used these principles again and again, their value will be recognized and a new reality of causative healing opened up. You will be able to watch what happens to the body of the patient when the different therapeutic agents (triangle circuits and center balancing) are used, and become aware as to what to apply next time, and so on, just like a doctor would when dispensing medicines. With practice, and especially if you attend a recognized and established esoteric healing clinic, you will learn how to speak to patients and to deal with those who come for your aid. What questions to ask are dealt with below. How to diagnose in esoteric healing must not be confused with a "labeling system." It is best to avoid telling anyone what you think of their condition, as the human mind is apt to exacerbate the condition by focussing on it. How to prescribe different triangles for treatment is best learned by repeatedly reviewing the triangles and practicing them on yourself or on willing "guinea pigs." What circuits to avoid when certain conditions present themselves is best learned at a training clinic (beginners should not work on pregnant women, for instance). What to do in emergencies will be discovered the more familiar you become with the circuits and with the routine of esoteric healing. Sometimes the disease seems to create further problems as a result of the treatment, sometimes called the "healing crisis." Treatment for the dying needs special care, and you need to be well experienced for that work.

How to balance the centers

To balance the centers is the very heart and purpose of the healing process. Where there is no balance, i.e., where the inflow and outflow through the centers is unequal, there can be no effective way of bringing the patient to an understanding of the illness, nor of changing the inward self and so bringing about healing. In esoteric healing it is always the patient who heals him or herself; the healer is but a reflector, a mirror, and an ideal, all in one. The healer is not—and this must be made clear—a reflector of himself or herself, but of the patient, i.e., within their soul interaction, the healer acts as a reflector to the patient of the patient's true purpose and nature, thereby causing change to become possible from that level. This makes for permanence. Healing has many nuances: it doesn't always result in physical healing. The physical body has laws which it must follow, and if these laws have been broken to the extent of becoming irreparable, then, it is clear, healing can only take place on a higher or more subtle level. The physical body is the least important in the sense that it is the automaton of the higher vehicles. The physical body is "not a principle," as the Ageless Wisdom tells us. The physical body has reached perfection in evolutionary terms and so all it needs to do is release any karmic imperfections. The new principle or goal of divine evolution "has entirely to do with consciousness."

To set the stage, let us first discuss some important components to healing through balancing the centers and through creating triangles: the hands, visualization and the breath.

SOME EXERCISES

1. To learn to balance the centers: First, practice by putting your hands nearly together without touching. Keep your eyes closed. Gradually, very slowly, move them apart. See if you can detect any feeling between the hands or in the hands. Where? Then, when they are quite far apart, move them inwards towards each other again, very slowly, stopping to notice changes of feeling, if any. Do this exercise a few times. Then try detecting different energy radiating from, say, your elbow and your knee, your hands and your feet, your left foot and your right foot, the different parts of your body, chest, abdomen and so on, and finally feel your head. You can also use your fingers as pointers of energy: point a finger at the palm of your other hand, moving it up the arm and down to the fingers, then change hands. Learn simply to feel by observation and detection. You might register feeling in your hands as heat or coldness, as heaviness, thickness, or in your brow center. Simply observe, observe, observe.

2. Another exercise to increase sensitivity: Hold your hands out in front of you. Using your brow center like a finger, point at one hand then the other, moving along the fingers and elsewhere, as you did when pointing with your finger. Notice the energy feeling. Do all these exercises thoughtfully and slowly and meditatively (in esoteric healing impatience is one of the worst hindrances to success), trying to assess their difference or similarity.

3. An exercise to experience your bodily organs: Sit comfortably in a meditative position and focus on an organ of your choosing, say, your liver. Be aware of its position, its bulk, its function, its relationships with the stomach, intestine, diaphragm. Notice your own feelings as you scan these different aspects of the organ. Use the same sequence with other organs—stomach, pancreas, intestine, kidneys, bladder, uterus (or prostate), spinal cord, heart, lungs, brain, ventricles, nerves, blood vessels, lymph glands, the ductless glands, ears, touch, eyes, taste, smell, and so on. Keep notes to help you clarify your thoughts and feelings as you do this every day. Images can be actual or symbolic; they can be seen as if from outside, or you can get inside them (microscopic vision); simply allow them to speak via your intuition, but do not allow yourself to get caught up with these pictures, losing your original focus. In esoteric healing we are not interested in psychic phenomena; this is worse than valueless and is a hindrance to healing. Keep detached and practice, practice, practice.

Over the weeks, cover the whole body by powering up your perceptions, visualization, and intuitive feelings. Repeat these exercises often. Be aware of their etheric quality, their astral quality, their mental quality; try even to go to their soul quality and higher. Even when one is said to be advanced, there is a place for such regular exercise. Do we want to be expert healers or just lukewarm channels? Any effort is repaid a thousandfold.

The hands in healing

Now that you have experienced how the energy can be directed, magnified, withheld, fired, charged, softened, absorbed, etc., by the use of the hands, we should again consider these amazing organs of creative (and destructive) energy manipulation.

I remember during my early monastic years, when I was being prepared to enter the novitiate from my period of postulency, I was put into "contemplative silence" for seven days. One of the assignments the Novice Master asked me to do was an active meditation on the use of my hands during each day. This meditation left a lasting impression on me, and I realized that the hands are almost alive of themselves, giving to and taking from each other, talking to one another, supporting, acknowl-

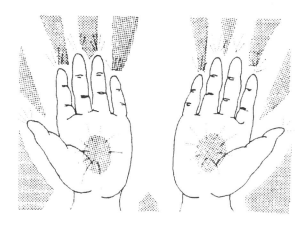

edging, serving one another. They seemed to me to be the perfect pair, a couple with whom you couldn't find fault, a marriage and bondage of love and beauty! During that week I also came to realize their power. The hands wielded the creative will just as the legs and feet controlled the animal will. The hand could offer the tribute of recognition, the gentleness of affection or the assault of hatred. The hands contain very powerful energy centers. My religious experience reminded me of my weeping heart when considering the nails through the hands of Christ on the cross.

Alice Bailey quotes a lovely passage which the Tibetan Master passed on to her (remember, please, that the word "man" here refers to humanity, male and female.):

> When the right hand of the man of matter
> grasps the flower of life and plucks it for himself,
> the left hand remains in emptiness.
> When the right hand of the man of matter
> grasps the golden lotus of the soul,
> the left hand descends seeking the flower of life,
> though he seeks it not for selfish ends.
> When the right hand holds the golden lotus firm
> and the left hand grasps the flower of life,
> man finds himself to be the seven-leaved plant
> which flowers on earth and flowers before the Throne of God.
>
> (Bailey, 1951–70, v. 1, p. 61)

When we shake hands, vitality or nerve force passes across from the meeting hands into the bodies of the individuals. A sensitive person can tell a lot by a handshake. An aware disciple can consciously encourage the soul of another just through shaking hands. Many of us have heard about the Masonic secret grips whereby one Mason may know another and know him as a brother, whether he meets him in the dark or in the light, and it also informs him how far he has progressed in the Craft. So also in healing, behind the outer forms of hand movements and finger flexions, there can be found an inner action, a movement initiated by higher mind. The use of the fingers as they are connected to the ethers and the subtle bodies has already been described in an earlier chapter. The hand responds to these according to the trained will of the skilled operator. "The healer must seek to link his soul, his heart, his brain and his hands. Thus can he pour the vital healing force upon the patient," says Rule Five of Esoteric Healing as it describes how we prepare ourselves for magnetic work.

Most centers in the body rely upon glands or organs or joints for the precipitation of subtle energy. The hands, however, rely on certain forms of molecular substance within which are conserved, and from which are expelled, streams of magnetic energy that are subject to the will of the healer. Usually unconsciously to the healer, this molecular substance of the corpuscles expands or contracts, unconsciously to those concerned, and so flashing their message of consent or denial to the brain. See how this connects with the Healing Triangle. The healing hands can also grasp at forces that are spiritual or rather more subtle than the gross physical, which are then transmitted to the brain, then relayed to the heart center and to the intuition for interpretation. In this way we can heal bodily and emotional ills, and even manipulate mental matter and currents. So we learn that just as the personality is the soul's instrument for expression, so the hands are a major means whereby the individual distributes energy and expresses intention. An ancient saying speaks of the means by which creative energy of the third aspect of divinity is made manifest:

> Seek to cooperate with the creative process,
> and learn to work with the eyes open,
> the voice proclaiming
> and the hands conferring.

This speaks of the open inner eyes, the discriminative voice of thought and instruction. Another text has this to say:

> The hand of man evokes a miraculous fire from space.
> You know that from a single touch flashes out a flame
> that does not burn.

Again, a different source says the following:

> Only the hands that have let slip all within the three worlds
> are free to carry the ultimate blessing to struggling humanity.

Phases of vital flow

To understand how to balance a center we must realize that there is throughout the body a constant circulation of vital energy. This movement has a flow that is fresh (directed into the body) and "spent" (or directed out of the body). These are likewise the two phases of circulation in and out of a center. A third phase is the actual circulation of the energy within the body. Furthermore, the condition of the centers reveals the state of evolution of their possessor.

Each of the centers themselves can be understood as to be in one of the five basic states according to the development of the individual. These correspond with the five races, planes and stages of consciousness:

1. Closed, still and shut, and yet with signs of life, silent and full of deep inertia. (Lemurian Race. Atmic Plane. Mineral Kingdom.)
2. Opening, unsealed, and faintly tinged with color; the life pulsates. (Atlantean Race. Buddhic Plane. Plant Kingdom.)
3. Quickened, alive, alert in two directions; the two small doors are open wide. (Aryan Race. Mental Plane. Animal Kingdom.)
4. Radiant and reaching forth with vibrant note to all related centers. (The Sixth Race. Astral Plane. Humanity.)
5. Blended they are and each with each works rhythmically. The vital force flows through from all the planes. The world stands wide open. (The Seventh Race. Physical plane. The Hierarchy of Masters.)[2] (Bailey, 1951–70, v. 4, p. 81).

The simplest method to balance a center as an initial stage to healing requires the healer to bring the center's inflow and outflow into balance, so that the inflow equals the outflow. Sometimes this imbalance is so noticeable as to immobilize the hands or one hand. The energy feels stuck, or feels as though it is being drawn through thick mud or molasses. Or the opposite may occur, where one feels as though there is a vacuum, offering absolutely no resistance. The hands as it were slip and slide. The incoming energy is pure, clean, fresh, new, like a breath of fresh air being drawn in, and the outflowing energy is devitalized, like our outbreath. But like our breathing, only a balanced flow in and out makes for health. In the subtle bodies, however, this flow is much more sensitive to change, like a finely tuned barometer.

Visualization

Visualization is a gateway and the secret to all true meditation work. Visualization is the use of the directing activity of the mind and the faculty of the creative imagination, which is the highest level of the astral nature and the counterpart of the intuition (buddhi). For just as discrimination is to the mind, so imagination is to the feeling nature. The image-making faculty is the result of the five senses plus the integrating sixth sense, the mind. In astrology, Mars governs the five senses, with its fire and energetic will, inaugurates the thoughtforms, while the ascendant integrates the imagery with a specific and impersonal purpose in view.

The exercises described above are the foundation to a creative imagination. This is because visualization is based largely on the sense of touch. In the tabulations in Chapter 7, p. 229ff. concerning the senses, note you will find that, when the sense of touch passes through the buddhic body or consciousness, it becomes true healing. This is the beautiful reality: when we touch another from within the buddhic field (the realm of pure reason or spiritual intuition), we perform healing. Nothing could be said more simply! This is certainly a most profound definition of healing, and it is the method of esoteric healing.

What happens when we creatively utilize the power of visualization? As you work with visualization, you will note more and more an emphasis on the sense of quality. Here you will experience the astral-buddhic approach towards the work at hand—a feeling, but a feeling directed by the discriminative or selective aspect of the mind, an experience of an interior process of a quality, or what might be called a sense of the patient's karma. This results in an identification with the realization of the problem and symptom, a vision of the purpose—what I call "spiritual prognosis." The final activity of this process is the projection of the realized quality: a very powerful but extremely delicate activity which actually RESOLVES THE PAST. We do this using the tools of esoteric healing, notably the many esoteric triangles within the human bodies or grades of consciousness. These particularly involve the whole system of chakras.

It is not difficult to understand in this description of visualization how that "energy follows thought." This is one of the greatest of the esoteric laws. From it hangs the whole structure of esoteric healing. Once visualization is recognized and experienced as an internal process, then we have taken the first step towards the direction of energy. When you begin to practice visualizing pictures, you should do so within the head center, between the ajna and crown centers. Here you acquire the facility to see in a higher or more subtle way. It is here also that you should focus when you intend to work with a specific triangle in a patient. In this way you gather energy, focus this energy under the power of intention, and then project it or distribute it (often by means of a pictorial process or as a symbol) in the intended direction—to particular centers and in the appropriate sequence.

There is no haste or rush during such treatments. As healers-to-be we must make these disciplines habitual, practicing them slowly, regularly and gradually. Remember what happened when you first tried to swim? You sank! But with perseverance and effort it became effortless and rewarding. Some exercises on how to visualize can be found below.

You will, I am sure, feel, as you read these words, the power and overwhelming Presence of this technique. One of the most influential teachers of healing this century said of it, "this constitutes one of the major healing techniques of the future" (Bailey, 1944, v. 1, p. 91). By correct visualization we have the superstructure for ascertaining the truth or falsity of all that comes to our awareness, and, what is more, what to do about it from the angle of the soul. We can make the future a present reality.

Breathing techniques[3]

The average person breathes about 1000 times per hour. Forcing the power of the breath is dangerous, both for yourself and the one you are trying to heal. Breath is related to the will, whereas healing is done through love. Hence the conflict and the difficulty. More potent than any pranayama technique available from a touring yogi is the development of an even, rhythmic breathing cycle. When you have balance and rhythm in your breath, you will have power in your words, and your thoughts will take on a new vitality and creativity.

Visualization is strongly related to the natural inflow and outflow of breath, uncontrolled yet even and profoundly rhythmical. Only with a focused mind can the breath play a part in healing.

Try the following safe exercise given by the Master DK in *Letters on Occult Meditation*: Withdraw the consciousness onto the mental plane at some point within the brain, then sound the Sacred Word (OM) gently three times. Picture the breath sent forth as a clarifying expurgating force that in its progress onward sweeps away the thoughtforms circulating in the mental ovoid. At the close realize that the mental body is free and clear of thoughtforms (Bailey, 1950a, p. 96).

Balancing the centers

There are two ways to balance the centers. The most common way is to have the patient sit in an upright chair while you, the healer, hold your hands on either side of their body. This method is fine to start with. You can then progress to the more advanced method. The other, more advanced method, which I prefer, believing it to be more in keeping with the esoteric teachings, is to sit or stand behind the patient (who is seated in an upright chair) with your hands outstretched in line with the center to be balanced. (If the patient is lying on a couch the healer stands to their side. If the patient is dying, the healer stands behind the head.)

To do the work of balancing you should be aligned and attuned and have already opened the Triangle of Healing. This will be described in the next chapter. For now, simply practice the technique on a friend without being attuned, so that no energies are actually being transmitted. You are able, nevertheless, to begin working with the energies of another person. This is an important safeguard for both yourself and your friend: no energies are being exchanged, and you can practice in complete confidence that nothing will happen.

SYNCHRONIZING TRIANGLE

To balance a center, the healer works with the Synchronizing Triangle as described in Rule Three of Esoteric Healing:

> Let the healer concentrate the needed energy within the needed center. Let that center correspond to the center which has need. Let the two synchronize and together augment force. Thus shall the waiting form be balanced in its work. Thus shall the two and the one, under right direction, heal (Bailey, 1951–70, v. 4, p. 534).

As the healer, you first align with your soul (a stage described in the next chapter), and then direct this spiritual energy from the head center via the ajna center to that center in yourself which corresponds to the patient's center that is going to be balanced (cf. pp. 155–57). The soul linkage is a major protective measure for the healer to prevent your center from becoming overstimulated as it connects with the patient's corresponding center. Practice this many times before you align with the soul as it is connected in higher triangles (see below) and before opening the Healing Triangle.

Having drawn this energy down from your soul (via the head center and ajna) to the center which corresponds to the patient's center, hold the two centers steady against each other. Here the healer uses both hands: one hand in the energy inflow and the other hand in the energy outflow.

Two other techniques may also be used with this triangle according to the intelligent intuition of the healer. Move slowly and with due caution even at the expense of being ineffectual and unsuccessful. One technique, called the expulsive technique, is used if the patient's center is overactive. To bring it back into balance the healer can expel the excess energy. As healer, increase the energy in your corresponding center to make it highly magnetic. You then draw off the excess overstimulating energy from the patient's center and the excess is transmuted in your (the healer's) head center and soul.

Synchronizing Triangle

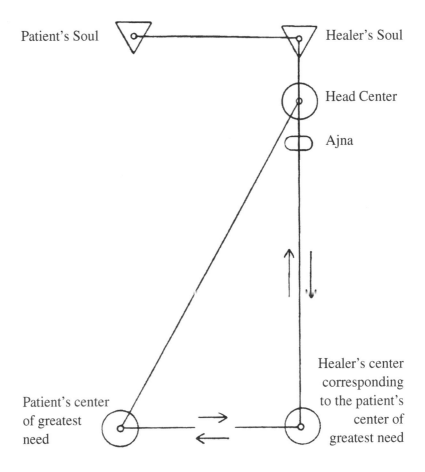

Patient's Soul   Healer's Soul

Head Center

Ajna

Healer's center
corresponding
to the patient's
center of
greatest need

Patient's center
of greatest
need

The other technique, called the stimulating technique, is used when the healer finds the patient's center exhausted and devitalized, contracted and weak. You, the healer, can empower the patient's center from your own corresponding center by sending a ray of your own energy. In this way the patient's center is amplified and strengthened.

Let us summarize these three techniques of the Synchronizing Triangle:

1. The Balancing Technique. The safest method. Hold the two centers steady against each other, to bring about a balance in the patient's center. The use of magnetic and radiatory healing together.

2. The Expulsive Technique. When the patient's center is overactive, you, the healer, empower your own center to strongly magnetize (draw out, draw back) energy from the patient's corresponding (overactive) center. This is using radiatory healing only. The hands are not needed. Balance of the center is then restored.
3. The Stimulating Technique. When the patient's center is underactive, as the healer, send a powerful ray of your own energy from your own center into the corresponding (underactive) center in the patient. This uses magnetic healing only. The hands are used to control the movement and lead to a balance (see Diagnosis, p. 157).

The whole aim of using these techniques, as is the purpose of all medical methods, is to bring the body into renewed or restored balance or homeostasis. In esoteric healing our intention is for etheric balance, on an ever higher scale. Of course, it is not a balance which is restoring a past integration, but a balance which has moved the patient on to a new integrity or larger whole. A karmic problem is released and resolved thereby; the secret is unveiled.

Such balance is easier to achieve in persons who are on the spiritual path, since they have already started the process of developing their seven major centers. It is less easy to bring into balance the centers of a person who is not spiritually oriented, as the major centers are still dormant (the minor centers are more active). Such a person may well be better advised to consult a practitioner in the orthodox or complementary medical field for quicker results. However, the Triangle for Undeveloped Persons (Bailey, 1951–70, v. 4, p. 430) may be used in conjunction with the Synchronizing Triangle to help the absorption of higher energy. To do this, hold the soul of the patient, directing the energy to the head center, then down to the solar plexus center—or perhaps you might prefer to use the Triangle for the Majority which may be used safely for the majority of people who are not on a spiritual path, and which involves the ajna center, the solar plexus center, and the sacral center—and then do the balancing technique with the Synchronizing Triangle. This may assist the balancing work of any particular center which is badly out of rhythm.

The method for arriving at which center in the patient is in greatest need requiring the Synchronizing Triangle technique shall be fully described in Chapter 7.

Practicing with the major centers

Begin a practice balance session by starting with the solar plexus center, which is the most active in humanity at this time and therefore easier for the healer to detect. Close your eyes and visualize energy streaming in through your one hand (at the back), through the solar plexus center, and out and through the hand at the front. If you wish, you can start balancing by holding each center from behind the patient only.

In all the centers the energy always moves from the etheric and entering the *back* of the body through the center to the endocrine gland (except for the ajna, and head of course). This is because five major centers are situated outside the spinal column in the vital etheric body about 2-6 inches (5-10 cms) away from the spine (linked to the endocrine glands which they vitalize).[4]

As you "hold" the inflow and outflow of the solar plexus center, see if you can feel any difference in actual flow: is the movement of inflow too fast or too slow? Is there congestion? If so, what form is it taking? How does it feel at the outflow of the center? Is it coming out in a weak stream? Or is it pouring out too quickly? Does there appear an irregular throb? Do you detect heat or cold? In which subtle body is the cause of the problem? Is it in the etheric solar plexus center, or is it in the astral solar plexus center or in the mental solar plexus center? What sort of desire or emotion is out of balance? Are you getting any sensation in your hands? How do you interpret that sensation? Does a picture, image or symbol arise in your mind? If so, hold this and, as you scan the center, observe what happens to the image you're holding. You can then visualize the picture or image or symbol changing for the better, improving, unfolding into ever greater beauty. Allow it to move towards perfection, for this is the way visualization works. As the image changes for the better, improves, this has a corresponding effect on the center (or triangle) being worked on. Never allow the image to get out of control or get negative in any way. You are in control; always work towards the positive, the good, the beautiful, the true.

Listen to your intuition as you become more and more sensitive to the subtle changes going on within the flow. Don't worry about not detecting a lot at first; it takes practice. As you think about the energy in this way, let your hands respond to the flow, very gently directing it towards balance and harmony and towards right radiatory resonance, or if you're using imagery and visualization, towards greater and greater perfection.

Your hands will move to bring this about, and when it does you will know at once that balance has been achieved. Movements of the hands or fingers might feel huge and exaggerated when you are in a meditative state, but they are usually minute and hardly detectable by anyone watching. Anyone using showy movements which are large and elaborate is not healing but pretending to heal, and pretending to be important. When indicated, hold the center in this perfect state according to the visualized image. Then you can move on to the next center (or triangle).

My first encounter

On a personal note, I remember that, when I first started to study esoteric healing, I went to "Brenda's Clinic" (run by Brenda Johnston, who founded the International Health Research Network for the dissemination of the use of esoteric healing. This Network, a registered charity in England, is now known as the International Network of Esoteric Healing.) I had hardly arrived when I was placed on a chair to "watch and feel the energies"! This was a remarkable first experience of their methods, for I saw beams of light coming out of the healers' hands and fingers and going into the patient; it looked as if the patient were attached by strings or threads or rays of light to the healers. I couldn't feel much myself except some sort of vague, profound movement on deeper, almost unconscious levels. Later, when I was learning some of the techniques, I felt as though I was the most insensitive student alive. I felt nothing at all, and in the early days I questioned the value of this form of esoteric healing. And yet, when Brenda was teaching me, she would demonstrate, for instance, by moving her hands over my legs at a distance of some three or four feet and point out that there was trouble in my left leg (I had broken it in a motor cycle accident a few years before) and in my right knee area (I had a series of dislocations from playing rugby and an operation there when I was at school). She did not say, "Aha! You had dislocation trouble in your right knee ... mmm, yes, that was when you were about 16 years old and I can see you lying in pain on a rugby field, and ... mmm, yes, you had an operation on it a year later!" That is for the psychics to see and enjoy. As indicated above, this work is not in the least related to psychism. We are interested only in the energy on soul levels as it streams to its mirror, the etheric body. Any psychic activity is simply ignored as an inconvenient interference. Anyway, I suppose I must have felt enough to persevere, for I joined the clinic at Brenda's (with Ann Higgins and Helen Frankland; Brenda had retired from healing by that time, although she did come in to do some work with us occasionally) and worked there for two years. The clinic was a very good training ground, for we were able to discuss the different aspects of healing and also encourage one another on this untraveled path. We all had to drive long distances to attend this clinic. I remain in close contact with both Helen and Ann, even though we all run our own clinics now. We also all teach esoteric healing, each giving upward of three courses a year both in England and in other countries.

But as you see from this little detour, nothing comes very easily or very quickly; it is only with regular practice and study that we can succeed (and this can be said for anything). In this work, we like to add one other requirement to the two above, that of meditation. So we have: practice (service), study, and meditation, each relying on the others for complete success.

Balancing the other major centers

Once you have practiced on the solar plexus center, you have the basis for balancing all the centers up the spine. The order is as follows: solar plexus center, base center, sacral center, heart center, and throat center. Practice on each, moving from center to center up the body. Before working on the head centers (alta major, ajna and head center), I strongly recommend that you balance the five centers up the spine until you are well acquainted with their different energies, and until you feel confident about this part of healing. It is very important to get this right, for it stands as the foundation of all future treatment on the subtle bodies. Through this sort of initial practice you will encounter your own doubts and insights; it will enable you to build up or empower your own healing forces for the future. Then you may go on to balance the alta major center and the head center, and finally the ajna center.

The ajna center

Start with this center when doing the balancing for real on a patient. The energy of the ajna center is drawn in from the front, which is different from the other centers where the energy comes in from the back. This flow moves in through the brow and then exits just behind the crown center at the top of the head. Start by feeling the ajna on yourself:

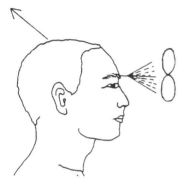

cup your right hand and place it in the energy stream a few inches in front of your brow. (When speaking of exits of energy, two things are being referred to: first, the exit of energy from the etheric center to the gland, and second, the exit from the gland both into the blood stream and associated organs and systems, and also from these back out into the etheric body as spent energy.)

Then using the index finger of your left hand raise your left hand above the top of your head. With your eyes closed, find the outstreaming ajna energy—it is often quite a "thin" stream of energy, hence we usually use the index finger to pick it up. When found, bring it into balance in much the same way as you have done when practicing with the solar plexus, base, sacral and other centers up the spine.

The ajna center governs the whole system of centers and actually has little inputs or centers in the brow itself (associated with the stalk of the pituitary gland) which relate to the different major centers on the spine. But don't worry about these at this stage; simply bring the whole center into a nice state of integration, being aware that this is the master center and influences all the other centers. When this center is in balance, all the other centers will be found to balance much more easily and more quickly.

Once you feel confident about this and the other centers, you may work on a friend to balance their major centers of energy—a wonderful experience for both of you, even if the outcome is unexpected. For, even though it may be relaxing, it is not a method for relaxation. The energy of the patient will be changed or charged, and this is not always acceptable or desirable insofar as the patient can see with the "eyes" of the personality. Often the soul has other plans!

So please practice on friends and on yourself as often as possible and be prepared to be called crazy or eccentric. Anything unknown, new, or different will earn this label. Try to be discreet and don't impose your newfound joy on your friends or family to make them feel used or uncomfortable! At this stage you may ask them if you may practice on them (I am afraid later this liberty is taken from you and you have to wait to be asked to give healing). So go on undeterred; the rewards are great. Or, if you can, get in touch with a clinic near you.[5]

Here is an exercise that will help with your diagnosis skills (see pp. 155–157); it was given by Master DK to "intensify the activity of the ajna center." It will also help to produce new vision and personal integration. He calls this an exercise, not a meditation.

1. Achieve quiet. Relax. Raise the consciousness to the ajna center.
2. Sound the OM, visualizing the integration of the personality with the soul. Link the ajna with the head center.
3. Pause.
    a. Take a long breath, drawing the energy from the throat center.
    b. Repeat the breathing, drawing the energy from the heart center, holding these two withdrawn energies imaginatively in the ajna center.
    c. Repeat the process in connection with the solar plexus.
    d. Repeat the process in connection with the sacral center.
    e. Recognizing then that four types of energy have been centered in the ajna, take another long breath and draw the energy of the base center to the ajna focus.
    f. Now consciously endeavor to hold all the energies there.
4. Now dedicate the energies of the personality (which express themselves through these five centers and the ajna, making six centers in all) and breathe them back again—by an act of the will—into the centers to which they belong. Do not do this sequentially and piecemeal but as one dynamic out-breathing; see these energies traveling down the spine to their respective resting places, carrying new life, pure stimulation and dynamic will to each and every center.
5. Now, as the soul informing the body, sound the OM.

You can follow this exercise with your daily meditation. It is an exercise that needs regular use to be effective (Bailey, 1944, v. 2, p. 604).

Balancing and visualization

While you are working on the centers, train yourself to visualize, to see the energy flow. (This does not employ lower psychic vision. Remember that in esoteric healing, psychic senses are actually more a hindrance than a help, so don't use them.) What we want is a creative use of the higher imagination. Here are some exercises in visualization:

i. Imagine a flow of water, pure white; see it flowing through your hands as you hold them about 18 inches (45 cm) apart.
ii. Now imagine a stream of air, clear but visible, moving in one direction through your hands.
iii. Now imagine the vital force, the etheric energy, as pure energy streaming through your hands.

In each of these exercises move your hands slowly in and then out to feel the different action of the hands on the stream of imagined force. Notice the changes that this action causes, both between your hands and in your hands, and also in your consciousness. Practice this at any time of day when you have a spare minute. It is a refreshing activity and can make for renewing a sagging concentration. Then, when you have become well-acquainted with the process, you can practice on a friend, with their consent, of course. And if your friend is interested, allow the roles to be reversed. It is good to be both a giver and a receiver, helping you to be more aware of the energies you are dealing with.

Transmittable force

Visualization is such that it is transmittable. That is to say, the limitations put on the physical world do not apply here. Through visualization the practice of healing can be done from a distance. Hence we have what is called absent healing, or, more appropriately, distant healing. My advice is that we use this form only when we are thoroughly versed in the art and technique of healing, and that we have done many years of work on patients that are present physically. The reason for this is that we need a sound foundation on the body first, where the patient's consciousness is close to us. In this way we can avoid mistakes and confusion. But what we can do is practice on a person who is present but on whose body you don't actually work. Let me explain. The patient sits in the center and the healer sits on the side but does not actually work in the patient's aura. Again, I would suggest you do this only after a lot of practice on patients who are physically present. Doing this will prepare you for healing from a distance. To repeat, distant healing should at first be used when a patient is there with you but on whose body you do not work. You will probably find this is easier if you practice in an organized esoteric healing clinic. Here is the technique:

Distant healing

Sit in an upright chair. Make your alignment, activate the Higher Triangle, and open the Healing Triangle and other triangles as usual when about to heal (see the description of this process in the next chapter). Now, since there is no actual patient physically present, imagine the person is there in front of you.

Remember, you have already achieved rapport with your patient on the soul level through the alignment and attunement, so the linking channels are already in place. This imagined presence is as real as if the person were present in his or her dense physical body—that's how strong the imagination makes it. In actual fact, the only thing that separates is what we call space and distance, whereas in meditation and in the activity of creative thought we enter the zone of timelessness. Where there is no time, the separation which distance or space causes no longer exists. Instead, all becomes immediately present. This is the nature of telepathic rapport; it is as if you are actually speaking to or possibly inside the person you are communicating with. Such a sense of identification can only be brought about after one has first acquired self-identification: a recognition and realization of one's "isness" and "beingness," based on the eternity and immortality of spirit.

With this in mind, do the healing as if the patient were there. It will surprise you how easy it is, and how effective it is. All it requires is a mind that is able to concentrate fairly well and the ability to stay aware of what you are doing at any given moment. Of course, we all will wander into other realms of thought, or into what we are to do after the healing is over, and so on. This is normal for beginners. If this happens, simply draw the mind back without any concern or irritation to its work. Gradually, in time, these deviations will occur less and less often. If you accept your own weakness, then you can build on your strengths. But if you get upset and cross with your weaknesses, you are actually strengthening them instead, while making your strengths more fragile. Deviating thoughts are as harmless as they are futile in the healing work, so the sooner you simply drop them—or turn them off or mentally say to them, "I will attend to you later," i.e., acknowledging them, but not following their lure—the sooner your focus will become clear and defined. Be interested in what you are doing to the patient. This will help to hold your thoughts on the process of healing.

The next chapter deals with the healing technique with a patient present. In absent healing or distant healing (although, as we have seen, distance does not actually exist in thought on soul level), we work with exactly the same process, all within the creative and vivid imagination, visualizing the energies bringing the entire organism into right balance and relationship with itself.

Appointments

Now we will turn to describe the actual processes involved in esoteric healing. The background knowledge essential for applying esoteric healing has been described. Now we can move into the practical use of esoteric healing. Before accepting your first appointment of a patient, we assume you have worked and practiced regularly at all these preliminary exercises leading up to your first consultation by a patient. We're going to be very practical and professional.

An esoteric healer's rule is that we will never use this form of healing unless asked by the patient, or the patient's parents if the patient is a child, or the patient's family or close friend if the patient is critically ill or unconscious. This rule never wavers, for it is through the voice that the patient's soul expresses itself and has the intention to change and be healed. It is normally best to have the patient present when you do the first healing, which establishes a close thread of energy between you and the patient that can be recalled if the patient is unable to see you personally on subsequent visits due to distance or for other inevitable reasons. Then you may heal via visualization and telepathy,[6] called "absent healing" or "distant healing."

THE FIRST APPOINTMENT

The first appointment should be assigned one hour. You will not actually be healing for an hour, but you do need time to talk a little to the patient beforehand. Allow the patient to verbalize their symptoms and needs. The healing will take something between fifteen to thirty minutes (no longer for first appointments) and then, if you can, encourage the patient to rest silently in an adjoining room for ten to fifteen minutes, to "absorb the treatment" and so be ready for the outside demands again.

PAYMENT

"The worker deserves his pay," says a Master. A marked donation bowl may be left in the waiting room so that the patient can, out of freedom, and without embarrassment, leave an "energy" exchange for the healing group. Money should always be regarded in terms of energy, and someone giving money for the healing should be seen to be exchanging energy, for "he who gives, receives, to give again." Such an aphorism should be thought about, as it has far-reaching implications. The spiritual server, says DK, seeks nothing for the self, save that which may equip for the work to be done. I know healers who accept "gifts" instead of money as payment, for example, a homemade loaf of bread, a couple of jars of homemade marmalade, a bag of homegrown greens, and so on. Esoteric healers are professional like other medical practitioners. They have undergone a long training and the work is often demanding and tiring. They deserve to be repaid for this. But they should not expect anything. The healing is not for money (it is not for sale), as it is actually a healing energy "exchange."

Where the healer works in a dedicated clinic, it is often more comfortable to patients and more professional to have a "recommended donation" as a guideline.

Preparation of the patient

ASKING FOR HEALING

Let's explore more deeply the issue of asking for healing, as it is important for the healer to understand. The patient who seeks your help comes to you out of individual need and freedom. This point is one of the most difficult for beginners to understand. There can be no "Let me do some healing on you" to someone who has not asked for it. The healer must wait until those who require healing make an appointment. This is that so-called magnetic quality where the healer "attracts those who can be helped." At first it is very tempting for the new healer to want to go out and demonstrate their skill, to show esoteric healing off, to test the methods on people who have real problems. But in this form of medicine, which is entirely based on the higher form of energy and on a deeper understanding of the human being, it is imperative that the initiative for the establishment of the healing energy between the healer and the patient be instigated by the patient. It must be the patient's will to invoke aid from the healer. The healing flow of energy is then evoked, being drawn by the patient from the healer. This would not be the case if the healer were to suggest to a person, "Would you like me to give you some healing?" or "I can see you could benefit from esoteric healing; may I do this for you?" As stated earlier, the imposition of higher, more radiatory, energies for the act of healing can only be transferred from a position of passivity and receptivity from the angle of the patient, whereas if the healer asks to heal someone, this imposition is made from the will. It is a subtle form of forcing the patient into acquiescence. Such manipulation can have dangerous, even disastrous, long-term effects, not only for the patient but for the healer as well.

As with all rules there are always exceptions. The exception relating to this rule refers to those who do not have the capacity to ask for healing, viz., babies and children, and also those in a comatose state, and others who cannot rationally seek your help, but who are, according to your own intuition, calling out to you for healing. Those who seek your help via friends or other people must not be given healing by you until they make the effort to ask you themselves. Those who write to you asking for healing but who cannot get to you, you may treat by using "distant healing." Afterward both of you have an obligation towards each other to regularly keep in touch by letter, telephone, or e-mail. It is useless and a waste of time and spiritual energy sending out healing to someone who is not aware of the fact, not interested, or who is already better! For this reason, generally, it is best to see the patient on the first occasion at least, even if the later appointments are given absently, where the healer works with the patient at a distance. Again, it is best that the patient comes to see you for healing every week, or every fortnight, or monthly according to your estimation of the patient's need. Keep an appointment book for this purpose.

SITTING OR LYING

To return to the discussion of appointments, on arrival the patient should get into a comfortable position which can be maintained for 20-30 minutes. (During later appointments, the person might have to remain stationary for even longer.) The patient might like to sit on a chair or lie on a couch. Either position is fine for doing esoteric healing, and each position has its own advantages. Usually the lying position is used only when the patient is too ill to sit or is not able to. In that event, the patient is asked to lie on one side, so that the chakras can more easily be reached by the healer. If the patient is sitting, however, an upright chair with a hollow back is best. Avoid lounge chairs where the posture of the patient is rounded and slouched. Of course, sitting on the more recently designed chair where the knees are on a cross bar and the feet are tucked under is excellent; so is sitting cross-legged on the floor.

QUESTIONING THE PATIENT

Put the person at ease and ask a few questions about the problem with which the patient is suffering. A few details should be recorded in note form for future reference on the patient's filing card (don't forget their name, address and telephone number and, if possible, exact date, location and time of birth).

The questions may be made to access certain information useful to the work of healing you are to perform. For instance, questions may be geared towards finding out what is the major influence of the person's personality as a whole at this time (find out what their major interest is, what literature is studied, what is the favorite pursuit). DK suggests the following questions:

What are the ordinary topics of conversation the person engages in?

Which body is the problem originating in? Is it physical, emotional or mental?

Which area in the body is the problem most closely related to? Which center governs the area of greatest need?

What is the major quality which the person's soul is expressing; what selfless service is the patient doing, if any?

What do you feel is the predominant color of the patient's emotional body?

Is the patient subject to sudden turmoils that throw the entire emotional body into disorder?

Does the patient show symptoms of devitalization or of congestion? Is there a lack of energy, does the person always feel tired, feel the cold, etc., or the opposite?

In relation to the condition of the patient, be aware of the following:

1. The symptoms of the disease and their particular nature.
2. Its location.
3. The primary center involved and its condition.
4. The acute or chronic nature of the difficulty, that is, is it recent or long term.
5. The psychological condition of the patient.
6. The danger of death or not.
7. The rays of the patient (Bailey, 1951–70, v. 4, p. 702).

As you can see, the esoteric healer should either have some direct scientific knowledge or else be developing the faculty of inner vision that sees the trouble wherever it may be, allowing the healer eventually to clairvoyantly view the entire frame and organs, and thus locate instantaneously any trouble (Bailey, 1950a, pp. 243–44). Try to keep these questions short and to the point and don't be drawn away by emotional responses; the patient has come to you as a spiritual healer, not as a psychologist or dietitian. Sometimes, it is true, we need to be flexible and allow some of the congestion to be released through words, but you need to keep a tight rein over this lest it become insipid. Be aware of what you want to know and why (and how it will influence your healing approach) and try to draw it out. This takes practiced skill. Keep notes on all your findings, both before the healing (the consultation stage) and after the healing (the treatment stage). Obviously, a healer's work is wonderfully rewarding to both parties, so keep your attitude positive and joyful as well as earnest and sincere.

Duality

It may be useful at this point, to understand the patient's two sides, their duality. There is a will of the personality and there is a will of the soul. These are not necessarily opposing but they are usually different. The simplest way to come to grips with them in a person is to realize that the personality is born under the sun sign, say, Aquarius, and the soul is born under the rising sign (or ascendant) say, Leo. An astrologer will be required to give this information based on the person's date, time and place of birth. By reviewing the indications for each sign and relating them to the present problem of the patient, the true will of the soul may emerge a little more clearly. Of course, this is not essential to know at first, but as the healer becomes more attuned with this art, this may help in the work. Any good basic book on astrology will give you the necessary information[7]; the person is to aspire to the rising sign's positive indications in their personality life, i.e., replace or unify that which is in the personality.

After all, esoteric healers do regard their work as being scientific, that is, a knowledge and method which is ascertained by observation and experiment, systematized and brought under general principles, producing knowledge and skill. But as we are dealing with the "esoteric," what we are doing is not yet able to be proven as factual. The esoteric relates to knowledge which is beyond the five physical senses at this point in evolution; later, in years to come, the esoteric eventually becomes "exoteric" and hence provable by scientific instruments which before were not invented or sensitive enough. This has happened right down the ages. There will always be two types of scientific knowledge, one spiritual and the other sensual; how else could man advance?

Confidentiality

The healer, after doing the preliminary attunement and balancing of the centers (as described earlier), will allow the information in the centers and triangles to be reflected up into his or her consciousness via the hands or ajna center; and through the established link with the group of healers and the patient the healer will be consciously informed as to what to treat. This, of course, takes practice and more practice.

And to preserve the force we have created and projected onto the patient (or yourself in self-healing), the esoteric healer is requested not to talk about what is found, what is done, and what is thought. Talking about the healing is seriously detrimental to its potency. Talking about the healing in any form dissipates the energy of the healing. For the keeping of records (which is important) the healer has a card index system noting down only what has been essential to that healing.

To summarize, amongst other things relating to your practice, the following should be mentioned to the patient before you begin the work of healing, somewhat as follows:

1. "Be receptive to your higher soul energies."
2. "You need to be aware that healing changes may not be immediately noticeable to you; nor will they necessarily occur in the way you expect."
3. "We are working on all levels of consciousness so as to bring about a closer alignment with your true self, your soul. The better the alignment is, the more sound will be the healing."
4. "Confidentiality is assured."
5. "We would ask you not to speak to anyone about what you experience in the healing (at least for a few days) so you can absorb the treatment. This is because talking about it can dissipate the energy."
6. "There is no standard fee but there is a donation bowl in the waiting room."
7. "You have a choice to lie down on the couch or sit on a chair."
8. "The healing is done in silence and we do not touch you until the end."
9. "When the healing is finished, I will place my hands on your shoulders."

Have a glass of water and some tissues on the side; sometimes they are needed. We do this work in silence and without distractions (music and incense are not required).

Allocating the work to be done

After the consultation the healer will begin the healing. But if there are a few of you as healers, or if there are students-in-training attending, the patient is best returned to the waiting room for the short time of allocating the work to be done; don't do this in front of the patient. If there is a group of you who are to give the healing (a group, the number is not restricted, has the valuable asset of being more impersonal, so that there is less chance for, "I am doing the healing," and more chance for, "We are doing the healing"), this is the time to decide who is going to do what. Normally, at each healing consultation a leader is chosen, and he or she then designates what each person should do during the healing session. When the group members become proficient, this becomes a simple matter and won't take long. But, at the beginning, it may require quite a lengthy outlining of what each member is to do. Until all the members or student practitioners are completely at ease with the procedure, the healer(s) who are more knowledgeable should be the leaders. Here is an example which will illustrate what to do. Say there are three of you to do a healing on someone who has a personality emphasis which is highly intellectual but whose emotions feel starved of expression. There are twitches in the body and there appears to be wasting in some of the muscles. You deduce from the initial interview that the main center involved is the throat center with secondary involvement in the solar plexus center and sacral center. The soul seems to have a decidedly scientific bent. This suggests, because it has become too strong, that you need to balance this tendency with the heart center. So one of the healing group is asked to work on the sacral system, and the second healer is asked to work with the solar plexus system. The leader works with the throat system because the leader will always take the highest center involved. Within these simple instructions there is enough work to occupy at least 20-30 minutes.

It is interesting to note that at the first healing each triangle will take a lot longer to balance than at subsequent visits, so don't be surprised to work on only two or three triangles at first. People who are healthy (and advanced) will permit a lot more triangles to be done. Of course, it is imperative that the members of the healing group understand each other and love each other so that there is perfect harmony. The strength and power of a group is the synergy or combined action which makes it greater than the sum of the individual parts. If, however, you are working alone, you will take these systems and work correctively on them one at a time, usually beginning at the solar plexus center.

Having allocated the work to be done, the healers will sit briefly in meditation, align themselves as a group, and then sound the OM three times, to focus and concentrate the higher energies for the group. The patient is then recalled into the treatment-room and sits down in the center. The healers take up their positions: the leader standing on the right side of the patient; the other healers stand a comfortable distance behind the patient (if there are four or more healers in the group, some must stand to the front of the patient, so a circle is formed) (see p. 146).

7.

HOW TO USE THE TRIANGLE CIRCUITS OF ESOTERIC HEALING

When all the preliminaries outlined in the last chapter are under-stood, the actual practice of esoteric healing can begin. But before we move into this the most practical section of the book, I want to mention a few things about the use of triangles. The art of esoteric healing is connecting with the right triangle at the right time.

Understanding the use of triangles

The most frequent questions I get asked at courses or lectures on esoteric healing are: Why triangles? How do triangles work in the body? Is it important which direction they flow?

These questions are important and they need to be clarified. In an-swering them I ask you to stretch your minds; better still, I appeal to your esoteric sense, something the lower mind can be baffled by!

First, we must realize that the understanding of triangle circuits as patterns forming the foundation of our bodies is just another way of looking at the body. Already we know about the Western medical view, consisting of cells, glands, natural bacteria, and various systems (car-diovascular, respiratory, hepatic, glandular). Many of us are also aware of the traditional Chinese approach comprised of the five organ theory, meridians, Chi or life force, acupuncture points, etc. Another perspec-tive is the Ayurvedic model involving three types of energy. And there are other approaches to the understanding of the human organism and why it gets ill. The esoteric approach respects all these versions and offers its own explanation known as the Science of Triangles. The ancient wisdom reveals that the triangle is the basic building block upon which not only the human being is built, but also the whole universe as well. This has recently been confirmed by physics—the triangles are known as quarks. For we are the microcosm of the macrocosmic whole.

This simply means that the human being is a replica in miniature of the Grand Man of the Heavens, or of the Living Totality of Existence, the Great Architect of the Universe, to use other names. This is a new idea for Western science, and it will be some time before it is recognized. But signs of this new approach are already showing in some of the more profound (or abstract) sciences, e.g., in physics and in the Anthropic Principle, in which there is a theoretical proposal that there may be seven dimensional planes in our universe.

DK says, "In the study of the science of triangles, the student must bear in mind that there is always a point of the triangle which—in a particular crisis or 'event of consciousness'—is the emanating, dynamic, conditioning energy. During the cycles ... in which it thus controls, the other two points express receptivity and are regarded esoterically as embodying forces. Every triangle is, therefore, the expression of one fundamental energy and of two secondary forces" (Bailey, 1951–70, v. 3, p. 460).

Now, it is clear both in my studies of this subject and in my practice of esoteric healing that the triangle works in two possible ways. Which way it works will be the one chosen by the soul of the patient. We are not to force one particular method onto the patient. The two methods are as follows:

1. The first method of triangular activity is somewhat two-dimensional. It involves sequential flow from point to point to point, i.e., from the first center to the second or middle center, to the third in ordered sequences laid down by the Tibetan. This form of directional movement usually takes place first before the second method described below. It is the way triangle circuits work in average people, in aspirants and in most disciples. A few touches of the second method may be felt in the life of these people, experienced in the form of conversions and in so-called little kundalini experiences, a pushing back of the ring-pass-not, a widening of consciousness.

2. In the second method, the triangle stands as a whole, the points of the triangle working together at the same time. This method has the triangle functioning "dimensionally" and not linearly. Here the power being released into the triangle pours through the threefold nature of the patient affecting the monad, the soul and the personality together at the same time. This is a very powerful form of healing. Changes and spiritual development will be secure and permanent. A deeper alignment will be established in the human being (patient). Of course, we are talking about one particular circuit being held by the healer. But if this triangle were the one especially needing help, the reverberation through all other circuits would occur and the patient would feel an immediate shift. The burden would lift. The person would feel more able to face and overcome the problem presented. In each case we work with visualization and the creative imagination.

So let us review how triangles utilize energy from an esoteric perspective:

A. There is the major conditioning energy, producing manifestation: This is the monadic expression, symbolized as the point in the middle of the triangle. It is the emanating center of the triangle, being the dynamic and positive aspect of the triangle being held. On the most occult scale this energy can be traced back to the Eye of the Father (Siva) carrying the light of the constellation of the Great Bear.

B. Next there is the qualifying energy, producing consciousness. This is the soul expression. It is the receptive force center of the three points. It acts as the evocative expression of the initial impelling energy, synthesizing the two forces, the emanating and the responsive or negative forces (A and C), producing the motivating secondary energy. This, on an occult scale, comes from the Eye of the Son, carrying the light from the star, Sirius.

C. Then there is the responsive point of negative energy mainly responsive to the second point of the triangle (B), producing "a source of violent interplay between the two points of the base line" (B and C), causing an expression of force and tangibility. This is the Eye of the Mother, carrying the light from the Pleiades.

DK goes on to say, "When the experience undergone in Virgo is consummated in Pisces and the tests of Scorpio have led to illumination in Taurus, then the effects of these four energies will be to make man the true triangle, expressing the three divine aspects as they come from the three major conditioning constellations: the Great Bear, the Pleiades and Sirius" (Bailey, 1951–70, v. 3, p. 481).

The astrological symbols for Virgo and Scorpio are triple in nature, the only two which are. Grasp the meaning of this and you will be ready to work with the new astrology and the significance of this abstruse science of triangles (p. 480).

Much thought needs to be given to this information and it would repay you to discuss it in your study group. Such knowledge greatly potentizes healing.

Contemplate the interesting succession of triangles that are to be found in the body and the way they must be linked by the progression of the fire before that fire can perfectly vivify them, and thence pass on to other transmutations ... bearing always in mind that according to the ray so will proceed the geometric rising of the fire, and according to the ray so will the points be touched in ordered sequence (Bailey, 1962, p. 169). For, once the fire has free passage along any triangle, it flames continuously (p. 170).

We are told that when we reach our goal, each triangle is a radiant path of fire, and each center a wheel of living fiery force rotating at terrific speed. Each center at this stage not only rotates in a specific direction, but literally turns upon itself, forming a living, flaming iridescent globe of pure fire, and holding within it a certain geometrical shape, yet withal vibrating so rapidly that the eye can scarcely follow it (p. 170).

It must be remembered that the inner web of light which is called the etheric body of the planet is essentially a web of triangles and, when the evolutionary process is completed, it will have been organized (Bailey, 1951–70, v. 3, p. 479).

At the end of our evolutionary Path the following occurs:

The secret of the Fire lies hid in the second letter of the Sacred Word. The mystery of life is concealed within the heart. When the lower point vibrates, when the Sacred Triangle glows, when the point, the middle center, and the apex likewise burn, then the two triangles—the greater and the lesser—merge with one flame which burneth up the whole. The fire within the lesser fire findeth its progress much impelled when the circle of the moving and the unmoving, of the lesser wheel within the greater wheel that moveth not in Time, findeth a twofold outlet; it then shineth with the glory of the twofold One and of His sixfold brother. Fohat rusheth through space. He searcheth for his complement. The breath of the unmoving one, and the fire of the One Who seeth the whole from the beginning rush to meet each other, and the unmoving becomes the sphere of activity" (Bailey, 1962, pp. 172–73).

With this introductory perspective of how triangles function and evolve we can appreciate the potentiality of each triangle we work with in esoteric healing.

Beginning the act of healing (see photo #1 on p. 329 and also p. 334)

Bring the patient in to be seated in the center of the circle of healers[1] (or simply in the center of the room). Have the leader come over to the patient and gently lay hands on his or her shoulders, saying something like, "We are now ready to start the healing. Are you comfortable? Please feel completely at ease; we do not touch your body at all, except at the end of the healing when I will put my hands here (indicate the patient's shoulders or at the back of the neck between the shoulder blades) to let you know that the healing is finished. Now, please, place your hands on your thighs and both feet uncrossed on the floor; gently close your eyes." Closing the eyes is important but not essential for the patient. It helps to cut out irrelevant material imagery surrounding the person. It is at this stage the healers also close their eyes as they stand in their positions. The leader (usually) stands at the right of the patient (if sitting) or at the head of the bed (if lying down); the other healers will position themselves either at the back of the patient or towards the front, in a circle.

There are five phases to the work of esoteric healing, summarized as follows:

    A. Alignment and attunement

    B. Diagnosis

        a) The Aura

        b) The 5 Centers in the Ajna

    C. Vitalization of the bodies of the patient

    D. Esoteric healing treatment

        a) Synchronization Triangle

        b) Balancing the Centers and Triangles

    E. Closing and sealing the Healing Triangle

A. Alignment and attunement

1. ALIGNMENT

The first and crucial stage when working with healing energies is for you as the healer to move away from the personality, from the personal reactions which one has, towards the more spiritual energies that are the source of all that is. The description might seem long, but with practice the process should take only a few seconds to do. To achieve spiritual alignment, each healer first gets in balance physically. Then become aware of the physical energies (the etheric or vital body), feel them empowered and radiating around you as pure white light; see these energies linked to the emotional body, the cloak of many colors and modes (moods). Let all these expressions become one balanced, loving response. Link this with your mental body as a clear, focussed, receptive sensitivity.

The mental body must be stilled by focussing on the work being done. This enables higher sensibility to be achieved from soul level. Now integrate the whole of your threefold personality by visualizing the three bodies as functioning perfectly together. Then raise your consciousness to the abstract mind, and here link in with your threefold soul, that is, intelligent activity, unconditional love, and dynamic spiritual purpose. See yourself as living and working according to the plan of divinity. You have now aligned yourself. It is worth noting that meditation is a technique of the mind which eventually produces correct, unimpeded relationship, which is another name for alignment (Bailey, 1951–70, v. 4, p. 620).

2. HIGHER TRIANGLE

Next, you are required to build the first triangle of light, by connecting with the soul of the group of healers. Link up telepathically with each of them on the soul level. Link up also with the wider group of healers throughout the world (for you will be working as a representative of this spiritual or rather esoteric organization, just as you would if you belonged to an institute or society of practitioners or professionals on the physical plane). Link in with the soul of the patient and with the source of all power and life and love (the Supreme Being; you may also like to link in with the Christ, the Buddha, and the group of Masters, at this point). Thus you have your first great and highest triangle of energy:

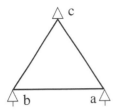

a. The soul of the group of healers (yourself, the group with whom you are working and the wider organism of healers);

b. The soul of the patient;

c. The source of all love, power and life (divinity).

Visualize this triangle of energy and light strengthening you as a group on this spiritual level of consciousness so that you may heal according to the will of the soul of the patient. At this point you may want to say together the group mantram—either aloud (softly) or silently:

"With purity of motive, inspired by a loving heart, we offer ourselves for this work of healing. This offer we make as a group and to the one we seek to heal" (Bailey, 1951–70, v. 4, p. 103).

This mantram is very powerful. Remember, it is not the sounding of the words alone that brings about the desired end, but also the mental concentration that visualizes the results to be attained (Bailey, 1950a, p. 189). Another mantram that can be sounded at this point is the Mantram of Unification (see Chapter 15).

3. OPENING THE TRIANGLE OF HEALING

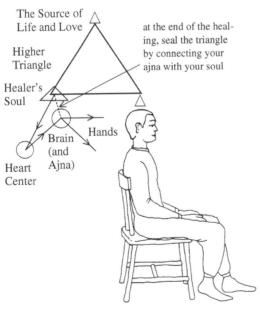

Now draw down the energy from the Higher Triangles to open the Triangle of Healing. To do this, the group visualizes the flow of energy from the Higher Triangle to the group's heart center and then to the etheric brain that has been integrated by the group.

The opened Triangle of Healing:

a. The healer's soul or the soul of the group of healers (connected to the Higher Triangle);

b. The heart center of the group (or to your heart center, if you are healing alone);

c. The etheric brain of the group (or to yourself if you are healing alone) (Bailey, 1951–70, v. 4, p. 648).

This is a very special triangle, for down and around it flows the soul energy for healing the patient on the etheric level, which is the source of the vitalizing of the physical body.

This is an open triangle, which means that the flow of energy from the brain does not return to the soul. [The return of energy to the soul is done at the end of the healing work, however, to close or seal the Healing Triangle, and so cut off any further (conscious or unconscious) energy transfer to the patient (see the illustration on the previous page).] During the healing the triangle is open so that energy can be transferred to the patient (via the hands of the healer), according to the will of the patient's soul.

At the stage of opening the Triangle of Healing (technically called Opening the Magnetic Healing Triangle), more advanced healers (those who have been trained in esoteric healing) will also open the Radiatory Triangle consisting of the soul, brain, heart center, and auric emanation, connecting you to the patient. Note the direction of flow compared to that of the Magnetic Healing Triangle (For more information about Radiatory Healing, see p. 111).

Having these triangles "installed" or "booted up" enables you to move from magnetic to radiatory healing at will. The Activating Triangles (see p. 153) were specially given to us by the Master DK for this very purpose.

ATTUNEMENT WITH THE GOVERNING RAY ENERGIES[2]

Leave this section out of your alignment procedure if you know only a little about the ray teachings. But if you are a healer who has immersed yourself in the teachings of the rays—and we must remind ourselves that DK wrote his book *Esoteric Healing* as the fourth volume of a set of five called *A Treatise on the Seven Rays*—then it is at this point that you will make your Ray Attunement. The objective before the initiate is to have every center in the etheric body responsive to the ray energy of the soul and to have all the other seven ray energies subsidiary to it

(Bailey, 1951–70, v. 4, p. 138). We must remember that the soul ray of the average aspirant is seldom in control to such an extent that it can bring adequate illumination and ray potency; until it is in control, these ray methods and techniques, determining the use and direction of the ray energies, are useless (p. 693). It is possible to determine whether the general trend of the healer is along the line of love or of the will, and then to act accordingly. The problem here is whether the relation between healer and patient will be from personality to personality, from soul to soul, or from personality to soul and vice versa (p. 702). Remember, the second ray deals largely with the soul's activity through all the centers and primarily the heart center (p. 130).

To heal using the rays, the healer should form the following triangles prior to the conscious act of healing (see the diagram on the next page):

1. The Greater Triangle. Here connect with your soul, and your soul ray. Then connect with either your mental or your astral vehicle (whichever is on the ray line of 2 - 4 - 6). Now, by an act of the will, relate the soul energy, via the desired vehicle, to the heart center (sometimes the solar plexus center). This is the triangle which affects the healer as a transmitting agent.

2. The Lesser Triangle. Now build the second triangle. Focus on the center of reception of soul energies, viz., the head center, then using the creative imagination, connect with the ajna center, and hold the energy there. Then gather into this ajna center the energy of that center in your etheric body which is related to your soul ray. This is the triangle which produces the effect upon the patient and through which you, the healer on the physical plane, work.

3. Now with deliberation, link the two triangles. When completed, you are ready to heal.

Practice this attunement on yourself first. Always work with love and through the second subray of the soul ray if you are not a second ray soul.

4. Protecting Triangle

After opening the Healing Triangle, another is "superimposed" on it. It is the Protecting Triangle. For this circuit, direct the flow of love from your heart center to your (brain and) head center and then out to the patient. (If you are a more advanced esoteric healer, start this triangle from

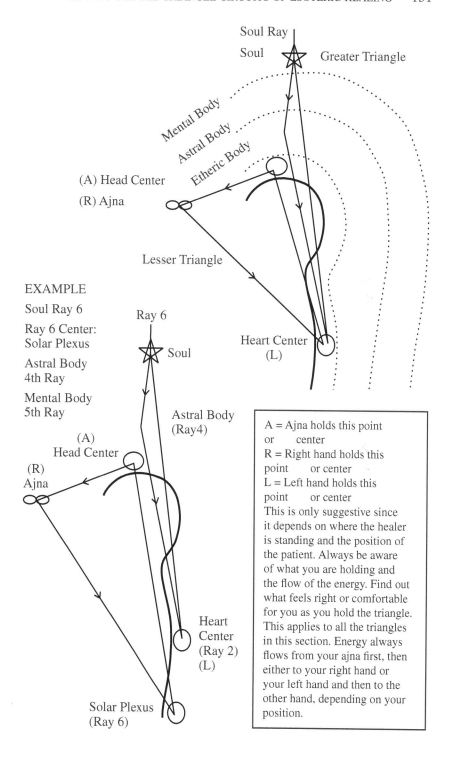

Soul Ray

Soul   Greater Triangle

Mental Body

Astral Body

Etheric Body

(A) Head Center

(R) Ajna

Lesser Triangle

EXAMPLE

Soul Ray 6

Ray 6 Center:
Solar Plexus

Astral Body
4th Ray

Mental Body
5th Ray

Ray 6

Soul

Heart Center
(L)

Astral Body
(Ray4)

(A)
Head Center

(R)
Ajna

Heart
Center
(Ray 2)
(L)

Solar Plexus
(Ray 6)

A = Ajna holds this point
or   center
R = Right hand holds this
point   or center
L = Left hand holds this
point   or center
This is only suggestive since
it depends on where the healer
is standing and the position of
the patient. Always be aware
of what you are holding and
the flow of the energy. Find out
what feels right or comfortable
for you as you hold the triangle.
This applies to all the triangles
in this section. Energy always
flows from your ajna first, then
either to your right hand or
your left hand and then to the
other hand, depending on your
position.

the heart-in-the-head center and continue as described.) This triangle has the effect of protecting you from taking on any of the symptoms of the patient (Bailey, 1951–70, v. 4, p. 556). It is particularly necessary to install this triangle when you first begin to practice the art of esoteric healing, and to make it a habit every time you begin the healing service, for, at these early stages, one is vulnerable to the glamor of curing others. This glamor sets up a vortex of negative flow towards the healer, causing the symptoms (but not the disease itself) to occur in the healer while still remaining in the patient. In fact, this happened to me soon after qualifying as an herbal practitioner. I so wanted to help a patient who had consulted me with acute extensive nervous eczema that for a week I had to endure both the itchiness and the inflammation of the skin, a disturbing experience. At that time I didn't know of the above transference protection triangle. I am glad to say it has never happened again. Sometimes one can get the symptoms without any physical effects. So as you light up this triangle, visualize a steady flow of the positive energy of love pouring out towards the patient. This will insulate you from the disease, but not from the patient.

Danger is a very real factor in esoteric healing, for we are dealing with energies not yet manifested, energies that are moving towards manifestation, with deep and subtle causes. And just as a doctor must know what effect a prescribed drug will have on the patient, we as esoteric healers have the responsibility to know what will happen to the energies we set in motion. I give warnings of danger not because I want to scare you or to make this form of medicine something mysterious or even exciting, but simply to protect you and to make you aware of effects which can come about. With deep inner love behind all of our work, we can rest assured no danger or harm can approach us (Bailey, 1951–70, v. 4, p. 555).

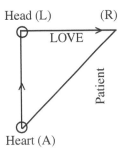

Head (L)   (R)

LOVE

Patient

Heart (A)

This Protecting Triangle may also be used to shelter the other triangles you use in the healing. There are often thoughtforms which hang over organs and around subtle circuits. These so-called entities can be very strong and highly magnetic, causing the patient to be vulnerable in similar circumstances at different times, perpetuating a condition or a fear or a set of symptoms, either continuously or cyclically. The Protecting Triangle can be used to ward off such imposing thoughtforms by pouring the energy of love (from your heart center [hold with your ajna] and head center [hold with your left hand]) into the triangle on which you are working (hold with your right hand).

5. ACTIVATING TRIANGLES

The next stage in our preparation to heal involves a sequence of three important triangles. They bring the directing flow of energy from your ajna under control for proper supervision and guidance via your hands. This series of triangles also links the two forms of healing, magnetic and radiatory, in one activity (Bailey, 1951–70, v. 4, p. 578). First visualize your triple soul energy of spiritual will (atma), intuitive love (buddhi) and higher intelligence (manas) as being "placed" on the Head Triangle (head center, alta major center and ajna center), then allow these energies to flow into the glands which are the physical expression of

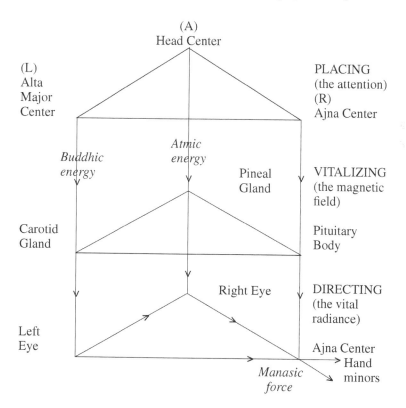

each of these centers, that is the pineal gland, the carotid gland and the pituitary gland, so that they become "vitalized" and receptive. Finally see these glands as radiating and directing their energies via the three inner "eyes of direction" (right eye, left eye and the eye in the middle of the forehead, the ajna center), taking their focus specifically through the ajna center (pp. 581–82). (Note the very interesting and significant connection with the Glamor Triangle). The ajna is used as the directing agent for a force called "dispelling radiance," which is particularly useful for drawing away or dispelling aggravating symptoms associated with a karmic condition, for example, fear, emotional imbalance and those psychological difficulties that enhance the problem facing the patient[3] (p. 581–82). But here into this alignment process we are drawing down the three high soul energies via the ajna for use in healing.

6. TRIANGLE OF TRANSFER (see photo #2 on p. 329)

In the brain the healer now visualizes the patient as whole, healthy and happy. Then focus your attention in your ajna center and create another triangle between this center and your two hands. This is the Triangle of Transfer, which takes the energy built up along the three connecting triangles and places it at the disposal of the two hands as directed by the ajna center. At this point, and not before, you are ready for healing.

The Triangle of Transfer is composed of the ajna center and the minor centers in the palms of the hands (Bailey, 1951–70, v. 4, p. 648). These two minor centers of force in the hands have a particular connection with the throat center (of selfless service) and with the ajna, the directing agent of all energy in healing.

At this juncture the healers are standing around the patient with arms bent, their hands at about shoulder level, their palms facing the patient. The forces are now all in place, ready for the act of healing transfer (according to the will of the patient's soul).

SUMMARY OF PROCEDURE FOR ALIGNMENT AND ATTUNEMENT

This is a summary of what a healer must do before entering the etheric field of the patient in order to heal:

1. Align your threefold personality with your soul
2. Create the Higher Triangle

3. Recite the group mantram
4. Open the Radiatory Healing Triangle
5. Open the Magnetic Healing Triangle
6. Build the Ray Attunement Triangles (if indicated)
7. Activate the Protecting Triangle
8. Construct the three Activating Triangles
9. Make the Triangle of Transfer

B. Diagnosis (see photo #3 on p. 330)

As with any medical system, before the practitioner can offer treatment, a proper process of diagnosis must be performed. A physician will ask all sorts of questions of the patient concerning the problem presented, the past medical history, and a number of physical examinations may be required to confirm or determine a diagnosis. In Esoteric Healing we do the same, but all in the energy field. First, we observe the aura of the patient, then we examine the ajna so as to discover the center of greatest need in the patient.

a. ENTRY INTO THE AURIC ENERGY FIELD[4]

After the Triangle of Transfer is completed, the healer is standing with the hands lifted. The hands are now turned towards the patient, and the healer becomes aware of the whole auric energy field of the patient— the emanation of body, soul and spirit. Then gently and slowly you push your hands through the energy barrier and into the auric field. Here you feel the whole patient as an integrated individual and get an initial impression of the condition of the patient's energy and needs. This can be in the form of an image, symbol, picture, or in energetic terms (graduated strength and weakness of the energy). This is done while standing some distance (about a meter) behind the patient.

b. THE FIVE CENTERS IN THE AJNA (see practical exercise on p. 130)

The healer now moves round to the side of the patient, usually the right, but whatever seems appropriate or comfortable. Place one hand at the outflow of ajna energy (back of the top of the head), and then from a distance (keeping well away from the forehead) bring the other hand in towards the patient's ajna. Become aware of the impression you receive.

Compare it to the impression you got from the aura. The former will be an impression of the integration of the personality bodies, giving important information for the treatment.

First assess the ajna itself. The ajna center is at the patient's brow. This center is the leader, director, or the conductor of the orchestra of centers all over the body. The energy passing through this center is attracted inwards from the front and passes through the pituitary gland in the head and then comes out at the top of the head a little behind the crown center. Remembering what we have learned about this center, we begin to assess its balance and integration. This means we hold the right hand in front of the brow and the left hand in line with the top of the head. We assess the energy moving from one hand to the other. This will inform you of the relative integration of the soul and personality of the patient. By this we will have some knowledge of the patient's stage on the Path (useful for certain activities and triangles). Sensing the balance of the ajna center brings into awareness all the other major centers before we assess their balance individually.

Now the time comes for each center in the patient's ajna to be held and assessed as to their balance. Here, still maintaining our objectivity, we "diagnose" the state of the personality of the patient via the centers as they are reflected in the ajna linked with the stalk of the pituitary (see p. 100). Now bring your hand closer to the brow and form a line with your fingers and thumb. Thus holding your five fingers of the right hand in the ajna energy field, connect each finger to one center (see photo #3 on p. 330) (cf. Bailey, 1951–70, v. 1, p. 290):

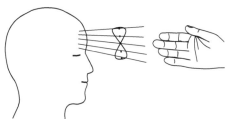

Thumb on the throat center.
Index or forefinger on
      the heart center.
Middle finger on
      solar plexus center.
Ring finger on the sacral center.
Little finger on the base center

Now being aware of the energy connection of each center and the linking center in the body (via the ajna), we sense which of the five centers has "greatest need." You don't "do" anything at this point, as the patient has not been properly prepared for healing yet. Once the center "of greatest need" has been established (diagnosed) (revealed itself), we know three things:

a. Where the source of trouble lies—the center of greatest need.
b. The center which must first be balanced using the synchronizing triangle.
c. Whether the center is overactive or underactive.

This preliminary diagnostic information will, in the fourth step, Phase D, of the treatment, be a springboard into the real, causative healing in the depths of subtle energy on the different levels of the subtle bodies linking and restoring damaged energy lines between the centers and systems. Remember, through the various centers of the body—especially the seven major centers—will come the power to heal the corresponding physical center, and as the centers are vitalized certain physical effects will be demonstrable, and in specific forms that work on and through the centers will come results that may throw light on this obscure matter of healing through the subtle bodies (Bailey, 1950a, pp. 161–62).

The leader (usually, but sometimes all healers present) will then also assess the balance of the alta major center and the head (crown) center.

Now gently withdraw the hands out of the aura of the ajna center. Hold the information you have acquired clearly in mind for later use (see p. 163). Now move round to the back of the patient so that the preparation of the energy body of the patient can be done so that the healing treatment can commence (Stage C).

We now realign ourselves with the original Higher Triangle whose three "points" are the source of love, power and life—the soul of the group of healers—the patient's soul. We are ready to move into the different electrical circuits and triangles of the patient's subtle body.

For this work the healer sits behind the patient (make sure a chair has been positioned in readiness). Most of the healing work is usually done from the back of the patient because the major centers are found outside the back of the body in the etheric spine.

C. Vitalization of the bodies of the patient—
The vitality triangles (see photo #4 on p. 330)

The four triangles that follow are placed in order of their use in the healing. These so-called "energy triangles" must be done at every healing session as they "empower" the patient with prana which is the healing force drawn on during the healing session. If we try to do any healing before doing these triangles, we are making demands on the body's own energy reserves which may not be adequately available and could deplete the patient instead making him or her more vulnerable.

1. THE PRANIC TRIANGLE

The Pranic Triangle starts the whole process of healing; it is the primary circuit for absorbing prana, the life essence of the beings who are using the planets and the sun as their bodies of manifestation. Solar pranic energy enters the body not only via the spleen but also via the minor center above the heart center (Bailey, 1979, p. 433). The Master DK is very specific regarding the activity of this circuit. He says we should be consciously aware that prana circulates three times round this triangle before entering the spleen (Bailey, 1962, p. 123). He goes on to say that these centers should be pictured as whirling vortices with a closely woven threefold channel passing from each center to the other. The energy finds its point of departure for the entire system at the further side of the spleen to that at which the prana entered. The vital fluid circulates through and between these three centers three times before it finally passes out from them to the periphery of its little system. The final circulation carries the prana, via the fine interlacing channels, to every part of the body, which becomes entirely impregnated by these emanations. The energies find their way out of the etheric system by means of surface radiation and as emanative human prana (pp. 99–100). This is due to the three centers of this triangle being *minor* centers—thus they primarily affect the etheric body. This prana has a triple effect in the body:

a. It preserves bodily health, protecting the patient from any deterioration during the demanding healing activity.

b. It constructs and builds in the body what is needed to replace the daily wear and tear.

c. It is the medium whereby one person comes into physical touch with another, known as physical magnetism (Bailey, 1962, p. 857).

The Pranic Triangle is the first of four vitalizing triangles for the movement of vital force (life energy derived from the monad) around and through the body. The Pranic Triangle stimulates vital force (prana) to move from above to below. That is, by holding this triangle we help the circulating energy to become more balanced between the centers above the diaphragm and those below the diaphragm, which can also signify

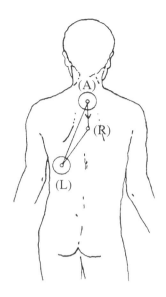

a greater harmony between the higher and lower self, between the spiritual and the material. Without doubt, this triangle, once lit, glows continuously, providing the patient with renewed energy and with increasing awareness as to purpose and direction. With its interconnecting triple channel this circuit forms a kind of separate circulatory system (Bailey, 1962, p. 98). We start the triangle above the diaphragm, at the vagus nerve center (which is governed by the heart center) between the shoulder blades, tracing the link with a minor center below the heart and near the diaphragm, and finally to the spleen minor center (p. 162, cf. also p. 135).

We will be able to understand how this triangle holds in balance the two sides of our nature, especially as we ascend the spiritual path and have to blend the higher with the lower or material self.

Prana is nervous force controlled by the mind from the brain itself. Prana brings into activity the sense organs, whether those of the most base people or of the most sensitive of persons who have raised their consciousness and widened their sense response to areas way beyond that of ordinary and average humanity. In each case this triangle of energy will help to relate the highest aspects to the outer and expressive part of the personality, linking rhythmically with the universal life stream of the soul centered in the heart. Prana is the planetary force which keeps us alive. We take it in through the air we breathe, the food we eat and sunlight, and at night through sleep. It comes to us via rays of harmony connected to the planet as a giant body; these rays will help us to integrate more consciously with the natural law of the earth so that the conflicts of our personal aspiration (towards a spiritual expression) are brought into equilibrium. Prana pervades all our bodies, from the physical right up to the most subtle and, according to the evolutionary development of the patient, will be their capacity to receive and utilize this energy. From the lowest point of view, the contact healer, through the laying on of hands, concentrates this energy (physical prana) and is thus able to heal "miraculously" and "instantaneously." Unfortunately, such healing does not last nor does it relate the higher aspects of the patient to the causes of their problem, but rather stimulates the natural processes of the physical body in cooperation with nature. Such healing does, however, have a definite usefulness for the personality of the patient. During esoteric healing, though, we never touch the patient, and so do not utilize this type of healing force by itself.

The pranic triangle in the body is peculiarly connected with two other triangles of which the healer ought to be aware. They have to do with the rising kundalini fire and so they act rather like channels in the subtle apparatus. The first circuit is in the head: the head center, the ajna center and the alta major center. The second is at the base of the spine (the secondary Kundalini Triangle), consisting of a point at the bottom of the spinal column and the two major sex organs in the male and female (Bailey, 1962, pp. 135, 137, 169; 1951–70, v. 3, p. 301). I refer you to the Kundalini Triangle for information as to how to handle possible premature raising of this energy.

2. SPLEEN TRIANGLE OF FORCE

This is the next triangle we do for vitalizing the body. It is a great triangle of force concerned with matter, with substance, form-building, creation, vitality and with persistence in form (Bailey, 1951–70, v. 4, p. 177). The spleen assimilates the vital energy given off by the planet in two ways.

First, it absorbs the sun's vital force, transferring it to the vagus nerve center where it is utilized via the circulation (see the Pranic Triangle above), and second, it takes from the food we eat that living vitality still in the food and sends it to the heart for use in the body's organs. Also in the spleen, the negative life of matter and the living energy of the positive etheric body are brought together, and then a "spark," as it is called, is made between the inner living bodies (through the medium of the etheric body) and the physical plane (p. 335). The spleen center (a minor center) is actually two minor centers superimposed on the spleen itself (p. 73). The Spleen Triangle of Force adds potency to this function of transferring energy and it permits a greater flow of energy into the body for the purposes described.

New healers should practice with the Spleen Triangle first. Here, healers draw the energy out from the solar plexus center to the double

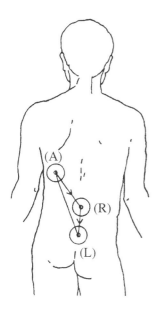

minor above the spleen and then direct the force to the etheric organ of the spleen itself. The action of this triangle is to prepare the spleen for the releasing of energy into the Spleen Triangle of Force, which is the first and perhaps the most important force triangle used to "ground" the patient for the reception of the creative and will-evoking healing energies. Experienced healers may go straight into the Spleen Triangle of Force.

The Spleen Triangle of Force consists of: spleen minor center (the organ of physical vitality coming from the sun), sacral center (the predisposing agent towards physical generation) and base center (the life-giving principle, the will-to-live, to all parts of the human frame (Bailey, 1951–70, v. 4, p. 177), and the Fires of Matter, connected to kundalini) (Bailey, 1962, pp. 136–37). Hold the major activating center of any triangle with your ajna center. Simply focus your attention, via your ajna center, on the major center involved in the triangle, in this case the spleen center. Then hold the sacral center with the left hand placed slightly below and to the right of the spleen. Position the right hand under the left to hold the base center. Merely doing this triangle circuit makes the patient's life more constructive (p. 137).

Once you have perfected this triangle in your mind and in your practice, you may perform the Triangle of Immortality (which is dependent on the Spleen Triangle of Force for its action) at the beginning of each session.

3. IMMORTALITY TRIANGLE

This triangle is a reflection of the Spleen Triangle of Force on a higher level and cannot be activated without the latter's relation. The Triangle of Immortality consists of the throat center, the pituitary body, and the pineal gland (the Fire of Mind or manasic triangle) (Bailey, 1962, p. 137; 1951–70, v. 5, p. 671). When these two triangles are related by the healer, it becomes the magnificent clue to the instinct of self-preservation (which governs the relation of spirit and matter, of life and form), to the survival of the subtle bodies after death and to the principle of immortality, which is seated in the soul and functions when self-preservation and survival no longer hold sway (Bailey, 1951–70, v. 4, pp. 177–78). These are important qualities of a soul striving for spiritual attainment. The Immortality Triangle is a grand way to begin a healing treatment, and one of the primary methods in the battle to transmute the miasm of tuberculosis (more about this in Chapter 8). We create this triangle by connecting i) spleen to pituitary, ii) sacral to throat center, iii) and base to pineal (higher life energies—higher creative/reconstructive forces—higher deathless qualities of consciousness, the state of Being).

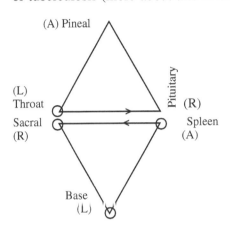

Pituitary Body (Spleen Center)
Throat Center (Sacral Center)
Pineal gland (Base Center)

4. Lower Prana Triangle

The last stage of energizing the patient's body involves the use of the Lower Prana Triangle, a circuit related to the energies running up the spine. The three points are the spleen minor center, the base center and the throat center (linking the alta major center and the head centers). Move your hands and ajna to the spleen minor center on the left; then, while keeping your ajna on the spleen minor center, move your two hands down to the base center, getting the stream of vitality moving at the same time. Next, with one hand draw the energy up the spine through the major centers in the etheric spine right up to the throat and alta major centers. Remember

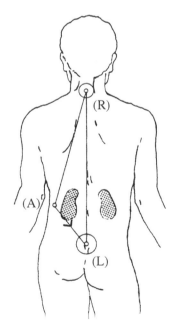

how the Spleen Triangle worked to generate primary energy for the use of the "engine room" of the body? Now we redirect this prana or chi into the spine and up to the throat and medulla oblongata, governed by the alta major center, covering all the spinal nerves, to energize the whole body of centers (major, minor and minute). This energizing triangle is also important to do before working on the spine. DK says that, when the spinal column is duly adjusted and aligned, and when the spleen is freed from congestion and is in a healthy condition, there will be little trouble in the dense physical body (Bailey, 1962, p. 57).

The energizing circuits are complete. The patient has been properly prepared and is now ready for healing. The healer can now safely enter the arena of karmic help for the patient who has sought his or her aid.

D. Esoteric healing treatment—Triangles used in esoteric healing: Options for each treatment

a. THE SYNCHRONIZING TRIANGLE (see photo #5 on p. 330)

The first triangle we always do after completing the four vitalization triangles is the Synchronizing Triangle. The healer recalls the center "of greatest need" discovered or diagnosed when assessing the patient's ajna as described earlier (cf. p. 155ff). That center is then balanced using the synchronizing triangle. Follow the method of doing the synchronizing triangle as described on page 123, selecting one of the three techniques appropriate for the healing of your patient's center of greatest need.

b. BALANCING THE CENTERS AND TRIANGLES

Now we are ready to choose which additional circuits might be called for. What follows are a number of triangles placed in order of the system of the body to which they are linked. It is for the esoteric healing practitioner to select by knowledge and intuition the appropriate triangles required by the patient, determined by the center of greatest need. What's more, each triangle selected may be treated from any of the seven levels of conciousness in the patient, according to the indications given to the healing practitioner by the soul of the patient. Each sitting will then be unique, since the treatment or healing will be "tailor made" for that specific person at that particular time in their life. It is highly unlikely that such a sequence would ever be repeated in the same manner.

The digestive system

5. LIVER TRIANGLE OF FORCE

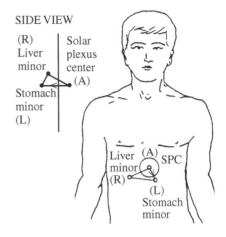

SIDE VIEW

(R) Liver minor | Solar plexus center (A)

Stomach minor (L)

Liver minor (R) (A) SPC (L) Stomach minor

The liver as we know is an organ of digestion, storing glucose and neutralizing toxins that enter the blood stream. One of the major functions of the liver is to supply the body with glucose, a principal source of energy in the body, especially the brain. All the blood from the spleen (and stomach and intestine) passes to the liver, where it is digested to form bile, which is stored in the gall bladder. This triangle on the etheric level helps these functions to be more efficiently carried out by absorbing and harmoniously distributing the energy required by the body.

Beginners should practice with the Liver Triangle, which is to be regarded as introductory to the Liver Triangle of Force. Using the former we draw the energy out from the solar plexus center to the minor center close to the liver and then connect with the etheric organ of the liver itself. This can set the energy flowing and is useful to newcomers of healing. Experienced healers may perform the Liver Triangle of Force itself. This triangle, which consists of the solar plexus center (which we know to be related to the pancreas and the Islets of Langerhans), the stomach minor center (this is, in fact, a secondary externalization of the solar plexus center), and the liver minor center. This triangle stretches over the right side of the body. All the three dense materialized organs (pancreas, stomach and liver) are fed and nurtured by the forces and energies of the solar plexus center. Djwhal Khul says about this: "I have here given a very important fact to those who are interested in the study of medicine from the esoteric angle; rightly appreciated, it will lead to an understanding of the healing art. Control of the solar plexus center, and the right reception and release of the energies focussed in that center, would bring about a major purification, an intensive strengthening and a vital protection of the three vital organs to be found in that area of the human physical mechanism" (Bailey, 1951–70, v. 4, pp. 173–74).

The Liver Triangle of Force can be adapted to include the gall bladder when indications show it needs work (gall stones or inflammation), which may simply mean that the patient has hard decisions to make, or cannot decide what to do next. People who are critical of themselves and of others cannot easily make decisions. In this case, hold the solar plexus center, liver minor center and gall bladder center (or the etheric organ—as on the gall bladder is a minute center, not a minor center, not difficult to find when you apply the principle of energy follows thought). When the patient is displaying biliousness, the healer uses this triangle to balance the attractive desires being held by the patient, for this condition is frequently an indication that there is too much desire for things one likes and a suppression of things one cannot cope with emotionally or control adequately.

6. STOMACH TRIANGLE

The stomach is the foremost organ of digestion; it breaks down food intake in preparation for absorption and excretion in the intestines. This Stomach Triangle is very much linked with the Spleen Triangle of Force, in that it helps the etheric body extract more efficiently the pure vital fluids from the food consumed, allowing them to be utilized by the heart and in the circulation. On a higher level this triangle affords protection against the solar plexus picking up too much negativity in the environment (the solar plexus' link with the heart center will help in its transmutation). The Stomach Triangle is also important in its absorptive capacity; in its vitalization the less pure vital energy is directed downward to the large intestine. Here again energies are separated, and from the impure the more pure is absorbed for use around the lower regions of digestion where absolute purity is not essential. The outer activity of this process is the reabsorption of the liquids and electrolytes from the colon. The Stomach Triangle governs all of these functions and is useful especially for those suffering from digestive diseases. For this triangle we hold the solar plexus center (hold with your ajna center), the stomach minor center (related to the hormone gastrin and found slightly to the left), and the etheric stomach organ or point.

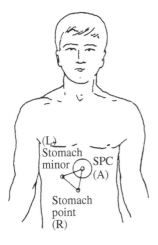

Both the Stomach Triangle and the Liver Triangle of Force can be used to address stomach trouble, since both triangles are governed by the solar plexus center. Difficulties in this center often lead to emotional imbalance, frequently due to worry, anxieties and temper. Prolonged irritation will cause disturbances in both the stomach and liver areas (Bailey, 1951–70, v. 4, p. 38; in this connection see the Triangle for Imperil, #10). Where the patient complains of acidity, the healer should work from the emotional levels of the Stomach Triangle, bringing into balance the criticism, personal dislikes and hatreds which have brought about a superiority complex in the patient. The soul cannot tolerate negative attitudes regarding other people and so "withdraws" (which simply means it is prevented from expressing itself in love and goodwill to all), resulting in digestive problems.

The stomach is the great symbol of desire in the body, so when working with this triangle, it is important to recognize that we all must desire. But it must be balanced with the heart energy of compassion and selfless love. Desire governs attraction and repulsion, sympathy and antipathy, love and hate. (Listen to children talking about food, who often say, "I love that" and "I hate that"!) Where the reception and release of desire energy is not being properly governed (for instance, feelings are suppressed and emotions are inhibited), stomach or intestine cancer or diabetes can result. In the healing of these diseases the healer can hold the Synchronizing Triangle (see p. 123) as well as the Stomach Triangle (see also Chapter 8 on cancer):

Synchronizing Triangle (for the solar plexus and stomach)

a. Head center of the healer

b. Solar plexus of the healer

c. Solar plexus of the patient via their emotional body.

The best way to energize this form of cleansing triangle is to balance the two energies between the solar plexus centers (of healer and patient) by silently sounding a mantramic sound through the interchange of energy (the safest and most effective mantram sound is OM, sounded as in "home"). Other techniques can be employed when the healer is much more proficient in the art of esoteric healing. One is "stimulating," which works on emotional energy that has become practically dormant, thereby causing a tremendous build-up of emotional force leading to stomach or intestinal disease or cancer. The other technique is "expulsive." This works on emotional desire energy, which has no resistance and rushes through the center with little or no control. Both techniques require the healer to draw off the energy or magnetize it using the hands at the solar plexus center level. The energy is then transmuted by the healer, and the patient is left feeling purified and in a lot more control of himself or herself (Bailey, 1951–70, v. 4, pp. 542, 602). Using this technique one can appreciate the importance of setting in motion that Protecting Triangle against transference (of the disease symptoms), described above when speaking about the opening of the Healing Triangle (#3). For safety, if you are a novice healer, do not attempt the stimulating or expulsive techniques. Use only the balancing technique. During all this work hold the ajna focussed, keep relaxed and calm, being receptive to soul intuition (i.e., soul tuition or instruction), working solely with the energy of love (see p. 122). Remember always that it is the soul of the patient that heals its form, which is the person on earth.

If there are problems which are specific to the subtle energy bodies, here are two triangles which can be used, the Astral Preparation Triangle and the Mental Congestion Triangle (see #7 and #8).

7. ASTRAL PREPARATION TRIANGLE

If the source of the sto-machic trouble lies specifi-cally in the emotional (or astral) body, as it often does when dealing with this area, the healing practitioner can use the Astral Preparation Triangle. The healer focuses as a soul in the head center, directs the needed energy, and controls the patient's

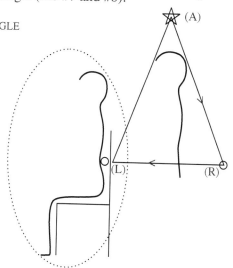

(A)

(L)   (R)

emotional nature via the healer's correctly oriented solar plexus center. The triangle, then, is head center of the healer, solar plexus center of the healer, astral body of the patient. In this way the center in the patient's body, owing to its emotionalism, is brought under control, causing it to be reorganized as a center for reception of the healing energies emanating from the patient's soul (Bailey, 1951–70, v. 4, pp. 554–55).

8. MENTAL CONGESTION TRIANGLE

The mental Congestion Triangle is used when a mental type of person is having difficulties due to energies coming down from the soul to the head (or other centers above the diaphragm). In this case it is important to instruct the patient to collaborate by directing their own energy downwards to *below* the diaphragm. The triangle involves the head center of the healer, the head center of the patient and one or other of the centers below the diaphragm of the patient (Bailey, 1951–70, v. 4, p. 554).

9. GIT TRIANGLES

The grand triangle for the whole digestive system is the throat center, solar plexus center and the solar plexus minor center (controlled by the base center). If the patient has digestive problems and if there is a clear indication that the gastrointestinal tract (GIT) is the major area where the energies are not flowing properly, then the healer should hold the throat center and solar plexus center while checking and clearing certain major points along the tract where congested force can occur. These are:

a. The swallowing reflex (for dysphagia) in the throat.
b. The esophagus, where stenosis or stricture can occur due to inflammation, growths, enlarged thyroid or aneurysm.
c. The stomach function for gastritis, peptic ulcer, or dyspepsia (indigestion). For these conditions esoteric healing asks to work on mental levels only, but we must expect results which are purely physical. Where there is stomach or abdominal cancer, we could say that it is due to an effort to control the astral body, resulting in direct inhibition and suppression of the solar plexus center. (Other stomach problems are usually due to temper, worry, and prolonged irritation, as we noted above.)

d. The pyloric sphincter, where the stomach joins the duodenum. This may be constricted or over-relaxed causing digestive upsets.

e. The whole of the intestine in case there are the beginnings of inflammation (enteritis) which can lead to other even more serious illnesses. Acidity often arises from a person being too critical, with violent dislikes and a superiority complex.

f. The ileo-caecal valve and appendix. This is where the small intestine enters the large intestine.

g. The three flexures (or folds) of the large intestine, viz., the hepatic flexure in the area of the liver, the splenic flexure in the region of the spleen, and the sigmoid flexure near the rectum. Here or along the course of the ascending, transverse or descending colon can manifest those common astral conditions, such as irritable bowel syndrome, colitis, ulcerative colitis, Crohn's disease, and diverticulitis.

h. The rectum and anal canal, for conditions such as hemorrhoids (use Force Triangles).

10. THE TRIANGLE FOR IMPERIL

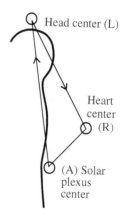

Head center (L)

Heart center (R)

(A) Solar plexus center

The effort to free yourself as well as your patients from irritation or from what is called "imperil" is particularly essential for the advance towards right service and right human relationships. Irritation and irritability are exceedingly prevalent during these days of nervous tension and stress. It most definitely jeopardizes progress and retards the steps of anyone who is the least interested in growing in consciousness and love. And, for those who are working in a spiritual group, it can produce "dangerous group tension" if present in any of the members, which can interfere with the free play of the power and light which the group is supposed to use, even when the other group members remain an emanating source. Irritation definitely generates a poison that locates itself in the region of the stomach and of the solar plexus. Irritation is a "disease," if I might use that word, of the solar plexus center, and it is definitely contagious to an almost alarming extent. So, you as healers should watch yourselves with care and remember that just insofar as you can live in the head and in the heart, you will end the disease of imperil and aid in the transference of the forces of the solar plexus into the heart center. The triangle for this transference vibrates from the solar plexus center to head center to heart center (Bailey, 1973, pp. 151–52). This triangle can be used also on anyone demonstrating stomach and intestinal problems as well as on any patient whose voice reveals the poison of irritation. It can be used to facilitate group healing and integration.

11. THE PSL TRIANGLE

This triangle, governed by the solar plexus center, involves the stomach as the main secondary externalization of the solar plexus center and the liver on the right of it, and the pancreas to the left. You will note that this triangle is similar to the Liver Triangle of Force, which uses the energy centers of the organs, whereas the PSL Triangle uses the etheric organs themselves. This triangle is governed by the solar plexus center but there is no need to hold that major center as these three organs are nourished and stimulated by it. However, this triangle is only done after three other activities have been performed: the solar plexus center has been balanced, the Liver Triangle of Force has been activated, and the Stomach Triangle has been magnetized. In this way the solar plexus center is under control and the energies focussed in that center are being received and released in the most balanced way. This process or sequence leads to a major purification, an intensive strengthening and a vital protection of the three vital organs. It is used to lift the lower energies of base and sacral centers to the solar plexus center. This triangle can reenergize the whole of the etheric body so that the incoming energy from the emotional life of the patient is immediately distributed rightly to the three organs, relieving the sort of pressure on the solar plexus center and pancreas that would cause so many problems. Splitting the astral energy three ways (through this triangle) has the remarkable effect of keeping the person's emotional life under control. It is a mental control even when the mind is undeveloped, making this triangle

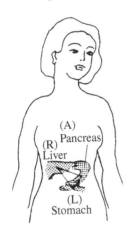

(A)
(R) Pancreas
Liver
(L)
Stomach

unique. For it is well known that most of the illnesses of mankind have their origin in the emotional body (also called the astral body).

When the astral energy is not being properly distributed, many physical symptoms can surface, for instance, bloating, indigestion, gastric ulcer, duodenal ulcer, Crohn's disease, diverticulitis, irritable bowel syndrome, and prolapse. This triangle, after the others have been done in preparation, is useful for these conditions, lifting the energies and protecting the organs for the future due to correctly circulating and sharing (or dispersing) the incoming solar plexus energies (Bailey, 1951–70, v. 4, p. 174).

12. DIABETES TRIANGLE

Diabetes is said to arise as a result of a violent suppression of desire through the wrong inner desires. The Diabetes Triangle, which should be used for all types of diabetic symptoms, consists of solar plexus center, stomach minor center, and the base center. This circuit will help the patient orient their desires toward aspiration and to a higher form of satisfaction more true to the soul.

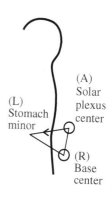

(A) Solar plexus center

(L) Stomach minor

(R) Base center

13. LOWER CLEARING TRIANGLE

The Lower Clearing Triangle involves the solar plexus center, the heart center and the ajna center. Its effect and purpose can lead the patient towards a stronger identification with some particular service in the world. But it is not done for a solo performance but for a work in cooperation with others who have the same inclination. This triangle helps lead to an increased sensitivity to group consciousness.

There are two forms of this triangle. One is for the average person just aspiring to the path of group consciousness (solar plexus center—heart center—ajna center), and the other, called the Triangle of Spiritual Facilitation, is for the advanced student of service to humanity. The latter triangle causes a downflow of energy from the ajna to the heart center, leading eventually to the heart-in-the-head center, as a result of the action of the first triangle, and of an advanced development of the solar plexus center (the ajna of the healer holds both the solar plexus center and the heart-in-the-head center). This latter triangle compounds and strengthens the disciple's mental approach and dedication to their chosen and known path of service in the world.

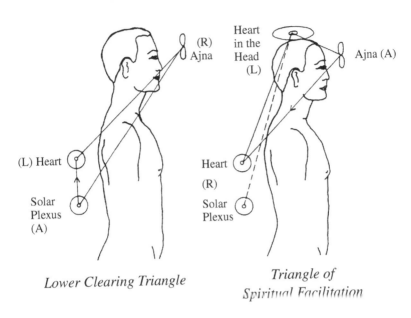

Lower Clearing Triangle   *Triangle of*
                                            Spiritual Facilitation

14. RESPONSIVE TRIANGLE

Having done the Lower Clearing Triangle (#13) and visualized the soul linking in with its own specific purpose on earth with others,

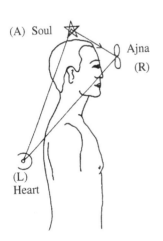

form another triangle to evoke response to service. Redirect soul energy downwards from the ajna to the heart center (i.e., soul of patient, ajna center and heart center), causing the heart's vibrational status to respond with more love to its chosen path of service. This triangle is called the Responsive Triangle, i.e., responsive to soul purpose. This important set of triangles (viz., the Lower Clearing Triangle, the Triangle of Spiritual Facilitation and the Responsive Triangle) is receiving much notice from other groups who are working in this way for the advancement of humanity, especially that group which is called the Hierarchy of Masters. Their interest suggests these triangles are for the quite advanced, and they are only really applicable to those who are on the spiritual path and who are having trouble with their health. The solar plexus center of these individuals should already have come under a great deal of control as higher development has begun (Bailey, 1951–70, v. 4, p. 170).

Another simpler set of triangles, called the Triangles of Stability and Right Group Relation, can help a person achieve integration, a sense of stability, and a feeling of being more grounded. These can be used for anyone, at whatever stage of consciousness:

a) solar plexus center, heart center, throat center, and

b) solar plexus center, sacral center, base center (p. 171).

These circuits resolve the problem of separateness, important for healing and for the process of spiritual and personal growth.

15. Triangle for Dispelling Astral Glamor

This is a useful triangle for groups struggling with the fogs and glamors of the astral or emotional plane: from the soul direct the energy to the astral body, then down to the solar plexus center, then to the heart center (Bailey, 1973, p. 143). New groups, or new members joining an established group, tend to bring with them impractical ideas. This can sweep the group into a confused state as it tries to sort and sift the input. The importance of the group to enter into inner alignment and then together permit this triangle to act on the group as a whole cannot be emphasized too much. It will help the group and its new members to refocus according to love, not desire or selfish glamor. The leaders or older group members should be aware of this problem and know of this triangle's use in dealing with it.

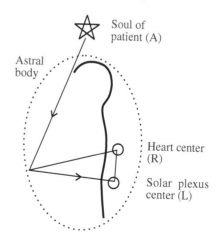

Soul of patient (A)

Astral body

Heart center (R)

Solar plexus center (L)

16. Consciousness Stream Triangle

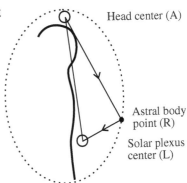

Head center (A)

Astral body
point (R)

Solar plexus
center (L)

This is another triangle which
is very useful, both to help resolve
glamor and also to help the healer
find the patient's place on the ladder of evolution: the points are head
center, astral body, solar plexus
center (Bailey, 1951–70, v. 4, p.
54).

The base center and the spine

This area involves the Base Center, the spine, and the kidney (or
renal) system (see chart, p. 233). Before entering this system I should
like to draw your attention to the esoteric healer's approach to the nervous system, since its entry into the body is via the spinal canal. This
involves what are called the Nadis. (Please refer to the section on the
nervous system on page 209).

17. The Basic Triangle

Since every healing session
begins with a sequence of four
energizing triangles (p. 157ff), including the Lower Prana Triangle
(#4), preparation has been made to
work in the spine area. Before going into the spine proper, however,
activate the Basic Triangle, which
will circulate the energies on a
causative level for use when clearing begins on the spine itself. This
triangle is also related to the Fear
Triangle, dealing with the fears
and phobias, shocks and "shilly
shallying" (lack of purpose and
direction in life) of the will-to-live.
The Basic Triangle is the key to

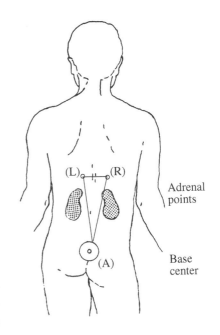

(L)   (R)

Adrenal
points

(A)

Base
center

getting the base note of the body vibrating, a motion and sound which is slow and intense. The three points comprise the base center, and the two etheric points on the adrenal glands just above the two kidneys on either side of the body.

When dealing with kidney problems or with bladder diseases, it is best to work on each side of the body, holding the base center, the adrenal gland (left or right) and the kidney (left or right). To work with the ureters, bladder or urethra, hold the base center, the adrenals, and the organ (ureters, bladder or urethra) as an etheric or vital force. Always we are working to get a balance between the three points in the triangle, bringing the balancing points in harmony with the rest of the body, and according to the will of the patient's soul.

18. THE SPINAL TRIANGLES

In preparation for work on the spine we should first activate that special circuit which is related to the energies running up the spine. It is called the Lower Prana Triangle. We met with this triangle when we energized the patient's body prior to the healing work. The three points are the spleen minor center, the base center and the throat center (linking the alta major center). Move your hands and ajna to the spleen minor center on the left, then keeping your ajna on the spleen minor center, move your two hands down to the base center, getting the stream of vitality moving at the same time, then with one hand draw the energy up the spine through the major centers on the spine right up to the throat/alta major center. Remember how the Spleen Triangle worked to generate primary energy for the use of the "engine room" of the body? Now we redirect this prana or life force into the spine and up to the throat and medulla oblongata governed by the alta major center, covering all the spinal nerves. This energizing triangle is important to do before working on the spine so that there is an abundance of lighted force available when one goes into the spine to balance it. The esoteric healer has been informed that when the spinal column is duly adjusted and aligned, and when the spleen is freed from congestion and in a healthy condition, there will be little trouble in the dense physical body.

The spine is a great resource area. The spinal column is the physical symbol of that essential alignment which is the immediate goal of directed relationships carried forward in consciousness by the spiritual man and brought about as a result of right meditation (Bailey, 1951–70, v. 4, pp. 202–3). Through it pass all the nerves to the body. It is in fact a reflection of the brain just as the body is a reflection of the head. We have already seen how the five major centers are found related to the different sections of the spine (the esoteric view reveals that they are right within the spine in a different dimension to space and time which might make us think a little differently of the spine and its cord). As noted above, esoteric healing is not particularly interested in the details of anatomy and physiology (although these details should be surveyed by and can reveal much to the intuitive healer), it is far more interested in general areas and how they relate to more subtle causes.

The etheric cord is primarily intended to be the channel through which the energizing of the centers and distribution of energy to the surrounding areas of the body is carried forward by the intelligent, integrated personality, acting under the conscious direction of the soul. But there are many inhibitions, blockages, unawakened areas, deficiency of vitality, lack of free flow and consequent lack of development with the "whole man," or also there is too much stimulation, a too rapid vibratory activity, a premature awakening of the centers leading to overactivity. These conditions can lead to nervous problems, psychological difficulty and disease in some form or another (Bailey, 1951–70, v. 4, p. 201–2). Therefore a chart is here included as a reference guide of the nerves from the spine and the areas they govern and the conditions they may cause if pressure or damage is caused (see p. 178). The Chart can be a useful tool to the new esoteric healer facing specific conditions involving the spine.

The spine is governed by the base center and is also related to the alta major center (at the top of the spine), which governs the spinal cord. When approaching the spinal area, one must do so very carefully; do not "jump in." There must be no sudden or harsh movements. The need for finesse applies to the whole of esoteric healing, more so when working on the spine. Low back pain is one of the most common complaints of patients due to severe stresses in daily living—lifting, twisting, walking, running, stretching, etc. Such a delicately balanced and sensitive structure as the spine deserves its possessor's consideration. Should a patient come to you for help, recommend exercises that keep the back supple, such as swimming, walking, yoga and massage. The patient may need to lie on their back, so have a couch ready, and be prepared to work above the front of the patient, visualizing the back. If she has no problem sitting, then work from the back of the patient.

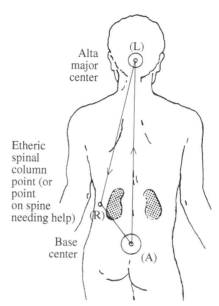

Alta major center

Etheric spinal column point (or point on spine needing help)

Base center

But whatever the condition, a primary treatment of the healer is to hold the Spinal Triangle: hold the base center with your ajna, the alta major center with your left hand and the whole spinal column (vertebrae and cord) with your right hand. Gently energize it and in visualization feel it coming into balance by clearing energetic congestion and blockages.

Remember when working on the spine to recall the base center's influence. For instance, the patient may have low back pain or a slipped disc due to deep unresolved fears or repressed anger and resentment which need to be cleared from the emotional level. This may call for a further triangle to be made between the healer and the patient similar to that which we did on the solar plexus center where we "draw off" the energy stuck and congesting the flow through the center (Synchronizing Triangle). But instead of using the solar plexus center we synchronize with the base center: the healer's head center, the healer's base center and the patient's base center. The base energy of the patient is then magnetized towards the healer's base center and transmuted in the healer's head center. You will need to know the condition of the center to use this technique. Please read about the dangers involved and the protective measures to be taken when using this particular type of healing triangle (see p. 123).

Remember also what I said about that initial Protecting Triangle, where we visualize a continuous stream of love flowing to the patient. With deep inner love behind all our work we can rest assured no danger or harm can approach us, or the patient.

Six triangles can be used in relation to the spine and any particular problem found there. Obviously, not all of them will be relevant to a particular patient, for they refer to different conditions.

CHART II
THE NERVES

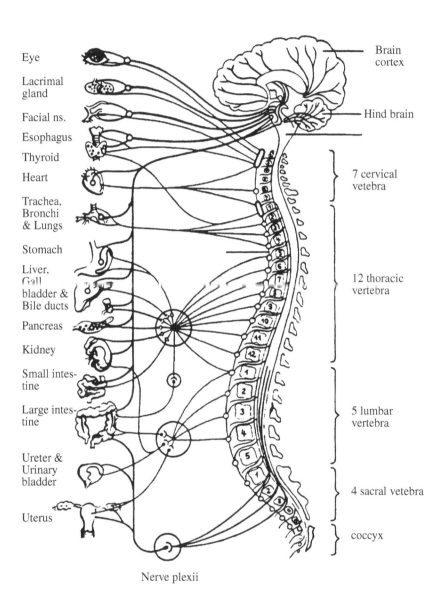

Eye

Lacrimal
gland

Facial ns.

Esophagus

Thyroid

Heart

Trachea,
Bronchi
& Lungs

Stomach

Liver,
Gall
bladder &
Bile ducts

Pancreas

Kidney

Small intes-
tine

Large intes-
tine

Ureter &
Urinary
bladder

Uterus

Brain
cortex

Hind brain

7 cervical
vetebra

12 thoracic
vertebra

5 lumbar
vertebra

4 sacral vetebra

coccyx

Nerve plexii

a. Base center—alta major center—spinal point needing help. This will help release trapped nerves. On the emotional level the person feels like a prisoner, trapped by their own illusions and fears.

b. Base center—spine—spinal area. This is for inherited (congenital) conditions, including fused spinal vertebrae, displacements or malformations. The healer is encouraged to work in the astral part of this triangle, for such a person feels the need to be somewhere else, is of two minds, and often has a sense of being stuck, and has a fear relating to these emotions.

c. Base center—throat center—spinal point needing help. Do this triangle to check whether arthritis is beginning to settle in the vertebral joint affected. If it is indicated, hold the triangle to cool the condition and balance and restore the energies of the area (Johnston, 1983). This person often is found to be creatively bound by their life's conditions, causing irritablity and resentfulness. Their will to be of use to the world is hampered by so-called "personal responsibilities" that do not really exist.

d. Base center—heart center—spinal point needing help. Used mainly for the spinal muscles which may become over-contracted or over-relaxed or a combination of these (a so-called spasm) in a particular area. More blood and more circulating vital energy is gathered at the area for use to restore healing. This triangle is often used in relation to the other triangles for this effect. Visualize the will-to-love streaming round this circuit; the person usually wants to help mankind in some way but is unable to motivate the spirit of selflessness (again, fear is the constraint).

e. Base center—sacral center—spinal point needing help. The sacral center is the generator of life force and creative building energies, so we use this center where we find an eroded spinal disc, or where trauma has caused injury. This circuit is also often used after the use of the above triangles to consolidate the building and repairing work needed for healing. This triangle also has other indications: you will usually find a relationship problem involved here, and most frequently it is in the family. Help the energy to flow more openly and freely. (Often the hips are tight, so after the healing suggest yoga exercises to loosen them). The will to express themselves sexually is often inhibited, causing this triangle to indicate poor flow.

f. Base center—spleen minor center—spinal point needing help. This is another triangle which is usefully employed in relation to other triangles on the spine to draw in an extra supply of prana or vital force to help smooth the way to healing. It acts like a balm to the area (Johnston, 1983).

When doing these triangles we always work from the causative area in the subtle bodies, allowing our intuition, which is the higher correspondence to the sense of touch, to direct our thoughts and actions, as we impose by love a new vibration and flow in the patient. This new vibration may not result in physical healing but may simply help a patient to see through the illusion of their disease and to live with it with head held high. Remember, the work of esoteric healing is multidimensional and is entirely controlled by the patient's own soul.

At this point I should like to illustrate how things can go radically wrong should a person, by the power of self-will or through an over-development of the mental side of their character, acquire the power to blend the three energies as they lay slumbering in the base center, driving them forward and upward. Such a person stands in danger of obsession (loosening of the physico-etheric connection) (Bailey, 1951–70, v. 4, p. 80; *see also* 1962, p. 127 & 1951–70, v. 2, p. 458), insanity,[5] physical death or dire disease in some part of the body. The person is also at risk of an overdevelopment of the sex impulse through the driving of the sacral force upwards in an uneven manner, or in forcing its radiation to undesirable centers. The reason for this is that the matter of such a person's body is not pure enough to stand the uniting flames. The channel up the spine is usually still clogged and blocked, and therefore acts as a barrier, turning the flame backwards and downwards. The flame (being united by the power of personality mind-will and not being accompanied by a simultaneous downflow from the plane of spirit) permits the entrance, through the burning etheric, of undesirable and extraneous forces, currents, and even entities. These can wreck and tear and ruin what is left of the etheric vehicle, the brain tissue and even the dense physical body itself. The unwary person, being unaware of their soul quality (or ray), and therefore of the proper geometrical form or triangle for the correct method of circulation from center to center, will drive the fire in unlawful progression and thus burn up tissue. This will result at least (if nothing worse) in a setting back for several lives of the clock of their progress, for much time will have to be spent in rebuilding what was destroyed, and with recapitulating on right lines all the work to be done (Bailey, 1962, p. 126). These are the sorts of forces one is working with in the base center. For such a person suffering from the above-mentioned premature "burning," triangles using the base center, especially the Threads Triangle (#60), can be very helpful.

19. TRIANGLE FOR ADDICTIONS OR OBSESSIONS

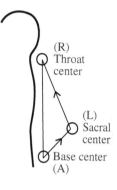

(R)
Throat
center

(L)
Sacral
center

Base center
(A)

To cure obsession, there must be a development of the first Aspect, goodwill, says the Master (Bailey, 1951–70, v. 4, p. 108; *see also* p. 80 & 1962, p. 127). The Triangle for Addictions or Obsessions consists of the base center, the sacral center and the throat center. The base center controls repetitive actions which can result in misdirected will. For example, autism could be a discipleship problem (abuse) of a former life (note that ray one governs the base center in the path of discipleship, see p. 76). The sacral center involves building, transforming, personal abuse. This center is also connected to plants (e.g., tobacco, pot, hashish, alcohol) and to opiates. The throat center directs this twisted energy upward and outward towards selfless service for humanity, the acceptable and intelligent "obsession and addiction," the "magnificent obsession."

20. FEAR TRIANGLE

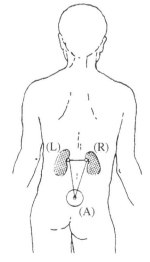

(L)   (R)

(A)

The source of nearly all fear is based on the fear of death. Fear = death = transformation. Fear is in reality the Dweller on the Threshold (Bailey, 1951–70, v. 4, p. 443), which is the sum-total of the personality fears. Fear and death form the Great Illusion. The Fear Triangle is very useful in all circumstances where the patient is in a state of unknowing. It can be used after someone has been diagnosed as having a terminal condition, or after accidents, or for children in distress, in fact, whenever there is fear or shock involved. The triangle may also be applicable for those with deep unknown fears that are hindering them from making decisions, or from taking steps to change their conditions or circumstances. The circuit involves the base center and two minute points closely associated with the interior of the kidneys (the "belly" of the kidneys where the input and output of the vessels and tubes can be found).

21. FEAR TRANSFORMATION TRIANGLE

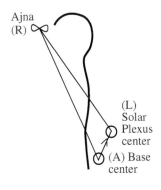

Having done the Fear Triangle, use the Fear Transformation Triangle to transmute the energies for the purposes of greater personality control and direction. This direction is achieved by transforming these subconscious energies through the solar plexus center of glamor and desire, right up to the ajna center which takes its personality direction from the Soul. Where the personality is being misinformed and misdirected (perhaps they're in the wrong social group), it is taking instruction from the solar plexus center (the animal brain). Use of the Fear Transformation Triangle will help to bring the individual back to a right relation to the Soul and to the planet and its kingdoms. This important triangle circuit goes from base center to solar plexus center to the ajna (*see* Bailey, 1951–70, v. 2, p. 529). The Glamor Triangle could then follow.

22. FIRST AND SECOND INITIATION TRIANGLES

There are two triangles involving the base center that can be used to help aspirants on the Path to greater stability and focus in their service of the Plan. I have put them together, but in reality they are worlds apart! To attain the second initiation after entering the first door may take many incarnations of work and training. However, in the service of esoteric healing, healers meet with people of all degrees, perhaps even those working for their higher initiations, although this is rare for beginners in this work. First-degree initiates are those who have just entered the Stream; they have just tasted the sweet wine of spiritual wisdom. It is the birth of the Christos in the cave of the heart. Such people always assume they know it all and want everyone else to be as clever as they! This first stage marks the beginning of a totally new life and mode of living; it marks the commencement of a new manner of thinking and of conscious perception (Bailey, 1951–70, v. 5, p. 667). The triangle for them to hold (or have held by the healer) is base center, solar plexus center and heart center (Bailey, 1962, p. 167). It is this triangle that is recommended to be held as the energy of the sacral center begins its slow ascent to the throat center (Bailey, 1951–70, v. 5, p. 678). What First-degree initiates have to understand are the following: beginnings; right discipline; relationship; sex magic. They are learning to work with the seventh ray.

Those who are working to control and transform their emotional natures are those of the second degree, symbolized in Christian teachings by the baptism. Transmuting desire to aspiration is a particularly difficult stage to master for most, and it may take several lives to gain complete control. The triangle recommended for these workers is base center, heart center and throat center (Bailey, 1962, p. 169). The circuit will stabilize their solar plexus center and harness the power of the sixth ray under which they will be influenced. These disciples should meditate on dedication, glamor and devotion (Bailey, 1951–70, v. 5, p. 340).

23. THIRD INITIATION TRIANGLE

This triangle is placed here for ease of comparison only; it belongs actually in the sections on the upper centers. It is used only with someone who has advanced mental and personality attributes who consults you regarding signs of problems in these areas. For it is at the third initiation that the person has a major triangle of energy comprising the heart center, the throat center and the seven head centers taken as one center. Such a student is working within the fifth ray, with the ajna center being the major focus of attention. The co-workers should come to an understanding of integration, direction, science. Such a person is gaining freedom from the ancient authority of the threefold, integrated personality as a whole (Bailey, 1951–70, v. 5, p. 686).

The reproductive system

Now we consider the triangles associated with the reproductive or building system. This is the area where work the building devas or lunar lords, they who hear color and see sound.

O Thou, Who givest sustenance to the universe
From whom all things proceed
To whom all things return
Unveil to us the face of the true spiritual Sun
Hidden by a disc of golden Light
That we may know the truth
And do our whole duty
As we journey to Thy sacred Feet.

This prayer, the Gayatri, is said to be the oldest invocation known. Its reference to the sacred Feet, links it to the sacral center of creative activity.

24. SACRAL TRIANGLE

In this center, creative life force is circulated, awaiting use. As we noted above, this triangle is useful for more than the reproductive system. We saw how this sacral force was utilized in one of the spinal triangles (#19).

In the same way, wherever in the body we want to draw in the building energies (devas) to establish some particular healing action having to do with the vital and physical body, the healer can call the sacral energy to help. Of course, its greatest usefulness is associated with the reproductive system, for that is its area of expression. The triangle consists of the sacral center (which the healer holds with their ajna), and the two minor centers on the gonadic glands (the two ovaries or the two testes), which the healer holds with the two hands. The form of the triangle is different for males than for females: in men the triangle has its apex pointing up, the opposite occurs in the triangle in women. Notice that this is one of the very few triangles which is different according to whether the patient is male or female. This difference is of importance only for the person further along the spiritual path, when the two sides of the sacral force (positive and negative, masculine and feminine) are required to drive certain other energies forward and upward. Where these glands have been removed, which is more usual in women than in

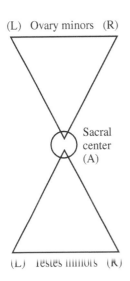

(L)   Ovary minors   (R)

Sacral center (A)

(L)   Testes minors   (R)

men—for instance in hysterectomies—the etheric organ remains. (This goes for any organ removal. The only time the etheric organ does not exist is when the person has been born without the physical counterpart, as in the case of unilateral kidneys.)

The work of the healer is to bring these sacral energies into balance. Generally speaking, the sacral triangle is very active because it governs the preservation of life and health in the physical body. Changes as to the strength and mobility of the circuit occurs as a result of over-use of the sexual function, or when sex is put to use where it was not intended, or when there is sexual suppression or neglect. Such changes are wide-ranging and may demand from the healer a great deal of patience and spiritual work. To help with difficult or perverse energy forms (especially where negative spirals are found in the sacral center itself), I recommend the use of the pastel shade of the color orange to be directed in visualization around the circuit. Another action in these circumstances is to tune into the throat center to draw the higher creative energy into the Sacral Triangle. To do this the healer "opens out the sacral energy" by forming triangles with the hip minors, knee minors (linking simultaneously with the base center), and finally with the feet minor centers. Do this opening up slowly and notice how the energy changes as it gets into the legs of the patient.

Energy travels from a center in gentle spiral movements round and through the nadis and meridians. Where there are sexual identification difficulties, there is often a reversal of this flow by the time it gets into the feet of the opened up sacral circuit, still downwards but in a different direction. Such a subtle switch of flow can be felt strongly or weakly, according to the karma of the person.

(A)
Throat center

(L)
Sacral center

hips

knees

feet
(R)

The whole work on the sacral center and these triangles is the most sensitive activity in the entire sequence of esoteric healing. Just as the base center establishes for the person what he does by revealing what he is, so the sacral center establishes who he is (the sacral expresses itself through the physical form). There is a subtle and important difference between the two triangles, sacral to the testes minors and sacral to the ovaries minors. These two triangles are possibly the most important in the whole of esoteric healing.

The healer will have to come back to them time after time to help them towards complete expression. They are subject to the most persuasive of illusions and delusions, and the healer on the subtle levels of these triangles will need to help the new rhythms to be imposed. These two triangles are in fact the personality of the person (either male or female), governed by the solar plexus center. When the three centers with their related circuits of energy are in harmony within and between themselves, then the higher circuits begin to function and become active in the life of the person. The Sacral Triangle works on the problem of personal relationships, on sexual fears, family relations, and personal tastes (see also p. 224). Wherever there are disorders or diseases in the reproductive system, the healer can work on the area by holding the sacral center, the gonad glands (together as one), and the point of trouble, e.g., ovarian tumor or prostatic enlargement. For a more specific approach to prostate problems, you may hold the Prostate Triangle consisting of the sacral center, the gonad glands as an etheric energy, and the prostate minute center.

25. THE TWO TRIANGLES OF FORCE (see photo #6 on p. 331)

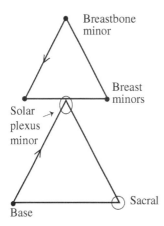

Breastbone minor

Breast minors

Solar plexus minor

Sacral

Base

These are probably the most important triangles to do in relation to damaged webs and violated etheric threads. Such conditions call for a combination of two triangles that must be held in mind and linked at the same time. The healer superimposes the upper triangle on the lower. Standing to the right of the patient, the healer first connects with the upper triangle by holding three minor centers with the right hand, thumb and two fingers at the front of the patient (no major center is directly involved). The centers are a minor etheric point just below the thyroid gland (and thus connected to the throat center) called the breastbone minor center (held with the thumb), and the two minor centers near the breasts (held with the index and middle fingers).

Once the trio of lines is flowing and steady, raise your left hand to the back of the patient to connect with the lower force triangle. Here hold the sacral center with the middle finger, the solar plexus minor center with the thumb (this minor center, despite its name, is closely related to the base center), and the base center (Bailey, 1951–70, v. 4, p. 73) with the index finger. You will find this very easy to perform even though it sounds complex. Now feel the lines of force connecting with each other right through the etheric body of the patient.

We use this triangle (the two circuits as one, connected through the body) whenever there has been trauma, be it a physical accident, an emotional upheaval or a mental shock. The upper triangle gathers and directs the energy downwards in a kind of involutionary spiral, while the lower triangle receives the energies and consolidates them in the personality. These energies are youth forces. (This is due to the major connection with the sacral center as it is linked to the throat center—bringing about constant creative regeneration. Hence God is called the Eternal Youth.) The linked triangles bring about stability and regained reasonableness. These words are used because, from the esoteric understanding of this condition, the etheric body has, due to the trauma, been punctured or displaced, usually somewhere between the lower centers, requiring the involutionary (consolidating or healing) energy of the minor centers to be utilized by the lower triangle of force (with its major centers) to enable mending to occur.

All the centers have "webs," or etheric discs, separating them one from the other. These webs act as transformers, either to upgrade ascending energy or to lower the vibratory activity of descending energy. These webs are the basic necessities for a balanced and harmonious life. On the path of spiritual development these webs are gradually and naturally destroyed; they become less functional as the person begins to handle force and energy more consciously. Higher energy acting on the web purifies the etheric form and cleanses it from "dross." Eventually, after the two fires of matter and mind begin to blend (which should be a natural, slow and gradual process), the web itself is destroyed. By the time the third initiation is reached, the individual can maintain continuity of consciousness. Breaking down the webs can even be resisted for certain specific ends by trained individuals, according to the Master DK (Bailey, 1962, p. 184). But if there is a sudden shock, for instance, in a motor accident, or the death of a loved one or even sudden financial ruin, a person may not be able to contain the rampaging energy surge, and a hole is blasted through one of the etheric webs. This opens the person out to a very strange world, a world full of phobias and misinterpretation. The person might suffer a nervous breakdown, or a temporary loss of personal control, or a state of panic and fear.

For supportive and more specific help with the webs, use the Threads Triangle (see #68). If there is fear, link in with the Fear Transformation Triangle described above (#21).

Technically and from the spiritual angle, the web naturally "burns away" when the person can sense and see the fourth ether. The webs are found midway between the third and second etheric subplanes (counting from below upward). After the webs disintegrate, the person merges with their astral vehicle. Viewed another way, the webs exist on each plane. They are broken down as the initiate develops—from the angle of spirit and of service—to establish that awareness called "continuity of consciousness," another understanding of the much misunderstood term "kundalini."

Build up the upper Triangle of Force and then the lower, and then link them as one to set in motion the "healing" of the webs. Once torn, however, these webs are never properly healed—their "scar tissue" is very thin and the person will always suffer from aftereffects. (This is never told to the patient, of course. Negative thoughtforms on an already torn web system could worsen the condition; hold the triangles and heal, according to the wisdom of the patient's soul.) On the other hand, the one sure way of healing, whereby aftereffects are no longer troublesome, is via a spiritual path whereon the webs are gradually broken down anyway and the person begins to handle the inflow of energy (physical, emotional or mental) consciously, without the need of these transforming units. It is really towards this end that healing tends, and in this sense such deep shocks can eventually be healed. It may take many years of attending a healing clinic, and even more years of individual spiritual effort and struggle for balance during this transition.

One feature of major importance is that the two triangles of force, when brought into synchronicity with each other, control the twenty-one minor centers and hundreds of minute centers of the body, bringing them into relation with the major centers via the sacral center.

By treating these two triangles in a patient, you will help to draw healing force into the etheric and physical bodies, carrying with it energies that are building materials for the rehabilitation and restoration of a patient's diseased organs. They are helpful for prolapsed organs and for menopause. The triangles are also particularly effective on one who is seriously ill but still has plenty of vitality. You can sense they want to live and they have plenty of fight in them to throw off the problem. Such patients are often young, but you can consider using this triangle for the older patient as well. Assess their trouble and be guided by your intelligent intuition.

Sometimes with the aid of these Triangles of Force, the required energy is supplied to a patient for the resolution of their problem. Otherwise it can be a force to help a patient ease into an "aware acceptance" of their condition and its inevitable consequences.

An elementary circuit called the Shock Triangle is sometimes employed for lesser problems involving trauma and shock. The triangle involves the solar plexus minor center (just below the solar plexus center), a minute point on the ileocaecal valve (between the small and large intestines, near the appendix), and the sigmoid flexure of the colon. This triangle has something in common with the "hara" (belly) so often referred to in Oriental systems of medicine and in the martial arts.

Another triangle very useful to hold the physical body in coherency is the Life Stream Triangle discussed on page 194 (head center-heart center-spleen minor). The stream of pranic energy vitalizes the individual atoms and cells of the physical body.

26. TRIANGLE FOR SEXUAL PROBLEMS

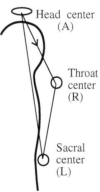

Head center
(A)

Throat center
(R)

Sacral center
(L)

This triangle is used for sexual inhibition or suppression, to balance and bring right control, and make the disciple creative in the worldly sense and of use to humanity: head center, throat center, sacral center (Bailey, 1951–70, v. 4, p. 215; *see also* v. 2, p. 528).

27. FERTILITY TRIANGLES

a) These triangles are useful for the patient who has consulted you for help with fertility—medical diagnosis having found there is nothing wrong physiologically, the patient or the couple who has not used contraception for a year, or, at worst, the male has a low sperm count. The healing work undergoes a number of stages, involving up to six weekly sessions or longer. This series of triangles are called the Fertility Triangles.

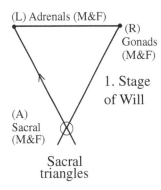

(L) Adrenals (M&F)

(R) Gonads (M&F)

1. Stage of Will

(A) Sacral (M&F)

Sacral triangles

The first stage is to work on the sacral triangles, relating them as one to the adrenal (yes, adrenal) glands of both mother and father and to the reproductive organs of the male and of the female. In other words, there are two triangles related as one. This is the stage of will. Here, the mother-to-be need only be present, although having both persons in the session is preferable.

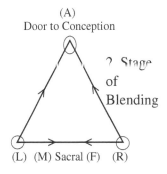

(A) Door to Conception

2. Stage of Blending

(L) (M) Sacral (F) (R)

For the second stage, have the couple present for the healing. The task of this phase is to relate this triangle to the subtle world of formative force or creative building, the so-called vital or etheric planes. For there is a need and a desire by the couple which is stopped or resisted at this plane. Put more esoterically and from a spiritual standpoint, the incoming child has been brought down to the place where conception can take place, but there is a block on the subtle etheric plane preventing the consummation. There is a relationship problem on subtle levels. It is at this point that the healer brings to consciousness the two partners, that is, the couple with the problem, and on the subtle level holds an esoteric triangle: the two sacral centers (of husband and wife) and the one incoming force which is the door to conception on the physical plane, an etheric point or "aperture" through which the child, the incarnating soul, will enter into physical incarnation. At this stage we do not link with the child. This stage is continued for a number of sessions. It is called the stage of blending.

The third stage results from the previous work and brings into activity another circuit called a Form-building Triangle: spleen center, sacral center and base center. The triangle of this stage involves the incoming soul only.

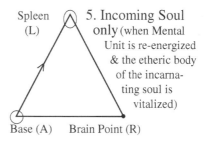

Sacral
(L)
3. Form-
Building
(Incoming
Soul only)
Spleen (A)   Base (R)

The fourth and fifth stages are only used when the healer considers the second and third stages to be related and completed.

This fourth stage concerns the souls of the three involved: father, mother, child (incoming soul). Since it links and works with the souls of the three individuals, there is a flow of "accepting energy" resolving the blocks and helping each of the three to take responsibility for the future relationships. Start of the fifth stage: Now the healer may connect with a triangle within the reincarnating ego. It is done when the two most vital moments in the work of this earth-seeking human are achieved—the very time when the mental unit is re-energized into cyclic activity, and when the etheric body of the incoming soul is vitalized. The fifth stage triangle's points are: the center at the base of the spine or base center, the splenic center, and a certain point within the physical brain (Bailey, 1962, pp. 181, 788). Throughout this work the ajna of the healer must control the progress and direction of the results. The results are never the same, so the healer is to assume nothing, but one thing is certain, there will be a greater understanding between the would-be parents. The healer can see that this is quite advanced work, but from the angle of esoteric healing, all work is advanced, for it all involves the future and the expressed intention of the soul governed entirely by the will-to-love.

Incoming Soul (A)
4. Resolving
Father (L)   Mother (R)

Spleen
(L)
5. Incoming Soul
only (when Mental
Unit is re-energized
& the etheric body
of the incarna-
ting soul is
vitalized)
Base (A)   Brain Point (R)

b) In relation to fertility, more advanced healers could use the Sixth Ray Technique (*see* Chapter 10; Bailey, 1951–70, v. 4, p. 711).

c) Another set of triangles to consider, if the healing group feels they are indicated: (i) From the sacral center open the triangle from the adrenals to the male gonads to the female gonads. (ii) Then link the sacral center, via the adrenal glands (as one) to the gonads (male and female, as one), to the base center (p. 179). These latter triangles are recommended only after the first sequence has been completed. They definitely materialize the fertility forces of men and women.

d) The Triangle for the Majority, using the ajna, solar plexus and sacral centers, is another triangle applicable to infertility. As its name implies, it is a triangle which governs the majority of mankind. It is to be used to balance those of the human family who have been selected to regenerate the race. Because this triangle is activated when regeneration occurs, it is essential for use when a couple has come to you for the healing of their infertility problem.

It is clear that the power and strength of the sacral center is wide and varied, and frequently extremely difficult to handle. The sacral is very active, so the healer must be ready to return to it often to relate it to the other work being done for the patient. For this is the creative and productive "virgin" of the body—a powerful and useful force when correctly applied by the higher centers.

28. TRIANGLE OF ENERGY

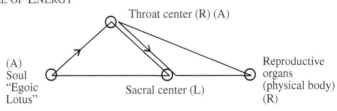

The sacral center is a necessary evocation between that which is high and that which is low, and between that which is sounded forth from the center in the throat and that which replies to a deeply sounded note. To connect these areas we do the Triangle of Energy consisting of: the egoic lotus, the throat center and the sacral center. The circuit produces a subsidiary triangle of force: the throat center, the sacral center and the physical body (symbolized by the organs of reproduction) (Bailey, 1951–70, v. 3, p. 428). This double triangle (or you can make it into a tetrahedron) can be used as much for helping to resolve relationship problems as for sexual potency or sexual identification difficulties.

29. TRIANGLE OF THE PRACTICAL MYSTIC

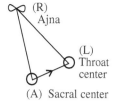

(R) Ajna

(L) Throat center

(A) Sacral center

This triangle is for the person who is a developing humanitarian, aspiring to be a practical mystic and to be an occultist in the highest sense of the word. Sacral center, throat center, ajna center are the points of this triangle.

30. TRIANGLE FOR CREATIVE ENERGY DISTRIBUTION

This triangle could have been called the triangle for the third ray centers in man (a hint for those who have some knowledge). Include the sacral center (creative thread of the personality) with the throat center (consciousness thread of the soul), and the ajna center (life thread or sutratma of the monad) (Bailey, 1951–70, v. 4, p. 153). Are you aware how this triangle is connected to the activity of creative energy distribution? When you do this triangle, you will observe it has a different emphasis compared to the Triangle of the Practical Mystic, even though the points are the same. Energy follows thought is the key.

31. TRIANGLE OF YOGA

This is an unusual and advanced triangle for experienced esoteric healers, having an important relation to sex on a higher level. For the three points, connect the buddhic body with the astral body and with the monad. Through the circuit, visualize the search for balance, aspiration towards harmony, union and yoga, and a longing for union with God (Bailey, 1962, p. 669). The triangle is used for disciples seeking a deeper meaning in their lives.

Above the diaphragm

This represents symbolically a step up in consciousness. Below the diaphragm is the metabolic area of instinct and of personality, will and purpose; above the diaphragm is a more sensitive area (signified by the protective cage of the ribs) where there is more imagination and feeling—a sensitivity to more conscious (and thus, controllable) rhythms and cycles. To experience this transition upward, we could tune into the heart center to feel this higher energy.

The heart and circulatory system

The heart of the body is where the person's innermost feelings are hidden and protected. We can enter only with love. The heart center in the etheric manifests in the thymus gland (via its hormone thymosin), a little above the heart. The function of the thymus is little known, symbolizing mankind's own undeveloped heart center. But it is known that the thymus changes its function several times in our life. In babyhood its function is to help break down mother's milk for assimilation. From eighteen months to puberty it is involved in the development of the sex glands, thereby working with the sacral center. At puberty another change occurs when thymosin influences the height of an individual (working with the ajna center, which controls the output of human growth hormone). At this time the thymus also acts as a balance between the higher and lower instincts, hence discipline is essential for correct development (connection with the vagus nerve center). The heart center also governs the lymphatic system, aided by a metabolic influence (thyroxine) of the throat center.

From the esoteric standpoint there are three causes of heart disease:

1. Overuse of the life energy.
2. The opening of the heart center, which puts a strain on the heart organ.
3. The premature lifting of the solar plexus energy to the heart (Bailey, 1951–70, v. 4, p. 238).

Another esoteric cause of heart problems has to do with the incoming seventh ray. People on that ray are more susceptible to the difficulties and diseases incident to the blood stream than are any other ray types (p. 128).

The heart center anchors the life stream (sutratma) using the Life Stream Triangle (head center, heart center, spleen minor) (p. 428), which rhythmically conveys life force around the body (from the monad through various transformers). This stream controls the pumping action of the heart and the circulation of the blood, feeding every cell of the body. The heart is not a pump, as has been pointed out by other esotericists (notably Rudolf Steiner), but rather an effect, manifesting the rhythmical pulse of universal energy pounding into our system from a higher power source. With this rhythm cranio-sacral osteopaths work.

Consciousness is governed by the heart center, which conforms with the Chinese understanding of this "organ." Esotericists are aware that the heart referred to is in the head center. The central whorl of energies within the thousand petalled lotus in the head is the heart, using the Consciousness Stream Triangle (see p. 174) (head center, astral body, solar plexus center) (p. 429). An opened heart center gives a sense of the whole, or hylozoism, which avers that all is alive and aware. A thriving heart chakra also conveys impersonality, healing, humility, responsibility, goodwill, tolerance, compassion. Distrust is a major key to the blocking of heart energy.

When working with the circulatory system or with specific triangles concerned with distributing heart energy, it is a wise preliminary to circulate etheric energy in five directions:

a. Head, neck and arms.
b. The hepatic (liver) system (note: anemias are due to excess energy through the liver).
c. The digestive system (which connects with the liver before returning to the heart).
d. The kidneys.
e. The rest of the trunk including the body and legs.

What follows is a brief description of the process. Hold your ajna on the patient's heart center. (a) Start the energy moving from the left ventricle of the heart, then draw the energy up to the neck, arms, head and brain. Next, move the depleted energy, traveling within the "blue" blood, to the right atrium in the heart, then down to the right ventricle. Draw it up to the "revitalizing" system (the lungs), releasing the heavy and taking on the light, then come down into the left atrium. (b) From the left ventricle again, along with the prana and meridian force, visualize the energy flowing to the next circulatory part (the liver system), and so on with (c), (d), and (e). This method definitely gets the vital force to every part of the patient's body and is useful for those with circulatory problems, including varicose veins and varicose ulcers.

32. HEART TRIANGLE

Where the patient is showing signs of coldness and a lack of love and compassion, we can use this triangle. It has other effects of a

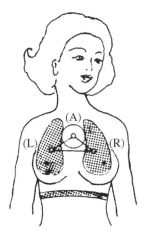

more physical nature as well. These include improving the cardiac circulation, varicose veins, insomnia, and conditions which concern the quality of the blood. This triangle vitalizes the energy in the blood and, as a result, works on cleansing it for more efficient use by the patient. The heart is the center of radioactivity; when this center is opened and active, the power of love that streams from it will affect all who come in contact with that person; people will feel the dynamic radiance of loving understanding pouring out from such a person. This center and the associated triangle expresses the intuitional qualities in the person, not, mind you, the psychic aspects of lower, more selfish love. To bring in this energy requires clear focus on the part of the healer—focus, that is, from the soul level, so that the response of the patient will be from the same source. The healer holds the heart center and the two lung minor centers (Bailey, 1951–70, v. 4, pp. 460–61). This has the effect of opening out the life force of the person, an opening out which will evoke a great deal of change in their life, probably including a deliberate and determined effort to work consciously in a group, which itself is selflessly and altruistically attuned. One energy that will be brought in by this triangle is what is called "harmlessness." It has a particular affiliation to the etheric channels of the body, clearing them and purifying the centers as a result, thus permitting entrance of those higher intuitional energies. Set in motion, this triangle immediately begins to activate the energies which will counter the causes of disease. Since it works from above to below, conditions such as thromboses and high cholesterol in the blood are reduced by degrees, making the process of change safe for the person. In esoteric healing, inasmuch as we are tuned in to the source of all love and to the soul of the patient, all the work is done by the patient, in relation to the soul of the healer. (One of the paradoxes of esotericism is that in manifestation each individual has a soul, but in its own nature that soul is a group entity connected to every other soul, forming one Oversoul.) So the progress of the disease and its cure is entirely under the control of the patient. This encourages humility in the healer and healing group, and responsibility in the patient. It does not mean that the healer is irresponsible or is without responsibility. The healer has been asked to help the patient; she is from that moment responsible regarding her words and her actions, and especially her thoughts concerning the patient, for all three are conditioning factors. Esoteric healing, we recall, is an act of directing the energy of love from soul to soul, using the intelligent mind.

33. TRIANGLES AT DEATH

a. An interesting alternative deployment of the Heart Triangle is its use at the time of death. For this application it can be combined with:
b. The Desire Triangle (soul—astral body—solar plexus center);
c. The Withdrawing Triangle (soul—head center—ajna);
d. The Triangle for the Dying (spleen minor—lung minors—heart center);
e. The Triangles of Force (see #25);
f. The Immortality Triangle (see #3);
g. The Samadhi Triangles (see #39);
h. (for the more advanced healer) the First and Fourth Ray Techniques of esoteric healing, discussed later.

The triangles can also be used more specifically to work with those who have died, to help them through later phases of the excarnation process, as the soul passes through its various sheaths to its monadic self.

34. IMMUNE TRIANGLES

Since the rampage worldwide of AIDS (Acquired Immune Deficiency Syndrome), the importance of the immune system has been brought home to us. Its strength protects us from infection, and its weakness opens us up to all kinds of diseases, illnesses and allergies. Even the common cold is due to a breakdown in our defenses, leading to an invasion by a "cold" virus. There are three triangles covering the whole immune system, involving the skin and mucous membrane bacteria, all the body fluids (blood, urine, digestive juices, tears, sweat, which all carry substances poisonous to most bacteria), as well as the phagocytes throughout the body, particularly in the blood (called white blood cells).

The first triangle of heart center, spleen minor center and bone marrow point (in the thigh bone) stimulates the production of white blood cells, building up specific chemical antidotes to infection called antibodies.

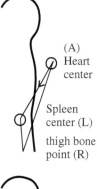

(A)
Heart
center

Spleen
center (L)

thigh bone
point (R)

A second triangle, from heart center, to thymus point and spleen minor, activates the immune system. From the esoteric standpoint, there is no greater protection against any kind of infection in any part of the body (physical, emotional and mental) than the power of love. This is not the emotional side of love, but rather the unconditional, selfless aspect. It is the "disarming love," for it completely negates all the past, putting it right so that there are no regrets, no resentments, no dislikes, no residual mistrust. All the anomalies of life are understood, really understood, as being part of the Universal Plan. It is the love "unto death," not of the personal kind, but of a kind that gives with no thought of return; the love

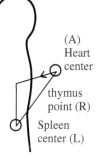

(A)
Heart
center

thymus
point (R)

Spleen
center (L)

that sees the oneness of all things and is able to say, "so be it." It is a love which accepts, identifies with, an altruistic activist and creative server, and is at the same time self-aware. With true love we become totally immune to all disease; we are totally given up to the present moment. It is this ideal state which we in the West refer to as "Christ consciousness," and in the East is called "Buddhahood." Of course, this is the ultimate state of love for a human, and in healing we must seek this ultimate. Love is the true protection; with love we have true immunity.

For the more advanced disciple, you can use a different version of the Immune Triangle, one formed by the linking of the heart center (connected with the thymus gland and with the T-cells, governing the lymphatics and the lymphocytes), to the spleen minor center (which plays a significant role in the immune system) to that representative of the whole system of protection on all levels, called the heart-in-the-head center—the central lotus within the head (crown) center, the

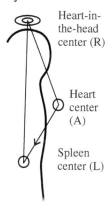

Heart-in-
the-head
center (R)

Heart
center
(A)

Spleen
center (L)

point where true Being and Love are made conscious. Around this circuit the healer sends spiritual love as understood by the soul, the true self of the patient. Visualize the whole system of immunity, that is, of mental health and balance, emotional control, and physical vitality, flowing through this third triangle to the heart-in-the-head center.

35. LYMPHATIC TRIANGLE

At the physical level the Lymphatic Triangle helps clear and vitalize a congested and overworked system, the lymphs. Notice that the lymphatics have an unexpected drainage system. The right lymphatic duct, just under the right clavicle (collar bone), drains all the lymph from the right brain, the right breast and the right arm. The thoracic duct on the left, however, just under the left clavicle, drains the whole of the remainder of the body. All the lymphatic fluid from these two ducts drains into the innominate veins. The lymphatics are important to

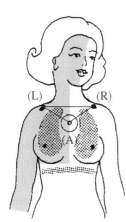

the circulatory system inasmuch as they drain all the wastes from the cells and destroy any cells that are threatening the integrity of the body. This triangle is energized by holding the heart center simultaneously with the minute etheric points on the two lymphatic drainage ducts. Visualize the whole system as being cleared and vitalized. This triangle has an obvious connection to the Immune Triangle, so in a group healing they should be done by the same person, who would see them as acting together.

It is of interest to note how DK links as one the endocrine and the lymphatic systems in the way they are conditioned by the etheric body, indicating that the lymphatic system is extremely important. This suggests the twofoldness of the etheric body, the endocrine system being the active, positive, masculine expression, while the lymphatic system is the passive, receptive, feminine aspect. He says: "The human body is an aggregate of energy units [and] in the vital body (thus conditioning the endocrine and lymphatic systems) are certain focal points through which energy pours into the physical body, producing an impression and a stimulation upon the atoms of the body and thus having a powerful effect upon the entire nervous system which it underlies in all parts" (Bailey, 1951–70, v. 2, p. 533).

36. ALLERGY TRIANGLE

Allergies are due to immunodeficiencies, so the Immune Triangles (see #34) are called for. A further triangle can be used as an adjunct: the vagus nerve center with the two minute points on the etheric adrenal glands.

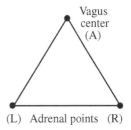

(L)　Adrenal points　(R)

37. BLOOD PRESSURE TRIANGLES

The first triangle has two uses: to balance and normalize blood pressure whether it is high or low; and to correct the causes of the rise or fall. So the healer, as in all these triangles, is required to seek within the subtle levels of the patient's being for the real trouble, and so allow the soul energy to flow. Remember, the basic law governing all illness and disease is an "inhibited soul life." For health the soul's life needs to perfectly express itself through the threefold personality of physical body, emotions and the thinking mind. Since high blood pressure is so often caused by stress in life, the healer seeks to balance the emotional effects coursing through the circulatory system. This general tonic triangle consists of heart center, ajna center (upper ajna, relating to the circulation), and spleen minor center. It bears repeating that none of these triangles is to be used simply symptomatically, i.e., by themselves, but in the course of healing they may be used as an adjunct to the other healing work. And the healer should remain "tuned in" to the soul and to the Higher Triangle (which is the source of all energy, life, love and power—the group of healers on the soul plane—and the patient's soul), for no work of a lasting nature can be accomplished without this link.

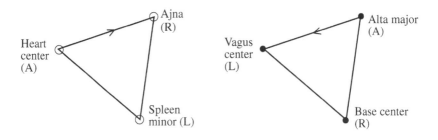

There is another triangle the healer can use for controlling high blood pressure: alta major center, vagus nerve center, and base center in its relation to the kidneys (as a single vital organ). This triangle has a more specific application for blood pressure problems, and should be linked with the first triangle for blood pressure described above. The blood stream is the instrument of the life force (Bailey, 1951–70, v. 4, p. 79). Where this life force becomes overstimulated due to pressures and demands the person can't handle, the heart cannot contract and relax properly, resulting in hypertension, the medical term for high blood pressure. If high blood pressure is an inherited condition, work on this triangle within the causal body.

38. KUNDALINI TRIANGLE

Listen to what Djwhal Khul has to say about the real kundalini occultly understood in his book, *A Treatise on Cosmic Fire,* p. 139: "Only when the fire has circled unimpeded up another channel is the complete merging with the fire of manas effected, and only when it progresses geometrically up all the three—with simultaneous action and at uniform vibration—is the true kundalini fire fully aroused, and therefore able to perform its work of cleansing through the burning of the confining web and of the separating particles. When this is accomplished the threefold channel becomes one channel. Hence the danger." "Kundalini Triangle" is an unfortunate name because of the connotations of "raising the kundalini" and so on, but it is an accurate one just the same, for it is just at this time in a person's life that the primary energy which underlies existence begins to stir. The triangle intends to balance and hold the rising energy on course and so preserve the person from any mishaps in these early and tender days of spiritual growth. It should be observed in connection with this triangle that there is another triangle using the same three energy centers but which is called by another name, viz. the Triangle of Being (#52) where we will become what we truly are (Bailey, 1951–70, v. 4, p. 47). This triangle revolves around the head center (not the vagus nerve center), enabling the healer to focus the patient on what the patient is now and will become in the future (p. 47).

This triangle originates from the vagus nerve center, even though that is not one of its three points. The vagus nerve center, found between the shoulder blades—a little above the heart center and the thymus

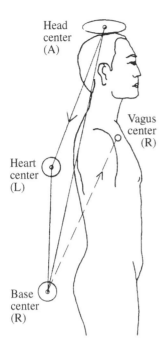

Head center (A)

Vagus center (R)

Heart center (L)

Base center (R)

gland—begins to vibrate and radiate as soon as the person starts to show an active and practical interest in working for the spiritual plan. Another name for this triangle could well be the Triangle of Aspiration, because all aspirants, i.e., those aspiring after the word of the spirit, set this circuit in motion. Here the directing force of the person's soul streams through the head center and brain to the vagus nerve center, affecting the rest of the body and personality. The bodies of the personality—physical, emotional and mental—begin the process of getting more closely focused, or fused, by the soul. The experience often takes the person by surprise, and can lead to relationship difficulties both with themselves and with those closely connected with them. Changes will result. The vagus nerve center affects the heart, with all that that implies. A second major center with which the vagus has powerful links is the base center, for when the soul begins its upward journey, a journey of purification and focused vision, the will is always involved. The will of the soul and the will of the personality are brought into increasing contact. Sometimes there is a clash, sometimes a cause for joy. The will of the soul works through the head center, and the will of the personality manifests through the base center. Thus, when the head center, the heart center and the base center have come into a preliminary alignment, the vagus nerve center begins to radiate and become dynamic.

The vagus nerve center, thus stimulated, causes the astral body and the nervous system to respond to the incoming energies—the so-called "call of the soul" to initiate the preliminary activities of spiritual growth. The doors that were closed to the person focused in the personality now swing open: entry is permitted. This triangle of centers—head, heart and base—with their effect on the vagus nerve center must be balanced during this green period. You might recall (the Kindalini Uprisings Triangle) that the spleen center is involved in the rising of kundalini fire in so far as the pranic fire (from the spleen) and the fire of matter (from the base center) rise together from the base center to meet the fire of mind (Bailey, 1962, p. 139) in the head center. The specific period where "kundalini awakes" refers to that period where the "point at the center" (the initiate's Life Essence) becomes vibrant, potent and active: its forces can then penetrate throughout the entire spinal area until the highest head center is reached. This, however, would not be possible had there not been three earlier "uprisings of the latent force of will." These uprisings serve to clear the passage up the spine, penetrating and destroying the etheric web which separates each center and the area it controls from the next above (Bailey, 1951–70, v. 2, p. 530) (more about the webs, see #25, p. 186). Nurture and correct growth depend on balanced attitudes and wide vision along with a goal-oriented aim. The Kundalini Triangle is an important one to balance when it is clear that such an occurrence has started, or if it is evident that such an experience is on the verge of occurring. The purpose of this triangle is not to "raise" the kundalini, but to balance the circulating energies so that damage (to the webs) or unstable development can be avoided. Obviously, we use this triangle to reintroduce rhythm and stability where these qualities are evidently lacking in the life of the patient seeking our help (Bailey, 1951–70, v. 4, p. 335).

Along with these two triangles, a third can be used (forming the Kundalini Tetrahedron) to support and strengthen the rising kundalini, called the Threads Triangle. For the latter, first hold the base center, bringing it into as great a balance as possible, and while continuing to hold it, activate the triangle of the solar plexus center, the heart center and the head center. For a full explanation of this triangle please see below (#68).

39. SAMADHI TRIANGLES

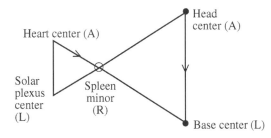

Heart center (A)

Head center (A)

Solar plexus center (L)

Spleen minor (R)

Base center (L)

This pair of triangles, fused as one, is usually done for the person who is dying, but it can also have a useful application for advanced disciples on the Path. The heart center has a close rapport with the spleen center and with the solar plexus. But once this primary triangle has been formed (heart center—spleen minor center—solar plexus center) you are asked to merge this with a secondary triangle (head center—base center—spleen minor center). Link the head center to the logoic plane, the base center to the physical/etheric plane and the solar plexus center to the center of the causal body. The result is communication, distribution, control and withdrawal, bringing about higher consciousness (samadhi) or death (Bailey, 1951–70, v. 2, p. 66).

The respiratory system

40. DIAPHRAGM TRIANGLE

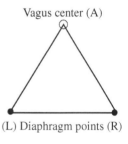

Vagus center (A)

(L) Diaphragm points (R)

This circuit employs the vagus nerve center and two centers on either side of the body, near the diaphragm. We use this triangle for the person who is seeking the truth in some form, who exhibits development along some line of spiritual work. For only at this time do the two centers above the diaphragm awaken and begin to vibrate and to circulate energy. Disciples at this stage are prone to heart and nerve difficulties. Frequently, such people, due to their yearning aspirations, become subject to over-stimulation, putting their centers into a state of imbalance, resulting in mental and cardiac problems. The Diaphragm Triangle can also be used to help restore the proper rhythm of breathing for such problems as asthma, bronchitis, and pleurisy (cf. Bailey, 1951–70, v. 4, p.137). Consider using this triangle with those employing the alta major center (breathing is controlled here) and with the Respiratory Triangle, the Purpose Triangle, and certain other triangles described below.

41. SERVICE TRIANGLES

This is a combination of three triangles which "open out" the throat center. They facilitate service and creativity in life (Bailey, 1951–70, v. 4, p. 151). Where a patient reports being blocked in the area of creativity and turns their focus inward, and where you hear faltering speech, and notice shoulders stiff and set, this patient could well be heading for arthritic attacks. The throat is governed by the planet Saturn, deliverer of lessons and challenges. Those who know of the

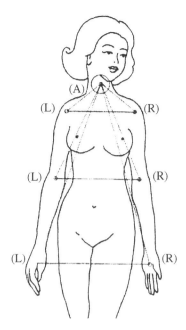

adverse use of this energy can more easily understand the problems associated with the throat center and the importance of this series of triangles. They use the throat center as the major center and then open out to the minor points connected with the shoulder joints, then out again to the centers at the elbows, and then out yet again to the minor centers in the hands (p. 72). The healer will feel the energy of this set of triangles being gradually let outward to the hands of activity and creativity. For this it is best to move to the front of the sitting patient so that you can draw the energy outward in a flow. Where the energy appears to be particularly resistent and blocked, often the case with those who are already chronic arthritics (those who have had arthritis for a long time and who have swollen painful joints), it would be useful to bring into more specific activity the Protecting Triangle that you established when opening the healing treatment.

Beyond their value in coping with arthritic conditions, the Service Triangles are helpful for people with creative blocks in their lives. On more subtle levels patients may be finding that life is not turning out as they had imagined, but they don't know how to change it, or even what to do. All their ideas and aspirations are gone, or seem to be locked in by other forces, obligations and responsibilities. There seems to be no way out. Menopause, both for men and women, has this quality, although the sort of feeling being described may come well before or after menopause itself. You can see how this series of triangles is related to the sacral center and to the Feet Triangle. The creative, generative force of the sacral center must be raised to the creative, service-oriented center of the throat. Of course, this has nothing to do with abandoning one's sex life. Expression through sexual activity continues, which is healthy and right. But if the sexual urge has gone or cannot be expressed for some reason, then what is needed is a transmutation of some part of the sacral energy to the throat center for use in a creative way on a different scale. The sacral center is never transmuted to a state of atrophy! In fact, all the lower centers involved in transmutation to their higher correspondences are never abandoned. Their usefulness continues. The only thing that changes is that one's conscious emphasis of that quality and expression becomes more sensitive. For instance, instead of being driven by desires and personal loves and hates (solar plexus energy), one gradually becomes aware of the heart center and expresses more selfless, unconditional attitudes.

42. PARATHYROID TRIANGLE

This triangle is not often used in healing physical conditions, since parathormone deficiency is very rare, but it has an important and more spiritual application. The circuit combines the throat center with the minute points on the two pairs of etheric parathyroid glands on either side of the neck. The thyroid gland (the manifested physical part of the throat center) backs up the parathyroid glands by balancing the action of the parathyroids. The action of the Parathyroid Triangle is to regulate the flow and production of parathormone, the parathyroid hormone, which affects bones, kidneys and small intestine insofar as the concentration of calcium in the body is concerned, mainly via the blood. From the esoteric standpoint, this triangle has value for persons who have a nervous tendency and muscular control difficulties, and also a sense of failure or inadequacy on the physical plane of life. Through this triangle a patient's sense of worth can be restored. Whenever there are symptoms of osteoporosis, teeth damage, kidney stones or bone fragility, this triangle may be found deficient, needing balance.

43. RESPIRATORY TRIANGLE

The throat center governs the only two processes which involve taking the external world into ourselves. In the first and more important instance, it is done through the breath, symbolized for us at birth when the first thing a newborn child does is draw in the air of our planet (and cry!). The second internalizing of the outside world and transforming activity looked after by the throat center is the whole ingestion and excretion of food. This second process is greatly dominated by the solar plexus center during life (under the triangles: throat center, solar plexus

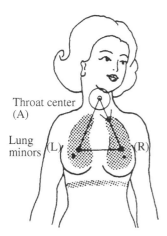

Throat center
(A)

Lung
minors (L) (R)

center, and either the stomach minor or the liver minor). So the Respiratory Triangle has fundamental importance. It is a circuit which is activated from birth, the first cry indicating its rotation around the points. The energy is circulated from the throat center to the two lung minor centers. Respiration problems can afflict people on the first ray of will or power (Bailey, 1951–70, v. 4, p. 132). This should come as no surprise since the will aspect manifests through the organs of respiration (p. 106).

The Master DK recommends that people who have lung or respiratory problems should "ponder the relation and distinction between the breath and the sound" (p. 132). One is related to time and astrology and the other to space and the rays.

We use this triangle when patients complain of lung congestion, for the condition is due to inhibited desire. The symptoms suggest that this circuit is having difficulty performing its instinctual function, breathing is difficult, there may be shortness of breath, or asthma, and a thick persistent cough. From the esoteric angle this triangle works as a pure transformer. The lungs are organs that draw in the vital etheric "fluid" embodying air. In fact, the lungs originally were built by the life substance or lives living in the air of our world. So these organs function by using the substance out of which they are made. It may be of interest that there are five lobes to the lungs (two on the left and three on the right), which may hint at the ancient wisdom's reference to the five pranas.[6]

The lungs are also connected to the blood and to the heart. To cover the exchange of air between the lungs and the blood capillaries, the two major centers—throat and heart centers—are also brought in, with the lung minor center held on both sides to make two triangles on either side of the chest. These triangles, also called the Lungs Triangles, are used to assist the air's vital force to enter the body and energize (oxygenate) the blood. While the healer holds these two circuits, become aware of the energy of love and purpose circulating through the patient's life stream.

For the person who treads the spiritual path, the respiratory activity as a whole, including the process of inhalation and exhalation, is governed by the heart center, rather than the throat center (as is the case with those who have not entered that path) (Bailey, 1951–70, v. 4, p. 130). The organs of respiration, however, are still under the throat center's control. Thus for particular people having respiratory problems, these two centers must be

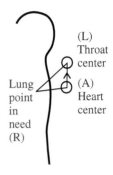

held, one for the process and one for the physical organs, along with the point in the respiratory system which is causing the trouble.

The only factor which makes the breath effective is the thought, the intent, and the purpose which lie behind it. The healer, when using the breath, knows how energy follows thought. Only when there is an alliance between breathing and thinking are results possible. But the healer also remembers that the healing should be according to the will of the patient's soul. For only the directed will, using the organized rhythmic breath of the patient as its agent, can control the centers and produce an ordered purpose in life (*see* Bailey, 1973, p. 256).

44. Triangle of Purpose

For this advanced circuit, the healer can use the breath by first linking in with the Triangle of Purpose, connecting the brain (as the receptor of thought), the mind (the agent of the will), and the

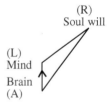

will aspect of the soul itself (Sacrifice Petals of the Causal Body). This abstract triangle gathers the patient's soul purpose, which the healer can conceive of as a clear thoughtform even though it may be totally unconscious. Remember, it is the healer's soul that is doing the work. With this circuit activated, the patient's life can be conditioned upon the vital levels, which in turn will eventually condition the physical plane life. We can now see how two important triangles can be linked and activated, the Respiratory Triangle and the Triangle of Purpose.

45. Sinus Triangle

The sinuses are governed by the throat center. From the angle of esoteric anatomy, we know that the senses built the sense organs. From

primordial times the sensitivity to light, for example, enabled the organ of the eye to be built
by the etheric workers called "lunar lords" and
"elementals" of our body. In the same way, the
sinuses are the result of two activities from past
times: firstly, the activity of sound reverberating from the organ of speech, and secondly, the

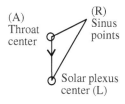

(A) Throat center
(R) Sinus points
Solar plexus center (L)

movement of air from outside into our lungs, which required warming
up. Both of these primary functions caused the hollowing out of the
sinuses. It is evident that this work came after the formation of the sound-
making organ and of breathing, which may be the reason why these
functions are not as efficient as other, more ancient organs. To help clear
the sinuses, use the following triangle: throat center, solar plexus center,
sinus points. The solar plexus is recommended because, more often than
not, the person's habits need correcting (good wholesome diet, regular
exercise, more intake of fluids). The fact that the person cannot smell or
taste does not primarily involve the sense triangles governing smell and
taste. More likely it is the astral or emotional force working through the
throat as it plays upon the secondary center under it, the solar plexus.
So on a higher level the Sinus Triangle can be used for regulating our
habits and for strengthening our belief in ourselves; the circuit empowers
speech and frees our flow in life.

46. SOUND TRIANGLE

This consists of the throat center, the ear minors and the vocal apparatus minute. It is used for all conditions of the voice and involves the
different levels. It is used for speakers, singers, and speech maladjust-
ment syndromes—a useful triangle to help to control speech (in this
connection it could be profitably used with the Fear Triangle and the
Triangle for Imperil). For the hearing triangle, see p. 219.

The nervous system

The student is asked to be especially focussed when working
esoterically on the nerves, for the nervous system is nothing short of
the manifestation of consciousness itself. Recall that the nerves are an
expression of the etheric body as it concentrates its energy in the seven

transforming centers or chakras, which then project its etheric force (embodied energy) into vital and unseen vessels or channels called nadis. Just as the etheric body is a mechanism of energy supply, the vital aspect of the whole outer form, and as the meridians of Chinese medicine are the vital aspect of the blood stream, so the nadis are the vital "jacket" of the entire nervous system. It is as though the nadis are the life or spirit of the nerves, the soul through which we gain consciousness and self-awareness. The more we meditate, study and serve other humans, the more our centers develop, resulting in a corresponding upgrade of development of our nadis, and vice versa. This is telling, for the less the nadis are in evidence or the more they are left in their slumbering state, the more likely the nerves (and consequently the endocrine glands) can become overactive, exhausted or express themselves in undesirable ways. Of course, this is primarily due to the state of the centers of the individual. Hence, disease is an obvious outcome of an unbalanced, un-controlled energy system. When healing, healers are called on to focus their attention upon the reality and upon the factors of primary spiritual importance (beauty, truth, goodness). Then the unfolding of the energies in the head, the spinal energies and the centers, plus the awakening of the basic center and its consequent fusion with the higher energies, will be an automatic and perfectly safe happening, says DK.

The nadis are channels for prana (vyana) reaching the nervous system, so the closer these channels can be brought towards the nerves and plexi, the greater chance there will be for healing and for throwing off the disease, the memories of the past and of the inherited thoughtforms, all of which can affect our senses and our sensitivity. The senses are a direct line of energy input from the nadis; therefore the more we act upon our centers through MSS (meditation, study and service), the more delicate will be our outer response apparatus. The impact of sound, contact (or trauma), sights, tastes and smells will be deep, to say the least. Nadis can be controlled as well as built by the mind; the brain is the outer symbol of the nadic network. DK informs us that the first two nadis to be loosened from the physical body before death are the eye nadis. Diseases and difficulties of the nervous system primarily affect second and sixth ray disciples (Bailey, 1951–70, v. 4, p. 130).

Problems or "dis-eases" of the nerves include the following: Parkinson's, epilepsy, neuritis, neuralgia, sciatica, multiple sclerosis, meningitis, encephalitis, brain tumors, tics, hiccups, headaches of all kinds, stroke, muscular dystrophy, and ME (chronic fatigue syndrome). DK lists the diseases of the mind as: diseases of the brain, disorders of the solar plexus, astral domination, premature clairvoyance and clair-audience, obsession, absence of mind, soullessness (p. 342). He then lists the diseases of the mystics: brain disease, mental imbalance, heart disease, neurotic tendencies (p. 342). Other problems are devitaliza-tion, delusion, delirium, and detachment (Bailey, 1951–70, v. 2, pp. 598–606).

So we can enter this field of triangles connected to the nerves and na-dis with a sense of anticipation—that, as we link these esoteric triangles, we are helping the fusion of two systems and thereby empowering the spiritual soul. Here we come face to face with the energy of conscious-ness in the patient.

47. TRIANGLE FOR THE NERVES

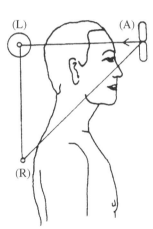

The ajna center, the alta major center and the vagus nerve center are the three points of this important triangle that co-ordinates the nervous system, linking it closely with the Head Triangle. Through the Triangle for the Nerves, the messages and impressions coming from the soul to the head centers and to the Head Trian-gle can be transmitted to the personality, viewed as a thinking brain and an acting body. The Nerves Triangle will be used for all diseases or problems concerned with the nerves. When holding the ajna, you will find it useful to link in with the lower portion of this threefold center. To reiterate, the upper ajna is con-nected with the blood and circulation, the middle portion or stem of the ajna connects with the major centers up the spine, and the lower ajna, as mentioned, is a vitalizing aspect of the nervous system. The ajna is linked with the hypothalamus (sympathetic and parasympathetic ner-vous system; their integration indicates personality control). Epilepsy is said to be a result of an overstimulated ajna center (Bailey, 1951–70, v. 4, p. 176). The alta major is specifically connected with the sympathetic nervous system, linked with memories "driving forward from the past." The vagus nerve center is specifically linked to the parasympathetic nervous system, leading to the first initiation. As you work with this triangle, visualize the whole nervous system vibrating with abundant energy and functioning perfectly. Should there be any part of the nervous system that has been damaged or is malfunctioning, hold the triangle like a tetrahedron (having a triangular base), focussing its apex

directly above the area in need. To do this, hold your hands in a triangle (index fingers and thumbs touching), palms facing down above the area, visualizing the downpouring energy from the soul, and, according to the soul's will, to the nerves of the area. To increase the potency, the healer often opens and closes the eyes rapidly but consciously, directing the energy as the eyes focus through the hand triangle to the area. Energy actually passes through the eyes and contacts the pineal gland, according to Soviet scientists (*see* Hopking, 1990). Such a practice can be incorporated in most of the triangles mentioned above. But due to its potency and because it involves the will, this amplification technique should only be utilized when the healer is definitely immersed in the love aspect of the soul.

48. CRANIO-SACRAL TRIANGLE

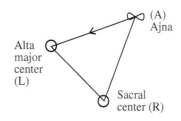

Another triangle connected to nerves and to thought involves the ajna, the alta major center and the sacral center. Here the cranio-sacral energies link, controlled by the ajna. Interestingly, the cerebrospinal fluid has a base rhythm of 16-18 pulsations per minute, just like the breath. The Cranio-Sacral Triangle can be used to re-establish right rhythm overall, achieve relaxation, release distorted or unwanted thoughtforms (often through visions, dreams, or vivid visualizations), and heal relationship problems.

49. MIGRAINE TRIANGLE

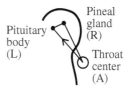

Migraines come in many forms, sometimes expressing as acute debilitating headaches. Sometimes they are creeping, numbing, disorienting. In every case they are disengaging, i.e., seriously affecting the etheric body. Those who are subject to migraines can be said to have too powerful an etheric body, which overstimulates the etheric centers. Frequently it is a result of fifth ray force (note that ray five rules initiates in the throat center, cf. p. 76) emerging in the person's ray make-up, causing a poor or absent relationship between the energy around the pineal gland and that around the pituitary body (Bailey, 1951–70, v. 4, pp. 87, 302). There is therefore a strong need for this triangle, formed by the throat center (the mental center under the fifth ray), the pituitary and the pineal glands. Link the circuit with the Immortality Triangle as it is built up using the Spleen Triangle of Force. Reestablishing the connection between the pituitary and the pineal glands should cure the problem (according to the will of the soul).

50. CREATIVE FUSION TRIANGLE

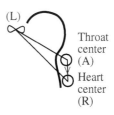

The ajna is an organ of idealism; since it is also closely related to the sixth ray, has a peculiar link to the third ray and to the third aspect of divinity as well as to the second ray and the second aspect, its function is one of fusion, anchoring and expressing. Exactly how the integrated personality should be! So the triangle involves the throat center (the ajna fuses these creative throat energies), the heart center (the ajna fuses the sublimated energies of desire with true love of the heart), and the ajna center itself. Since most patients are at the stage of seeking personality integration, this can be a good triangle with which to conclude a healing session.

51. THE HEAD TRIANGLE

The Tibetan Master tells us that the head center as a whole consists of 1068 petals (96 in the ajna, 12 in the heart of the crown and 960 subsidiary petals of the highest head center), forming 356 triplicities (Bailey, 1962, p. 168). This makes the head center more complex than an electronic

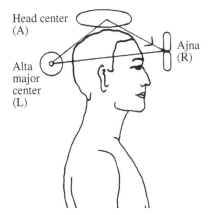

Head center (A)

Ajna (R)

Alta major center (L)

computer board! We are not told how many petals are in the alta major center, probably because it is so intimately related to the throat center and its development. When working with the major centers of the head, we notice they make one of the most subtle triangles in the system of esoteric healing. And, since most people rarely live in the head, preferring to think via the solar plexus center, we mostly do this circuit in a dimension far from the physical and vital bodies, in the hope that we will at least be impressing patients with healing energies they'll reap perhaps in the distant future. This triangle, signifying the connection between the three aspects of man—body, soul and spirit—as well as their unity, consists of the head center, the ajna center and the alta major center (Bailey, 1951–70, v. 4, pp. 578, 581; see photo #7 on p. 331). It is a triangle of force, a triangle of light, of living fire. When this triangle is rotating, the disciple is then soul-controlled and governed by the Law of Magnetic Impulse (Bailey, 1951–70, v. 2, p. 117). This Law governs relationships between souls in the soul world. It is also the law which relates the soul of a group to the soul of other groups. The symbol of this law is two balls of fire and a triangle (pp. 109–117).

Stand facing the right side of the patient. Hold your ajna on the head center of the patient, place your right hand in front of the forehead to hold the ajna, and use your left hand to hold the alta major center at the back of the head. See how this feels. If, however, it feels uncomfortable, try other ways of holding this circuit. The head center is a symbol of the spirit, ajna of soul, and the alta major of the body. By holding and balancing these points, the person's life might well precipitate before our eyes, first as a spiritual life image, then as a personality, and lastly as an integrated expression of the spirit on physical levels. Round these centers much light can be poured. Furthermore, we can create this triangle as a higher expression of the centers of head, heart and throat. The head symbolizes the consciousness and the awareness of will and of thought before they are expressed. The heart center (here related to the ajna) is the prototype of love and brotherliness, of selflessness and a real sense of the livingness in humankind and in all things. And the throat center (the alta major point of the Head Triangle), which fuses with the alta major center in the latter stages of spiritual advancement, symbolizes the strength of creative thought and activity in bringing about greater unity, sharing, cooperation and beauty in the world.

52. TRIANGLE OF BEING (see photo #8 on p. 332)

At this stage of human evolution, little can be said of this triangle, which is associated with the Head Triangle. It is a circuit important to do even if the person being healed doesn't feel able to respond to its far-distant vibration. In fact very few people will have this triangle even remotely vibrating. But its energies lie in the future for all of us, a triangle which will express us as we are essentially. It expresses that we will become that which we really are (Bailey, 1951–70, v. 4, p. 47). For this reason we light it up from a soul level so that the lower energies can be allowed to begin to respond to the soul intention. It is a triangle of tri-

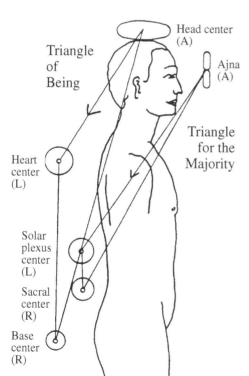

Triangle
of
Being

Head center
(A)

Ajna
(A)

Triangle
for the
Majority

Heart
center
(L)

Solar
plexus
center
(L)

Sacral
center
(R)

Base
center
(R)

adal radiation, like a spiritual satellite focussed on the primary "dish" of the body. It consists of the head center, the heart center, and the base center. As you work with this triangle, you will be able to see how these three energy points are fundamental to our life on earth and that they have a unique connection and relationship for a life of complete fulfillment and control and service to the planet and man.

Notice that this triangle has exactly the same trio of centers as the Kundalini Triangle (p. 201) while having different effects. To be sure, from one level their effects could be seen as complementary, even identical in essence. The Triangle of Being, however, is not associated with the vagus nerve center as is the Kundalini Triangle. The former circuit stands alone, by itself and isolated; it leans on no one and nothing; it is ready for a greater phase while not wanting it or resisting it. It is truly a triangle of becoming (which has not yet arrived).

This triangle can be allowed to superimpose itself on that very active triangle which governs the majority of people today, called the Triangle for the Majority: ajna center, solar plexus center and sacral center (see #63; Bailey, 1951–70, v. 4, p. 38). In this way the patient will aspire towards soul control, and if the patient is ready or at the relevant stage, the Kundalini Triangle may also be activated at the same time.

Another circuit, which has become popularly connected to the Triangle of Being, is called the Triangle of Becoming. This is also done towards the end of the healing work and helps the energies of the patient to focus forward to what the person eventually will become. The triangle consists of base center, head center, and ajna. This powerful axis of energies between base and head centers is focussed in the ajna for right direction and eventual fulfillment.

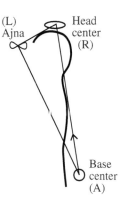

53. TRIANGLE OF THE WHITE MAGICIAN

The Brother of Light always works through the inherent force of the second aspect, Love. Only after the third initiation does she work increasingly with the spiritual will energy, the first aspect. "He impresses the lower substances, and manipulates the lesser, building lives with the vibration of love and the attractive coherency of the Son, and through wisdom the forms are built." In this way she learns to work from the heart and therefore to manipulate that energy which streams from the "Heart of the Sun," until, when she becomes a Buddha, she can dispense somewhat the force emanating from the "Spiritual Sun." Therefore, the heart center in the brother of the right-hand path is the transmitting agency for the building force, and the triangle she uses in this work is: the center in the head which corresponds to the heart, the heart center between the shoulder blades, and the throat center (Bailey, 1962, p. 986). The white magician works always in cooperation with others, and is under the direction of certain group leaders. The basic conditions for entry upon the path of white magic are: pure motive (comprehension of the nature of man, devotion to the cause of humanity), clean body (abstinence, right continence, clean living, vegetarian diet, self-control) and high aspiration (altruism, love of mankind, negation of lower desire). DK says that whoever seeks to work consciously with the forces of manifestation, and who would endeavor to control the energies of all that is seen, "needs the strong protection of purity" (p. 993).

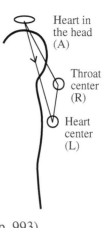

Heart in the head (A)

Throat center (R)

Heart center (L)

We are informed as to the triangle with which the brothers of the left-hand path work (those individuals, ignorantly blinded by personal power, who are working against the evolutionary purpose and the children of the Light): the center in the head corresponding to the throat center, the throat center, the base center (p. 986), called the Triangle of Matter. Such persons manipulate the forces of matter only (the third aspect). They achieve their ends through the method of pranic stimulation or of pranic devitalization. Their methods are specifically and spectacularly physical. The Dark Forces are intensely individualistic, often using inferior cooperators, who work blindly and unconsciously. About this, the healer on the side of evolution, the Path of Return, ought to be aware. To keep this triangle of matter in proper balance, the advancing healing practitioner may link it with the Triangle of the White Magician and then to the Triangle of Being (#52), or the Triangle of Purpose (#44). This will focus the right purpose to our triangles of matter.

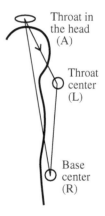

Throat in the head (A)

Throat center (L)

Base center (R)

54. SYNCHRONIZING TRIANGLE

This triangle has been indicated in various places before (viz., in the section on balancing the centers (p. 121) and in relation to the Stomach Triangle and Service Triangles) without much detail. To do it, the healer must focus the consciousness in the head center, then re-tune the attention on his or her own "eye of direction" (the ajna center) before turning it onto the center in themself corresponding to the needed center of the patient. In this way the healer's center evokes response from the center in the patient. The healer now endeavors to balance the inflow of energy coming from the patient, and which is immediately transmuted in the head center. This has great benefit to the patient who has a center which manifests continuous imbalance despite other efforts to correct it. It is a technique that needs a certain amount of concentration and practice, preferably on oneself, before using it on a patient. It will release congestions and blocks in the patient's center, sometimes bringing about almost immediate relief. The diagram of this triangle is on page 124.

55. GENERAL HEALING TRIANGLES

Another method available to esoteric healing practitioners is the use of the General Healing Triangles. Just as the Radiatory Triangle and method is a specific form of healing for more advanced or more spiritually developed patients, so the General Healing Triangles are more specifically used for the drawing down of a much hindered ("inhibited") soul life into the etheric body. We can do this in the following way:

(a) Establish a triangle of light between your soul, the patient's soul and your own etheric body.

(b) Next link your head center with the patient's head center and heart center. When this triangle is functioning smoothly and a measure of response is coming from the head center of the patient, then by an act of the will and the use of an invocative mantram (OM, or by intuition),

(c) Seek to implement this increased flow of life, from the head center via the heart to the diseased area, using the center which controls that area of the physical body, whichever this may be. Do this with great gentleness and care (Bailey, 1951–70, v. 4, pp. 541–43).

And let us recall what the Tibetan says in connection with this, "The magnetic aura around the head is that which is truly sensitive to the highest impressions [telepathy] and is the point of entry to the head center" (Bailey, 1950b, p. 117).

The senses

We now turn to the triangles for the senses, remembering that the senses are the gateways to higher consciousness, since they operate on multiple levels in the energy field. We are a sense body, and everything we do is but a mode or an adaptation of our senses on one or other level. These triangles are more to do with raising consciousness than curing disease.

Here are five triangles related to the senses described in the order of their evolutionary development.

56. HEARING TRIANGLE

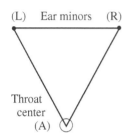

(L)   Ear minors   (R)

Throat
center
(A)

Obedience for the disciple is not enforced, it is contingent upon hearing. The process of learning by hearing is always slow and is one of the qualities or aspects of the stage of orientation (Bailey, 1951–70, v. 4, p. 681). We must learn to respond to the inner Sound through the sense of hearing and its higher correspondences (p. 689). The Hearing Triangle, related to the fourth ray technique of healing (p. 709), involves the throat center, and the two ear minor centers. (In some texts you may find it referred to as the Ears Triangle.) If one ear is in particular need, then hold the throat center, the ear minor involved, and the tympanic membrane or auditory nerve in etheric matter. Using the Hearing Triangle we can expand the capacity of hearing to an ever widening field of sensitivity.

The mind is called our sixth sense, bringing all our senses together and controlling them; it is our common sense. Making our senses more and more acute widens our perceptions and deepens our insights and our awareness. There is only a certain limit perceptible by the senses, whether it is of color, sound, taste or other. Then the range of perception stops, or appears to stop. However, higher than sight is clairvoyance. A wider range of hearing ability is called clairaudience. Our senses may well be as infinite as the Universe. So holding the Hearing Triangle may involve the hearing or balance faculties of the physical body, but we can also use this triangle to help a person become more aware of the opportunities that may and do present themselves to us on a regular basis. It is also a triangle to bring the patient more in touch with the inner voice, true sound and expression. Through this triangle we can work to clear the false noise surrounding and distracting the patient, whether it be in the emotional plane or in the mental life.

Where the patient has balance problems for instance, motion sickness, vertigo or dizziness, or Meniere's syndrome, the Balance Triangle is used. We hold the ajna center, the ear minor center and the cochlea in the ear (as an etheric organ). Do this triangle on each side of the head. Physical imbalance is a signal that there is a more subtle problem needing help which is affecting the brain and consequently the cochlea. It is for the healing practitioner to discover the deeper cause and facilitate its resolution.

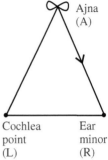

Ajna (A)

Cochlea point (L)   Ear minor (R)

57. TOUCH TRIANGLE

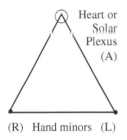

Heart or Solar Plexus (A)

(R) Hand minors (L)

This triangle is under the control of the solar plexus center in the average person and of the heart center in the patient who is endeavoring to live a spiritual life. The other two apexes of this triangle are the two minor centers in the palms of the hands. These represent the skin as a whole. This triangle can be used for gross physical problems such as skin cancer (see also Chapter 8 on cancer) and psoriasis (or more specifically a triangle with Heart Center-Base Center-Sacral Center), through to the more subtle problems of frigidity and inability to respond, including problems of contact and relationship, shyness, embarrassment and guilt-complexes. In fact, this triangle overlords all healing done in whatever form, since Touch on the highest level governs healing as a whole. On the spiritual level, touch is selfless service, divine healing—something beyond most of us at this stage. But we do try to heal from the buddhic or intuitional level of consciousness; this is what is meant by esoteric healing. All those in the medical profession work with the sense of touch and all work (mostly unconsciously or instinctively) with an aspect of psychometry. It is the ability to touch patients and understand what treatment or medication they need, called "according to discretion" in the code of ethics.

So, through the balancing and deepening of this triangle's parameters, patients can understand themselves better as an influential force touching those they meet, and as they impact the environment. Those who are active on behalf of the environment often have this triangle in strong vibrancy.

I know, O Lord of Life and Love, about the need.
Touch my heart anew with love
That I, too, may love and give.

Called the Noontime Recollection, this mantram, used throughout the world, may take on a new meaning and value in this context.

58. THIRD SEED GROUP TRIANGLE

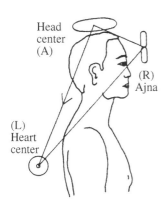

Head center (A)

(R) Ajna

(L) Heart center

Another triangle of particular value to hold if your patient is connected to the health profession, or if you wish to strengthen your connection with the energy overlording all the healing arts and sciences, is the one related to the Third Seed Group of Magnetic Healers. This group of individuals works intelligently as souls with the vital forces of the etheric body. The triangle involves the head center, the heart center and the ajna center (Bailey, 1944, v. 1, p. 41). This triangle is extremely important to work on whenever groups get together, particularly at times of national and international conferences. Consider the implications of these three centers as they are connected within the framework of the greater group of world health. The head center as the recipient of soul information regarding the work of healing and medicine; the heart center as the pivotal point from and to which radiates love between practitioner and patient; and the ajna center which is the precise focalizing attribute of every trained medical professional of whatever discipline. The purpose of this triangle is to facilitate the work of transmutation of substance according to the understanding of the cosmic Plan. The medical department (the third "Seed Group") is at the forefront of this activity.

59. Eyes Triangle or Sight Triangle (see photo #9 on p. 332)

Learning by sight is connected with the Path of Discipleship. These students have heard the Word and are developing the spiritual correspondence of sight. They are susceptible to the vision (Bailey, 1951–70, v. 4, p. 681).

The eyes are governed by the head center, so the healer may hold the head center and the two eye minor centers as a triangle, which will circulate energy and help the eyes in a general way. Moreover, use this triangle to help a patient "see their way through life," clearing away the mists and fogs hampering their vision. Worry and irritation literally prevent true vision. They shut out the view, and in this condition, no matter who the person is, his associates or colleagues are hindered (p. 70). Why is this? "As long as the eye of the person (who is representative of the Creator) is upon that which is created, just so long does it persist, for vitality or energy follows the line of the eye. Just as long as the 'eye' is directed to the created form, the current of force will be transmitted to it, and the more one-pointed the man may be, the more this energy will be centralized and effective. Ineffectiveness of people is due to the fact that their interests are not centralized but very diffuse, and no one thing engrosses their attention ... therefore no thought they think ever assumes a proper form, or is ever duly energized.... It accounts for much of the diseased condition of the human family at this time" (Bailey, 1962, pp. 974, 975). As you can see, this is a triangle to do with the general vision of one's life and purpose. It helps a person to have more clarity about a situation and about which way to turn. The circuit concerns the more subtle aspects of perception and "seeing."

For specific eye problems, there are four other possible triangles to activate, depending on whether or not the patient is on a spiritual path. A person not yet on an inward spiritual journey has two triangles to be lighted. These are: for the right eye—the head center, the right eye minor center, and the optic nerve of that eye (in etheric matter); for the left eye, hold the ajna center, the left eye minor center and the left optic nerve (in etheric matter). The ajna governs vision (Bailey, 1951–70, v. 4, p. 44). The right eye here will be looking through the emotional window and the left eye will be looking through the intellectual window.

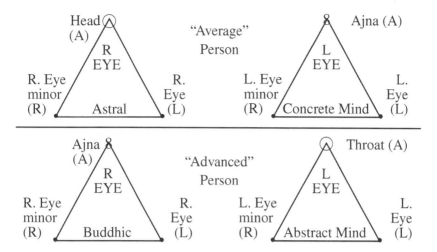

If the patient is aspiring to a spiritual way of life, the right eye triangle should then consist of the ajna center, the right eye minor and the optic nerve minute point. For the left eye, hold the throat center (linked to the alta major center), the left eye minor and the optic nerve minute point. The right eye, in this case, is beginning to see intuitively, rather than emotionally, and the left eye is beginning to see things more from an abstract understanding than from the intellectual.

There may be specific problems related to the eye or eyes either on the physical level or on the more subtle levels of a person's aura. It is up to the healer to test out each level to discover the cause. Seeing is actually performed through the window of the third ether. If there is etheric "dust" in the vital body, usually as a result of a malfunctioning or unbalanced Liver Triangle, then it would be necessary to bring these two triangles—Liver and Eye—into some kind of coordination in order to circulate the energies and clear the "dust." If, however, the problem with sight is more an emotional one, then it would be necessary to link in with the centers on the emotional level so that the glamors or emotional distractions could be cleared from view and clear vision restored. Likewise, if mental illusion is creating thoughtforms inhibiting the patient's vision, the healer needs to tune into this level to activate the triangles. Look at the chart about the senses and try to use it creatively, using your intuition while you work.

Right Eye	Buddhic Wisdom	Vision	Father	Light of the constellation of the Great Bear
Left Eye	Mind, Common Sense	Sight	Son	Light of the constellation Sirius
Shiva Eye	All-Seeing	Directs will and purpose of Deity	Mother	Light of the constellation Pleiades (Bailey, 1951–70, v. 3, p. 429)

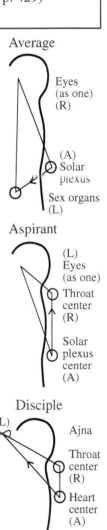

Average

Eyes (as one) (R)

(A) Solar plexus

Sex organs (L)

Aspirant

(L) Eyes (as one)

Throat center (R)

Solar plexus center (A)

Disciple

(L) Ajna

Throat center (R)

Heart center (A)

Patients who are little evolved do not employ the third eye for the stimulating of their thought-forms. Such people stimulate their thoughtforms by using solar plexus energy, which works in two directions, either via the sexual organs, or through the physical eyes. The negative circuit of this triangle causes the individual to see everyone just as sex objects. These three points—sex organs, solar plexus center and the eyes—form a triangle of force which can greatly aid the one seeking your help. As you become proficient, you can link this triangle with those more specifically connected with more evolved vision.

Work is similar with patients of greater evolutionary development. For instance, in the aspirant and in the intellectual, the Eyes Triangle may need to go from the solar plexus center to the throat center to the eye minors. Notice that this is the result of the sublimation of energy from the centers of the little evolved, viz., from the sex organs (sacral center), to the throat center. And in the person already living a life dedicated to spiritual service, the so-called disciple, the triangle of energy will have the heart for its lowest point (instead of the solar plexus), and the third eye will begin to do its work, though imperfectly, while the throat center forms the third point (Bailey, 1962, p. 973).

Let us summarize the three triangles to awaken higher sight:
1. For average people: Solar plexus center, sex organs, eyes.
2. Aspirant: Solar plexus center, throat center, eye minor(s).
3. Disciple: Heart center, ajna center, throat center.

60. DISSIPATING TRIANGLES

In connection with the eyes, there are three other triangles well worth learning and putting into practice. They are called the Dissipating Triangles, for they rid the patient of mental and emotional hindrances, which darken and weaken our powers of discrimination and implicit soul purpose. Note the reference to dissipation in the Radiatory Mantram, viz., "...and dissipate all that hinders service and good health." Remember also that the problem of "transference," about which I spoke in the section on opening the healing triangles (the Protecting Triangle, #4, p. 150), where a healer takes on or even takes over the condition of disease or discomfort, not in fact but symptomatically, of the patient, incapacitating them as a healer, is a glamor and an illusion in the healer (due to wrong identification), and desire (misdirected will) to bring relief (Bailey, 1951–70, v. 4, p. 555). To relieve this situation, these triangles can be of great value.

As a further deepening of your work with these three triangles, consider the following tabulation:

Hindrance	Effect	Ray	Counteractive Energy	Inspiring Being	Beings of Integration
Illusion	Separateness	I	Synthesis	Avatar of Synthesis	Christos- Silent
Glamor	Distortion	II	Love	Spirit of Peace	Watcher
Maya	Materialism	III	Creative Knowledge/ Intelligence	Lord Buddha	

Further connections with the dissipating triangles:
i. Illusion (head center - right eye - ajna) (to clear illusions from the mental body), then connect with sacral center - throat center - Soul to transform the mental body to be an expression of the soul-mind.
ii. Glamor (right eye - left eye - ajna) to clear glamors from the astral body, then connect with solar plexus center - heart center - Buddhic

body to transform astral into the buddhic body so that the astral is an expression of buddhi love and intuition and feeling.

iii. Maya (the tetrahedral whole - by connecting head center - left eye - ajna) to transform the matter/substance of the physical to be an expression of the atmic body so the physical on earth is directed by the will of the soul (spiritual triad).

a. Triangle for Dissipating Illusion

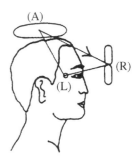

The first, the Triangle for Dissipating Illusion, can dispel the illusions of the mind. Its points are the head center, the ajna center and the right eye minor center. Through this eye the highest activity of the personality can be directed upon the physical plane. It is this complete circuit which protects us from illusion. Should energy get "stuck" anywhere along the circuit, mental illusions occur. Thus we can, when this triangle is flowing, see things as they *are* and not just as they *appear.*[7]

b. Triangle for Dissipating Glamor

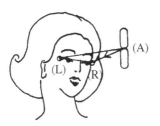

The second triangle, the Triangle for Dissipating Glamor (linked to the last Activating Triangle, p. 153, with all that that implies), can disperse glamor, namely, those emotional desires and aspirations, hopes and fears, persuasions and allurements which have nothing to do with reality, a charming force which weakens the mind (and often empties the purse!). Use the ajna center and the left and right eyes in triangle form to dissipate the glamor of the emotional plane of desire and false attraction. Let this triangle sit like a torch on the forehead, enabling the patient to see through superficiality and glittering innuendoes which have allured (and injured) them. Then, connect this glamor triangle with another that will help the process of dissipation by building higher and stronger threads of spiritual association, viz., awakening the love petals of the soul body and lifting the patient out of the astral body into the body of pure reason on the buddhic or intuitional plane. The latter circuit, engaging the throat center, the solar plexus center and the heart center, is called the *Triangle of the Second Thread*.

Do these triangles of illusion and glamor one after the other, and then allow them to stand in the etheric light of the person, for it is "when these two triangles are under control and are beginning to function properly that the seven centers in the etheric body are brought under clear direction" (Bailey, 1973, p. 252).

c. Triangle for Dissipating Maya

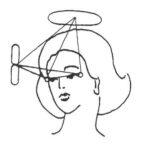

With the formation of the Triangle for Dissipating Maya we establish a tetrahedral form of dynamic transformational power. It must be built and experienced to understand. It is composed of four points and four triangles:

i. The base: head center and the two eye minors (the main triangle that governs the eyes and seeing on all levels).
ii. Illusion: head center, ajna center and right eye minor.
iii. Glamor: ajna center and two eye minors.
iv. Maya: head center, ajna center and left eye minor.

This last triangle involves the physical and etheric vehicles and their embodied energy blocks and debris. These deeply embedded energy wastes are the etheric toxins which severely damage the energy circulation, inveigling the will more intensely into materiality. It takes a serious student to lift their boots out of this trench. Release involves something more than just meditation (which stimulates the love petals of the causal lotus); it also involves the building of the rainbow bridge, called, in esotericism, the antahkarana. Here, the student or patient (and are we not all both, or at least the latter?) must work in mental matter to bridge the energies from the etheric body to the atmic plane (the spiritual dimension of divine will), necessitating a link with another triangle, viz., the throat center (the creative center of building), the heart center and the spleen center, called the *Triangle of the Third Thread*. Only in this way can maya be finally overcome; the result will be the fourth initiation, a crucifixion of the whole of one's personality achievements. This sort of advanced work on the part of the esoteric healer will presuppose the use of ray words of power, according to the soul request of the patient. The healer wishing to pursue this spiritual activity is asked to study the two books by Alice Bailey concerned with the antahkarana, *Education in the New Age* and *The Rays and the Initiations*.

Summary of Treatment

First Thread: throat c + ajna + head c – Illusion – sacral c + throat c + higher mind

Second Thread: throat c + spleen + heart – Glamor – solar plexus – heart c + buddhic body

Third Thread: throat c + heart + spleen – Maya – base c + head c + atmic body

These triangles will take a lot of practice to perfect, but the effort will be repaid a thousandfold. I consider the senses, particularly the eyes, the ears and the skin (touch) as primary areas to address in a healing. But they should only be worked with after a lot of balancing has been done on the other many triangles.

61. TASTE TRIANGLE

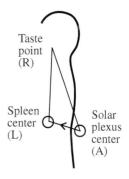

From the esoteric angle the taste and smell triangles are not as developed as the other three and are regarded as coming under the director-ship of the touch sense. And symbolic of this, medical science tells us that taste is only fully developed after we have reached forty years old. Taste is governed by the solar plexus center (assisted by the spleen center). When we say a person has good or bad "taste," we are referring to their judgment and discriminative capabilities. It is in this way that we work with the taste sense. If the patient has physical problems with tasting, however, or has tongue ulcers, or if there is nervous deviation of the tongue due to a stroke or accident, then we can employ the Taste Triangle to try and balance the escaping energy. The triangle consists of holding the solar plexus center along with the spleen center and linking the third point of the triangle with the tongue minute center (where the four cranial nerves, the fifth, seventh, ninth and tenth find expression). (A variation of this circuit: solar plexus center, point at the taste area in the brain, called the parietal opercular-insular area of the cerebral cortex, in the lateral margin of the postcentral gyrus in the sylvian fissure, and the tongue point. Knowing energy follows thought, as you think of this point in the brain, you immediately connect with it.) This triangle helps a patient to be more creative in the imagination and less caught up in impractical imaginings and dreams. And on the mental level, the intellect can be helped to sharpen its wits and be more discriminative in its use of thought and commitment, i.e., to avoid being taken in simply by "taste," but rather by what is truly valuable.

62. SMELL TRIANGLE

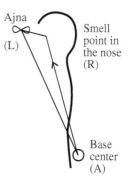

The last and least developed of the senses is the faculty of smell. It is governed by the base center, by an energy point in the nose (the olfactory nerve—the first cranial nerve ending in the nose) and by the ajna center (for the ajna center rules the nose and vision) (Bailey, 1951–70, v. 4, p. 44). (A variation of this triangle: the base center, the point in the brain [the medial and lateral olfactory areas], and the point in the nose [the olfactory nerve].) We often say, "he followed his nose," or "I smell a rat," or "he has a nose for it." All these suggest direction and focus, or some sort of idealism, realization or discernment. Frequently, however, our sense of direction is poor, and our ability to know the difference between the true and the false is equally weak. This triangle helps us to rise to the greater powers of knowledge and to the recognition of truth.

TABULATION RELATING THE SENSES
TO THE SUBTLE BODIES (Bailey, 1962)

Sense	Physical	Emotional (Astral)	Mental (Manasic)	Intuitional (Buddhic)	Spiritual (Atmic)
Hearing	Hearing	Clairaudience	Clear sound	Comprehension	Beatitude
Touch	Touch	Psychometry	Planetary Psychometry	Healing	Active Service
Sight	Sight	Clairvoyance	Pure seeing	Divine Vision	Realization
Taste	Taste	Imagination	Discrimination	Intuition	Perfection
Smell	Smell	Emotional Idealism	Spiritual Discernment	Idealism	All Knowledge

TABULATION RELATING THE SENSES
TO OTHER FACTORS IN HEALING

Sense	Cranial Nerve	Body	Main Center	Lower Aspect	Higher Aspect	Ray
Hearing	8	Physical	Throat	Sound	Divine Response	7
Touch	6, 10	Emotional	Solar Plexus or Heart	Contact	Understanding	1
Sight	2	Mental	Head	Perspective	Vision	3
Taste	5, 7, 9, 10	Buddhic	Solar Plexus	Discernment	Intuition	6
Smell	1	Atmic	Base	Emotional Idealism	Spiritual Discernment	4

TABULATION OF THE EXPERIENCE OF THE SENSES

SENSE	PHYSICAL	ASTRAL	MENTAL	BUDDHIC	ATMIC
HEARING	I hear	I sympathize	I listen (I hear clearly)	I comprehend	I am That
TOUCH	I touch	I feel	I feel touched (I feel exposed)	I balance (heal)	I serve the One
SIGHT	I see	I witness	I know	I see as I am seen	Reality is
TASTE	I taste	I imagine	I discriminate	I discover	I am Perfect
SMELL	I smell	I sense the ideal	I discern the Path	I experience the ideal	I am omniscient

MANTRIC AFFIRMATIONS OF THE SENSES

Through hearing I listen and comprehend that I am That.
Through touch I feel and heal: I serve the One.
Through seeing I know, and see as I am seen—reality is.
Through taste I can discriminate and discover the Perfect.
Through smell I sense the ideal and know I have all knowledge.

A WIDER TABULATION FOR THE SENSES

	Hearing	Touch	Sight	Taste	Smell
Organ	Ear	Skin	Eye	Tongue	Nose
Organ of Action	Mouth	Hands	Legs	Anus	Genitals
Effect	Speech	Grasping	Walking	Excretion	Procreation
Form	Sound	Tactility	Color	Taste	Aroma
Cranials	8	6, 10	2	5, 7, 9, 10	1
Center	Throat	Solar Plexus or Heart	Head	Solar Plexus	Base
Triangle of Healing	Throat-Ear minors	Solar Plexus/ Heart-Hand minors	Head-Eye minors	Solar Plexus- Spleen minor Tongue point	Base-Nose point- Ajna
Ray	7	1	3	6	4 or 7[8]
Quality	Word of Power	Finger/Hand of God	Eye of God	Desire of Nations	Beauty of Revelation
Expression	Magic	Destroyer	Vision	Idealism	Art
Root Race	Lemuria	Atlantis	Aryan	6th Race	7th Race
Plane	Physical	Astral	Mental	Buddhic	Atmic
Plane Span	Atmic- Physical	Buddhic- Physical	Mental- Physical	Astral- Physical	Physical Only
Planet	Mercury	Saturn	Jupiter	Mars	Venus
Color	Black	Yellow	Blue/Green	Red	White
Highest Attainment	Beatitude (Being)	Service	Realization	Perfection	Omni- science
Buddhic Attainment	Compre- hension (Telepathy)	Healing	Divine Vision	Intuition	Idealism
Mental Attainment	Clear Sound	Planetary Psychometry	Pure Seeing	Discrimi- nation	Spiritual Discern- ment
Astral Attainment	Clair- audience	Psychometry	Clairvoy- ance	Imagination	Emotional Idealism
Awareness of	Direction	Quality	Proportion	Value	Innate Quality
Responds to	Voice of Conscience (The WORD)	Control or Vibration	Recognition	Sensitivity	Knowing

(Table continues on the next page)

	Hearing	**Touch**	**Sight**	**Taste**	**Smell**
Psychic Powers	Telepathy/ Inspiration	Understanding/ Spiritual Impression-ability	Mystical Vision/ Spiritual Identifi-cation	Intuition	Spiritual Discern-ment
Planet (the sense now being evolved)	Mars	Venus	Earth	?	?
Logos	3rd Aspect	2nd Aspect	1st Aspect	Closely related to 3rd Aspect	Closely related to 3rd Aspect
Laws	Economy Unity Involution	Attraction Duality Evolution	Synthesis Triplicity -	- - -	- - -
Elements: Average Man	Ether	Air	Fire	Astral Light	Ether[9]
Advanced Man	Akasha	Ether	Air	Fire	Astral Light[10]
Planes: Average Man	Atmic	Buddhic	Mental	Astral	Physical
Advanced Man	Monadic	Atmic	Buddhic	Mental	Astral
Subplanes (physical & astral)	Gaseous	4th Ether	3rd Ether	2nd Ether	1st Ether
Subplane (mental, buddhic, & atmic)	Solid	Liquid	Gaseous	4th Ether	3rd Ether

(*Mind* is the 6th Sense, using the 5th Ray with the Quality "Knowledge of God." *Intuition* is the 7th Sense, using the 2nd Ray, with the Quality "Understanding of God," expressing Love/Wisdom.)[11]

TABULATION RELATING THE CENTERS
TO THE SUBTLE BODIES[12]

Centers	Vital Body ETHERIC BODY	Emotional Body ASTRAL BODY	Mental Body MENTAL BODY	Intuitional Body BUDDHIC BODY
BASE CENTER	Bones & Spine; Will to Stand	Will to Have	Will to Think	Will to Be Oneself
SACRAL CENTER	Generative; Life Force	Desire to Regenerate; Protective	Personal Responsibility	Group Love
SOLAR PLEXUS CENTER	Nervous System; Assimilation/ Excretion	Desire for Pleasure	Thinking of the Self	Desirelessness
HEART CENTER	Circulation; Love	Impersonal & Unconditional Love	Justice	Intuition; Pure Reason
VAGUS NERVE CENTER[13]	Disciple of the Physical Body	Discipline of the Astral Body	Mental Discipline	Awareness of the Possibility of Soul Control
THROAT CENTER	Respiration; Creativity	Desire to Serve; Speaking Well of Others	Adaptation	Pure Ideas
ALTA MAJOR CENTER	Spinal Cord; Acquired and Conscious Control Leading to Memory	Pleasurable Memories	Memories of Thoughts	Memories of the Past as a Whole
AJNA CENTER	Endocrine System; Energy Direction	Directing Desire	Directing Thought	Directing Intuition
HEAD CENTER	Brain; Consciousness	Spiritual Aspiration	Spiritual Search; Study	Group Conscious; Soul Aware

Useful triangles in more advanced esoteric healing

63. TRIANGLE FOR THE MAJORITY

The ajna center, solar plexus center, and sacral center form a triangle which governs the majority of mankind (Bailey, 1951–70, v. 4, p. 47). It is to be used to balance those of the human family who have been selected to regenerate the race, i.e., any couple whose karma permits them to have offspring (see the illustration of this triangle with the Triangle of Being, #52). Therefore, this triangle is essential for use when a couple has come to you for the healing of their infertility problem. It should be included whenever the Fertility Triangles (#27) are used.

64. TRIANGLE FOR AVERAGE HUMANITY

Average humanity is largely emotional. The triangle controlling them is: the soul, the head center, and the solar plexus center (Bailey, 1951–70, v. 4, p. 430). It may be used for all human beings who are ruled by their emotions as a means to help them connect more with their soul impulse.

65. TRIANGLE FOR IMBECILES AND ANIMALS

A triangle for those who are mindless, senile and imbecilic can be used, called the Triangle for Imbeciles and Animals. Some groups of human beings still live a low-grade emotional life. They are not yet, as such, individuals, or rather, individualized. They still belong to the region of the soul, living in the realm of sexual desires, and they have not properly "descended" fully into the body, to take hold of their own centers in the body. Such people are rather like animals, although animals are governed by a different triangle which may also be used by the healer when helping or comforting animals: animal group soul, solar plexus center and spleen minor center (Bailey, 1951–70, v. 4, p. 430). To this latter triangle people return when unable to hold onto their center of consciousness. They have, as it were, lost their minds and have become insane or imbecilic, or completely senile. Unlike animals, however, the group soul to which they are connected is to the soul of the human race as a whole.

The head center, the heart center and the base center is that which will govern when we become what we really are (p. 47). This is the

Triangle of Being, which I have already spoken about. It is a good triangle to do alongside any of the above three triangles (Majority, Average Humanity, and Imbeciles and Animals) as it grounds them in what they really are and will be.

66. TRIANGLE OF SPIRITUAL FACILITATION

Two triangles are connected with the solar plexus center, which facilitate a stimulus to the heart center to enable one to become aware of the purposes and plans of the spiritual personnel working for and directing the spiritual progress of humanity. These two triangles are particularly important for those with this awareness but who are ill with heart problems, circulatory insufficiency, or nervous illnesses.

To set up this circuit of energy, focus your attention on the solar plexus center using your ajna and two hands as you stand behind the patient. Now, keeping your ajna on the solar plexus center, move your two hands to the heart center, and then, holding one hand on that center, move the other to the ajna of the patient (this you will recognize as the Lower Clearing Triangle which is used with so-called "average" people, those who are on the verge of the Spiritual Path). The final thing to do is to hold the heart-center-in-the-head with your ajna (so your ajna is now holding two centers, the solar plexus center and the heart-in-the-head-center of the patient). The heart-in-the-head-center is simply the heart center as found in the head center, for the head center is the unifying center of all the centers (Bailey, 1951–70, v. 4, p. 170). So the triangle consists of the solar plexus center and the heart-in-the-head-center (held as one point by the ajna), the ajna center and the heart center. Note that the flow of this triangle goes from ajna to heart to heart-in-the-head. It is a circuit for more advanced patients. (See an illustration of this triangle with the Lower Clearing Triangle, #13.)

67. TRIANGLE AIDING SELF-CONSCIOUSNESS

This triangle has more of a planetary use, but it can still be applied to an individual. After all, individuals make up humanity! The triangle has connections on a grand scale, a scale beyond most of our mental capabilities. Its cosmic origin means it will help mankind awaken, for its own protection, to its responsibility to the environment. For instance, the plight of humanity as a result of the industrial misuse of chemicals with

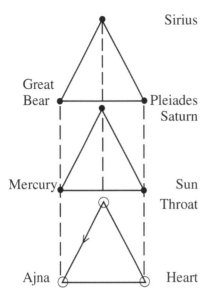

Sirius

Great
Bear ●————————● Pleiades
                    Saturn

Mercury ●————————● Sun

                    Throat

Ajna ———————— Heart

the resultant ozone depletion has led to urgent consultations and conferences on an international scale. These have steered governments to form such organizations as the International Panel of Climate Change and the International Geosphere-Biosphere Programme. The ozone "hole" is nothing but the result of ignorance and irresponsibility. Industrialists claim that they did not know of these effects. Then there are those destructive emissions that come from burning forests; from power stations and exhaust fumes; from fire extinguishers, microchip degreasers and so on. All are taking their toll. To stop all this is essential but virtually impossible. To stop it would not even mean a permanent cure. There are constant dangers to the environment due to the thoughtless actions, selfish desires and short-term gains of man. To cure such mental inertia and emotional greed, we must work on the inner planes of consciousness so that we can attain an awareness of a greater purpose and plan for the world of nature of which we are a dependent part. There is a need for the awakening of self-consciousness, or soul-consciousness (also known as Christ-consciousness). To help in this awakening we may be inspired during the healing session to hold a triangle that has cosmic origins. From the inner nature of certain constellations or stars, an energy flows to the earth and to people as individuals and as members of the human race. This energy is that of self-consciousness.

Using this triangle is advanced esoteric healing, but I think it is appropriate to introduce it in this book. (The healing of the future will be more related to the esoteric aspects of life, which means that advanced healing deals more with the higher causes of conditions.)

The Triangle Aiding Self-Consciousness consists of the throat center, the ajna center and the heart center. These points relate to the planets of Saturn, Mercury and the Sun, which are in turn related to Sirius, the

Great Bear and the Pleiades (Bailey, 1951–70, v. 3). And if the healer can hold these nine sources of energy flow, directing the stream right down to the individual, the power of more spiritual, planetary and unseen healing is performed. This triple triangle can also be done as an act of world service for mankind as a whole.

68. THREADS TRIANGLE

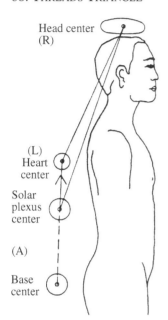

Head center (R)

(L) Heart center

Solar plexus center

(A)

Base center

The Threads Triangle is very useful for patients in spiritual emergency. It is used for those souls who have suddenly tasted the sweet wine of God and immediately want the whole heavenly vat! Their awakened vision is certain, their sincerity unquestionable, their urgency immense, but their methods can be menacing, malicious and self-destructive. They want Truth and will stop at nothing. The result can be an implosion, seriously rupturing their etheric web, with a consequent loss of energy and with telltale symptoms. In extreme cases, they might display erratic behavior—strong spiritual fervor then black depression and inertia, inspired creativity and selflessness followed by listlessness, lack of confidence and self-denial, and so on, always a high spiritual ideal coupled with material torment. This triangle, consisting of holding the base center first and then holding the triangle of the solar plexus center, heart center, and head center, is especially useful as a protection against the premature raising of kundalini (Bailey, 1951–70, v. 4, p. 181–87), which is the endeavor to incorporate energies into the etheric body which have not yet undergone proper or adequate development and transformation. Premature raising of the fire always results in burning; the web is either scorched, left "threadbare" or irreparably damaged. Compare the use of this triangle to the Kundalini Triangle itself. Note how this triangle is more advanced than the Kundalini Triangle.

Once this initial triangle is brought into active radiance and balance, you should connect with the Threads Triangle and the Dissipating

Triangles. This involves the three energies of the kundalini as they flow down (but not as they flow up, for that is under the soul's direction); and the three fundamental anchoring points for the spirit in the body, the threads themselves, via the Threads Triangle.

These three threads triangles are part of the building of the creative thread itself, hence the use of the throat center in each case. The creative thread is triple in form (Bailey, 1954, p. 147). This is what you do when the Threads Triangle is being held (this describes how each center in the Threads Triangle is connected to the threefold channel in the etheric spine. It is not a description of how to connect with the first, second and third creative thread):

   a. While holding the head center, link in with the central energy of sushumna as it connects with the base center, and with the conscious-ness thread which is anchored in the head.
   b. From the heart center, transfer to the ajna center and, as you do so, link in with the nadic energy of ida and with the life thread which is anchored in the heart center.
   c. From the solar plexus center, transfer to the alta major center (at the back of the head) and link in with the energy of pingala and the creative thread which is anchored in the throat center.

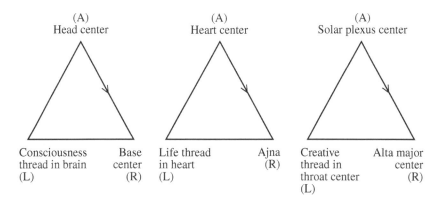

With these various triangles here mentioned, which link with the primary nadis up the spine and also the three major centers in the head, you can also enter three other circuits to which I referred earlier, the Triangle of the First Thread, the Triangle of the Second Thread, and the

Triangle of the Third Thread (see #60). These are the transforming force circuits of the creative thread itself (pingala). They form the first stage of the antahkarana, gathering each of the three major nadis (or threads) themselves. They have their own varying benefits both for the patient and for humanity (note the Eyes Triangle, #59).

The Threads Triangle is also a very important triangle in relation to those who are living an ordered spiritual life so as to control the process of awakening the centers. It gives protection and facilitates correct opening of the centers as the three major energies begin their rise up the etheric spine.

In my seminars on the reappearance of the World Teacher, I have found this triangle to be of particular benefit and potency for the group as it works together to open a channel for the coming of the Christ. I usually get the group to do it near the end of the workshop. This protects and orders the group kundalini in relation to the channel which humanity has to the fifth Kingdom.

E. Closing and sealing the healing triangle

Most healings take about twenty to thirty minutes to do, so it is obvious that you will not be required to do all the triangle circuits listed here. The healer is directed to work with different triangles by his or her active and intuitive intelligence. Some triangles may need to be worked on and balanced at subsequent visits. Keep a clock clearly visible in your treatment room, because in this work, just as in meditation, time seems to stand still. At first you will need to glance at the clock to keep within the time limit. Use this awareness of time to help you maintain your therapeutic awareness and sense of discipline. Guard against all dreaming and drifting in consciousness in esoteric healing. Train yourself to be alert and mentally active and aware of subtle impressions (diagnosis) and appropriate therapeutic response right through the healing treatment. At first this is difficult, for the mind loves an excuse to meander in and out of will-o'-the-wisp thoughts and feelings and perhaps tries to get some exciting psychic phenomena to boast about. Do your best to avoid these experiences and to maintain clear and conscious mental activity.

Balancing the pairs of centers

On completing the last triangle of your healing treatment, move back to the right side of the patient. Put your hands into the energy inflow and outflow of the ajna center, and bring it into a renewed balance in response to your work in and around the patient. Then balance three pairs of centers against each other to bring all the centers into integrated functioning. They lie above and below the diaphragm. In a healing this is the final act. It symbolizes the great fact of the transference of energy, when the lower centers will be in direct communication with their higher counterparts. The solar plexus center (for the average person) and the throat center (for the aspirant and disciple) will act as important transferring centers, one for the lower centers and the other for all the spinal centers into the head. Furthermore, each of the lower three centers will be directly linked by a specific nadi to its higher center. If you are healing in a group, the leader will balance these pairs in the etheric field in the head, while the other healers work on the major centers up the etheric spine.

HEAD–BASE

The first pair we take is the head center and base center. To do this correctly, the energy of the center at the base of the spine (the organ of the personal will) must be raised and carried up the spinal column to the head center, via the ajna center (Bailey, 1951–70, v. 2, p. 523). Put your right hand about six inches (15 cms) above the patient's head, palm downwards, and your left hand a little way out from the base of the spine. According to Law IV of esoteric healing, the good controls us via the head center, and "friction" or disharmony (dis-ease) is due to the inactivity of the base center (Bailey, 1951–70, v. 4, pp. 568–69, 593). These two centers control the will, soul will, and personality will, hence the conflict in many people. Using the creative imagination, visualize the energy flowing right through the base center around the body and, via the ajna center, through your hand at the head center and down again to your hand at the base center. Visualize the flow to be clear and smooth. In esoteric healing we work with white light; should any other color present itself (the white light has sacrificed itself for your information and instruction), do not resist it or become infatuated by it; let it flow until the white light returns by listening to its diagnostic and therapeutic guidance. When these two centers feel harmonious and rhythmical, gently withdraw your hands and take them to the next pair of major centers.

HEART–SOLAR PLEXUS

The heart center and the solar plexus center are the next pair to be balanced. Remember that the solar plexus center is the most active of all the centers, thus we must be careful to properly balance this center with the heart center. Hold your right hand in front of the chest (holding the outflow of heart energy) and the left hand at the back about half way down toward the waist, to hold the inflow of solar plexus energy. The heart expresses love and true beauty, which is distorted by the desires and passions of the solar plexus. As indicated above, visualize the energy circulating through the two centers becoming balanced and in harmony, taking on a beautiful form. The energy of the solar plexus, that is, the organ of self-conscious personal desire, must be raised to the heart and there transmuted into group service (Bailey, 1951–70, v. 2, p. 523). When you are ready, gently withdraw the hands and move them to the last pair of centers.

THROAT–SACRAL

The throat center and the sacral center are last because they are the creative, building expressions in life. Place your right hand in front of the throat (here you are holding its outflow of energy) and your left hand at the sacral center near the lower part of the spine. This pair is important to balance and integrate because these centers are esoterically concerned with one's relationship to Truth. The soul is endeavoring to bring about a creative interplay between these centers via the personality of the individual. This creative interplay is what is necessary, the True, for the person to express in this incarnation. Visualizing the flow as described above, see the flow moving round in a circle through these centers, integrating and refining their relationship.

Balance	Quality	Energy	Body	Ray	Miasm	Manifestation	Resolves	Problem	Method
Head/ Base	The Good[14]	The Will[15]	Mental	1	Tuberculosis	Life & Death	Fear & Maya	Omnipotence	Service
Heart/ Solar Plexus	The Beautiful	Desire,[16] Love and Wisdom	Astral	2	Cancer	Quality & Consciousness	Glamor	Omnipresence	Meditation
Throat/ Sacral	The True	Speech & Active Intelligence	Physical	3	Syphilitic	Appearance & Form Expression	Illusion	Omniscience	Study

Problems of a secondary nature result from the disharmony of the energy between these major centers above and below the diaphragm. This may even affect the ajna center (Bailey, 1951–70, v. 4, p. 593). When the upper centers (above the diaphragm) have an interplay, and when the lower centers impact each other, or when the transmutation process from the lower centers to the upper centers is involved, this is an expression of radiation. When the upper centers impact energy on those below the diaphragm, we see demonstrated the potency of magnetism. This could be an important point for those technically-minded esoteric healing practitioners.

Put simply, so that we can take advantage of the information the Master Djwhal Khul has so painstakingly given us, if the patient is not on the path of conscious spiritual development, then balance these centers from below up, viz., from base center to head center, solar plexus center to heart center and sacral center to throat center. Such a patient will respond more to radiatory healing and be aspiring towards the soul (unconsciously). If, however, there is sufficient evidence that the patient is consciously working for further spiritual advancement, then you may draw the energy down, from the soul contact, via the upper centers to those below, that is, head center to base center, heart center to solar plexus center and throat center to sacral center.

Let us continue with the closing procedure.

Return to the ajna center to balance it again, for the last time. Then visualize the patient in a bubble of light. See this pure, radiant, white light surrounding the patient and, as you do so, take your hands down to your sides, and, visualizing the light around the feet, move your hands upward, sealing and protecting the energies all round the aura and body of the patient (see photo #10 on p. 333). This sealing and protecting activity is not to isolate the patient from outside forces, but rather to strengthen their discriminative faculties and so help the mind from being led astray. Healing with white light can help the person be more responsive and responsible to the forces and energies from both inner and outer levels of being and to opportunities and relationships. The bubble of light will begin to act like a divine filter, rejecting the waste and auric toxins and unnecessary encumbrances, yet accepting helpful, enhancing and elevating influences and contacts.

When your hands reach the top of the head, hold them in a triangle, palms down with thumbs and forefingers touching (see illustration, p. 212). Visualize the light of divine purpose, divine love and divine activity (and at the very heart of the triangle visualize the Life Principle or Thread streaming from the highest levels [from the original Cosmic Universe, cf. p. 272ff] into every center, cell and atom) flowing through the head center. This is a conscious use of the Radiatory Triangle and radiatory method of healing (soul–brain–heart center, and then out to the whole aura of the patient). Then you may silently, or in a soft whispering voice, sound the Radiatory Mantram. Notice how this mantram is linked to the dissipation of the three primary glamors (illusion, glamor and maya).

"May the love of the One Soul, focussed in this group, radiate upon you, my brother, and permeate every part of your body—healing, soothing, strengthening, and dissipating all that hinders service and good health" (Bailey, 1951–70, v. 4, p. 105).

Now sound the Sacred Word, OM, three times silently or together softly with the other healers. The first integrates the mind of the patient, the second integrates their emotions and higher intuition and the third integrates their etheric body and spiritual will.

Now withdraw your hands, palms together, to your heart. By an act of spiritual will via your ajna center, seal the magnetic Healing Triangle (see photo #11 on p. 333). The healing force is literally "turned off" and redirected; it is no longer available (p. 651). Remember this was opened for healing, soon after your attunement with the patient right at the beginning of the treatment. It was a two-sided triangle, from the soul of the healer to the heart center to the brain, but not back to the soul. Within this open triangle we performed the service of esoteric healing. Now, at the completion of the healing, you turn off the energy flow by definitely visualizing the triangle circuit as flowing from the ajna center and the brain directly back to the soul (Soul–Heart Center–Brain (Ajna)–Soul).

If you had opened the Radiatory Healing Triangle at the beginning of the healing, now is the time to close it. You do this in the following way. The healer "shuts off" soul contact and reassumes control of the aura as a medium of your own spiritual expression; it becomes no longer an instrument for healing by radiatory activity, and leaves the patient alone (Bailey, 1951–70, v. 4, p. 658).

By this "sealing" and "shutting" process the healer is specifically empowering each patient by leaving them free and independent and having no dependence on the healer. Both healer and patient can then reassume their independent and unique spiritual path.

Next, give thanks to your fellow healers on soul levels and to the higher powers or beings for their help and for the opportunity to work with the energies of healing and to be of service to the Plan of the Great One.

Then when you feel you are ready, gently bring the patient back to everyday consciousness by lightly touching their shoulders and back of the neck (between the shoulder blades). This has the effect also of grounding their energies back onto the earth (see photo #12 on p. 333).

When the patient is ready, take them to the waiting room to rest quietly for a while. It is very restful to the patient to see fresh flowers and herbs as they quietly think about the treatment and come back to their physical reality. Plants have a profound healing effect on the inner bodies, their colors and fragrance giving hope and strength to the person.

At this point, make a few notes on the major findings during the healing, including the triangle you found important to the healing.

After about five to ten minutes, bring the patient back to the world with a little constructive chat. But remember that speaking about the healing dissipates it, diluting much of your valuable work. It is a good idea to remind the person that speaking about the healing to anyone should be avoided. (One great spiritual teacher recommends the following: "Say nothing to anyone about one's spiritual experiences, yea, be silent about them even to one's self" [Steiner, 1947]).

Let the healing do its inner work of adjustment ... and then send the patient on their way with a smile!

Summary of the healing procedure

Here is an outline of the stages of esoteric healing, from start to finish.

1. Ask the patient to relax and to close the eyes.
2. Align your threefold personality with your soul.
3. Establish the Higher Triangle. Now sound the Group Mantram.
4. Attune yourself with the patient by opening the Radiatory Healing Triangle, then open the Magnetic Healing Triangle, (open the Ray Attunement Triangles, if indicated), do the Protecting (against transference) Triangle and Activating Triangles (Placing-Vitalizing-Directing Triangles), finally do the Triangle of Transfer to complete this important stage of preparation for healing. (With a little practice this should not take more than two or three minutes.)
5. Diagnose the centers (ajna, solar plexus, base, sacral, heart, throat, alta major, head, ajna again) in the ajna to find the needed center (*see* pp. 155–57).
6. Light and activate the four primary vitality triangles (#1-4).
7. Do the primary diagnostic triangle, called the Synchronizing Triangle (*see* p. 123 & 163).
8. Visualize and activate the triangle circuits as diagnosed intuitively by the creative intelligence. (The sequence is similar to that of balancing: start with the solar plexus triangles, then go to the base triangles, sacral, heart, vagus nerve, throat, head triangles, and triangles involving the senses.)
9. Balance the pairs of opposing centers against each other (p. 240).
10. Create the circle of protection with the Radiatory Mantram (p. 242).
11. Seal (or close) the Radiatory and Magnetic Healing Triangles (p. 243).
12. Restore the patient to their normal waking consciousness.

8.

TREATING THE THREE INHERITED PLANETARY INFLUENCES

The spread of cancer

Any unusual growth of cells in the body can be called a "new growth" or "neoplasm." Most of these are simple local growths with no serious consequences and are therefore called "benign." The common wart is an example of such a "benign tumor." Sometimes, however, a "new growth" becomes malignant, behaves in a very different manner, and causes the frightening and serious conditions called "cancer."

Most people think of cancer as a single disease. This is true only in the sense that all cancer is characterized by an unrestrained growth of cells. In most cases these cells build up into tumors that compress, invade, and destroy normal tissues. If left untreated, these conditions usually lead to death. Whatever the specific form of cancer involved, these "malignant" tumors generally share some common characteristics. These are:

1. A higher rate of cell growth (or lower rate of cell death) than the normal tissues from which the cancers are derived.
2. Failure to maintain the boundaries of normal tissues.
3. Appearance under the microscope of immature rather than mature tissues, and
4. A tendency to spread to parts of the body distant from the original site of the cancer.

Not all of these features necessarily accompany every malignant tumor, but they are characteristic of most forms of cancer.

Over the course of a lifetime, the chances of developing cancer, according to present statistics, are approximately 25 percent.

We need not go into the specific ins and outs of these conditions; there are many excellent books which can explain it very well. What we do want to explain is some of the more esoteric aspects of this disease.

An esoteric view

Cancer has been around for a long time. Long before records were kept, cancer has been afflicting humans, probably for millions of years. Strangely, cancer cannot really be understood except from the angle of another disease. Teachers of the Ancient Wisdom say cancer grew out of the syphilitic diseases. So there is a strong connection between cancer and human sexual activities. The disease was a reaction to the awful horror of syphilis. This reaction was taken to such a degree, however, that humans refused to have sexual intercourse. A fear overtook the people of the time, a fear of death by syphilis. By repudiating sexual intercourse, these ancient people stifled the natural flow of energy rhythmically moving through the centers of generation (the sacral center of both men and women). In time this resulted in a counter disease to that of the over-expression and use of the sacral center, a disease of inhibition, called cancer (Bailey, 1951–70, v. 4). The inhibition was of such persistence that the energy that flowed into all cells to direct the process of replication instead caused mutation. In this way, not only the reproductive behavior of the cell was disturbed but also that of its progeny. The altered cell breeds true.

Countless millions have been killed by this disease (today it is statistically shown that one in three get cancer, and one in four die of it—BBC radio 27th September 1990). And countless millions have been buried, hence the "germs" of cancer can now be found in the soil of the planet itself. The Ageless Wisdom suggests that our dead bodies be burned so that this so-called germ should be destroyed, gradually cleansing the planet. It has been heartening to watch how church after church has been changing its emphasis from burial to cremation. But the healer knows that in every atom of the body is to be found a point of light. We know that the nature of the soul is light. We know about the light of matter and about the light of the soul. And in working with disease and cancer we learn to fuse and blend soul light and material light to bring about healing (Bailey, 1973, p. 196).

Cancer is a disease of the misuse of desire resulting in inertia, and the lack of right emotional control resulting in fear.

"One of the main sources of cancer as related to the sacral center, and therefore to the sex organs, has been the well-intentioned suppression of the sex life, and of all thought connected with the sex life, by misguided aspirants; they are those who find the teaching—monastic and celibate—of the Middle Ages the line of least resistance. In that period of time, good people taught that sex was evil and wicked, something not to be mentioned, and a potent source of trouble. Normal reactions, instead of being controlled and transmuted into creative activity, were violently suppressed and all thoughts about the sex life were refused expression" (Bailey, 1951–70, v. 4).

For many people, this "Middle-Ages attitude" still prevails. Usually the center which governs the area where the cancer has taken hold is overactive. This shows that the disease is deep within the structure or genetic life of humanity. We are no longer fearful of syphilis; it is contained and controlled by modern drugs. We now fear the "big C" instead, and the fear, sadly, is one of the sources of the overactivity.

Esoteric healing and cancer

Cancer involves the will-to-live, but where new life is generated, there is only distortion and malfunction. The proper functioning of the body through the cells is threatened and overstimulated. In fact this very overestimation can be said to be the rampant absorption of the life-force of the cell (and of the person). The patient's will is sapped. It takes a different kind of will energy to stimulate a cancer victim to fight for life. A few patients do achieve success, and their testimonies of how they did so can be found on the health shelves in all bookshops.

Cancer is caused by an inhibited emotional body and by an etheric body that is overstimulated in certain areas. It is an illness of the masses; more advanced people generally do not suffer from cancer. The so-called average person (one who has not entered the stream of service to humanity) has a low or slow vibratory rate. Cancer is an imposed hastening of this rate, causing an increase in cellular reproduction, leading to "malignancy." From an esoteric understanding the soul wills to have a faster vibratory rate to conform with its own plan for the person's incarnation; the person resists the new rhythm and the opportunities in life which would lead to a more mental polarization rather than an emotional expression, and this resistance, this damming of the flow towards the next step in consciousness, results in what we know as cancer. The suggestion is that the person who gets cancer should have already developed a higher consciousness. This higher consciousness has been held back by the personality and it forms a focus in one or more areas in the physical body. This develops as a tumor, which can spread to other tissues. The person has chosen to remain locked in the body and its lower desires. The consciousness of a Master or an Initiate of high degree vibrates in the whole body analogously to the way a cancer vibrates in the body of those who prefer not to move on in spiritual consciousness.

For this reason, in esoteric healing the cancer patient is always asked to consciously participate in the healing treatment (Bailey, 1951–70, v. 4). Explaining the process to the patient might take time, and require much effort on the part of the patient (who is often not interested in medical matters, still less in esoteric healing). The involvement of the patient can be limited to the actual work on the cancer. Therefore, the healer will do all the preliminaries—attuning, balancing, doing the various triangles necessary for that patient in preparation for working with the patient on the cancer itself. When it is time to work on the cancer, it is best to give instructions to the patient during the process of this treatment. For example, if the patient has bowel cancer (cancer of the large intestine):

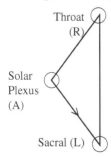

Throat (R)

Solar Plexus (A)

Sacral (L)

Before speaking to the patient, hold the solar plexus center, sacral center and throat center, the Triangle of Transmutation used for all cancers. Whenever directing others in healing, the healer should create and hold the triangle before instructing others to do so. Say to the patient something like the following: "With your mind's eye visualize the energy of pure white light flowing through your solar plexus center to your sex center (sacral center) and up to your throat center." Balance the Triangle of Transmutation (a word that is symbolically and also technically and scientifically correct [Bailey, 1951–70, v. 4, p. 61]), then move the ajna that was holding the solar plexus center to hold the energy of a healthy part of the colon, while continuing to hold the other two centers. Then say to the patient, "Now visualize the energy of pure white light flowing from your healthy colon through your sacral center to your throat center. Let this energy circulate round these three points." We never focus on the cancer itself, but always on the healthy tissue in the same organ. This is an important point, for if the cancer itself is held, it will be further stimulated, making the problems even worse. Now you have coordinated the will of the patient with your own (or with that of the healing group). The final stage is to visualize the whole organ as healthy. Do this first yourself. Then say to the patient, "Still visualizing the flow of pure white light from the healthy colon to your sacral center and to your throat center of creative service, visualize your colon as being whole and healthy and bathed in light." Then, after a while, say, "Allow pure love to flow in light through those three points." For only when the primary and ancient fear that has got into the cellular codes is replaced with love and light can right function return. When you feel ready, go back to holding the Triangle of Transmutation, and ask the patient to do the same. Next, ask the patient to release the triangle and relax. You will then complete the healing by balancing the centers of polarity, circling the patient with light and sealing the Magnetic and Radiatory Healing Triangles as usual (see pp. 240–244).

In more advanced esoteric healing, the healer will use the Synchronizing Triangle while the patient and other healers in the group continue to work with the Triangle of Transmutation. The healer should be certain they know what they are doing before employing the Synchronizing Triangle in this work. Unless you know what is specifically required (see pp. 124–25), this advanced form of the Synchronizing Triangle is best left to better qualified esoteric healing practitioners.

Syphilis, cancer and tuberculosis

These three disease miasms are within all of us. I am using the term "miasm" in the sense of an inherited planetary malfunction which no human can avoid. Our purpose is to transmute these miasms and so make the planet sacred. I do not plan here to go deeply into the understanding of these esoteric miasms (for this, see p. 255ff). The approach is slightly different to Hahnemann's and homeopathy's understanding. But the miasms are worth reviewing, since they are foundational to all our woes as well as to our role in spiritualizing the planet.

Syphilis, cancer and tuberculosis are vortices within our personality energy structure, set there at a time when we entered this planetary organism hundreds of millions of years ago. They act as precursors to disease, resulting in the myriad illnesses known to modern pathology. Syphilis is the earliest evil emerging from this planetary form (Bailey, 1951–70, v. 4, p. 58). It is related to the satisfaction of physical desire (p. 312) as shown by the excesses indulged in aeons ago during the middle period of the Lemurian epoch (p. 58). In that era began a primary misuse of the sex life and a primary misuse of the energy of substance itself (p. 59). We know, of course, that syphilis is caused by an entity called the spirochaeta pallida. I believe we can also say that when the collapse of the planetary life occurred, another alien entity entered, not exactly alien in itself but alien in that it was subservient to the life of the planetary being. And then due to a fundamental breakdown in the management of substance, this entity gained an undesired and consequently undesirable dominance. That is to say, the entity which we call the planetary disease of syphilis is unwittingly in control of the planet, simply because the planetary life (Logos) is in a chronic state of collapse or devitalization. Instead of the energy of light and love controlling and dominating, the opposite does, namely, hatred, darkness and so-called evil. This is the undreamt-of nightmare of the One About Naught May Be Said, in which the whole basis of creation has degenerated to a partial cosmic chaos, a cosmic form of a mentally handicapped person. To grasp these thoughts is not easy for one not versed in esotericism and occult meditation, but they ought to be grasped by the esoteric healer, for it is on this entity, the planetary spirochaeta, that we are working when healing the form. We can recognize this syphilitic miasm wherever we see breakdowns in structure, separatism, chaos, factions and wars, whether in the human body, in nations of humans, or in planetary events.

Tuberculosis, on the other hand, is more of a mental type of illness, which was "rampant in Atlantean times ... and generated principally in

Aryan times" (Bailey, 1951–70, v. 4, p. 59), gathered, as it were, from the astral world and forced into the mental world, using the air as the primary route of access. This forced rising in consciousness resulted in a starvation of the astral body of desires and feelings. The body of emotions became suppressed. The Tibetan Master says the tuberculosis planetary influence was "imposed by the Great White Lodge as a penalty ... [forcing] two issues and confronted the race with two hitherto unrealized problems. The first was that psychological attitudes and states of consciousness can and do bring about physiological conditions, these being both good and bad. Secondly, for the first time the people recognized the phenomenon of death" (p. 232). This problem or miasm makes many people desire eternal life, and they often have dreams of never dying. This is certainly not uncommon in children, and, personally speaking, I was very clearly aware as a child that I did not want to die, and I looked with contempt on those who were succumbing to death. This is a clear indication of that primary miasm. You can recognize this planetary disease wherever you hear references to living forever and "dicing with death," or where you encounter people wanting to acquire more and more physical things, resulting in possessiveness, spiritual inertia, even thievery and crime. Cosmetics and especially cosmetic surgery such as face-lifts are outward manifestations of this miasm, expressing a person's desire for youth and endeavor to defy the ravage of time (p. 61). This miasm is a mistaken use of the love force (for more about the source of these primary fractors, see Appendix A, pp. 255 ff.).

Notice how this links with Law II of Esoteric Healing (see p. 25).

"Ancient error"	"Tainted streams"	"Shares with all natural forms"
Illusion	Glamor	Maya
Mental Body	Astral Body	Physical/Etheric Body
TB	Cancer	Syphilis
Sacral/Throat/ Alta Major	Solar Plexus/ Heart/Ajna	Base/Head

Tabulation of the three planetary conditions

Let's end this brief survey by making a tabulation of these three primary planetary conditions, a chart which can be useful to the esoteric healer:

Clearing the Tuberculosis Miasm	Clearing the Cancer Miasm	Clearing the Syphilitic Miasm
1st Initiation	2nd initiation	3rd Initiation
Ray 2	Ray 1	Ray 3
Problem of the Aryan Race	Problem of the Atlantean Race	Problem of the Lemurian Race
Desire for Eternal Life/ Possessiveness	Desire of Doing/ Leadership	Desire for Separation/ Indulgence
Mental Body	Astral Body	Physical Body
Connected to the Planetary Solar Plexus Center	Connected to the Planetary Sacral Center	Connected to the Planetary Base Center
Complicated by Illusion	Complicated by Glamor	Complicated by Maya
Healing: Tuberculosis Triangle: Throat Center-Solar Plexus Center-Heart Center	Healing: Cancer Triangle[1]: Solar Plexus Center-Sacral Center-Throat Center	Healing: Syphilis Triangle: Sacral Center[2]-Base Center-Throat Center
Concentration	Meditation	Building the Antahkarana
The Beautiful	The Good	The True
Transference	Transmutation	Transformation
Ahriman (Devil)	Asuras (Tempter)	Lucifer (Satan)[3]
Sin	Temptation	Evil
Love	Power	Light

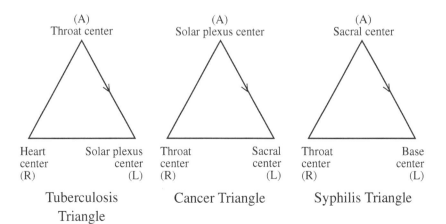

(A) Throat center	(A) Solar plexus center	(A) Sacral center
Heart center (R) Solar plexus center (L)	Throat center (R) Sacral center (L)	Throat center (R) Base center (L)
Tuberculosis Triangle	Cancer Triangle	Syphilis Triangle

It is of interest that the throat center is implicated in all these planetary forms of healing.

It is of interest that the throat center is implicated in all these planetary forms of healing. This is due to the fact that the creative thread is manufactured there, and the building of the antahkarana leads to the fourth initiation and to the healing of the planetary personality.

Jesus, the Anointed One, was put through three major tests at the beginning of his ministry: to cast himself from the pinnacle of the temple, to turn stones into bread, and to kneel before the ruler of the World (Satan, or Lucifer). Each of these incidents or tests represent for us a confrontation with one of the great entities of the human group personality. Even in the original Greek of the New Testament this is shown:

1. In Mark's Gospel, the Greek original of the English translation of "devil" is Satana. This entity, also known as Lucifer, the fascist arch-ruler of the earth planet, is humanity's elementary archetype of the physical body. The Christ was tempted to kneel before this entity and was promised "all the world will be yours," a physical glamor of life unending along with ownership of the planet.

2. The next temptation, mentioned in Matthew's Gospel, is by the entity, called in the Greek, Peirazon, the Tempter (the Asuras of the *Secret Doctrine*). It was the lure to capture the desire body within the forces of matter, by simply turning stones into bread. The Tempter is the entity of the astral body.

3. The last temptation, mentioned in the Luke Gospel, was by the being called, in Greek, Diabolos, the Devil (Ahriman). His effort was to tempt the Christ to cast himself from the pinnacle of the Temple to secure command over life's destiny (and thus kill the life of individual aspiration), the entity and the illusion of the mind.

You can now see the link between the great deed of Christ and the inherited planetary influences affecting the very genes of the human race.[3]

The first exoteric demonstration of the "overcoming" of temptation, sin and evil, has been performed by Jesus the Christ and revealed for us in the New Testament Gospels. Here, outside the secrecy of the Mystery Centers, this man undertook the tests of initiation without the security of hierophants. Jesus' lower bodies were transformed, the miasms of planetary inheritance, which conditioned and held captive the true light of the Monadic Self, merged and fused with their higher counterparts (the spiritual Triad), and in that instant (at the crucifixion or fourth initiation) two events occurred following the destruction of the soul, the causal body:

1. Planetary (Universal) salvation was achieved.
2. Personal salvation was made possible for ordinary man.

This means that no longer was it necessary to enter the sanctity of a Mystery School of Initiation to reach occult enlightenment, that is, the recognition of the Monadic Self, thereby attaining liberation from this Cosmic Order (in a state of Dis-ease or occult Imperfection) and the literal reunion of the Matter of the Planet (which formed the Enlightened One's body) with its Original Purity. This is what is meant by the clearing of the miasms or planetary influences; it is the purpose of esoteric healing; it is the way of every esoteric student.

Appendix A: OUR COSMIC PURPOSE

PART I. THE ESOTERIC PURPOSE OF HEALING

The Esoteric Cause of Disease and Purpose for Treatment
A Cosmic Perspective

It was said, "When the Avatar comes, He will convey to humanity something for which we have as yet no true name. It is neither love nor will as we understand them. Only a phrase or several words can convey something of the significance and then only feebly. This phrase is the principle of directed purpose. This Principle involves three factors:

A. Understanding (intuitive and instinctual, but intelligently interpreted) of the Plan as it can be worked out in the immediate future.
B. Focused intention, based on the above and emphasizing an aspect of the will, hitherto undeveloped in man.
C. Capacity to direct energy (through understanding and intent) towards a recognized and desired end, overcoming all obstacles and destroying all that stands in the way ... a destruction brought about by the greatly strengthened life within the form" (Bailey, 1957, p. 302). This destruction is not what we think. Esoterically, this "greatly strengthened life within the form" is the transformative power that is seen as destruction by the personality eyes but as restoration by the eyes of the spirit.

I would like to try to keep what I say simple (Bailey, 1950b, p. 129). The thought of what is to be written is very simple, but justifying it is the not-so-simple part. The simple formula of thought is as follows: There are many cosmic universes. The one in which we find ourselves went through a fault and collapsed. A whole range of "kingdoms" came into this universe from another to return it to its former state. The human kingdom is one such kingdom helping in this process.[4] To elucidate this thought, as stated above, can be undertaken via the law of correspondence in any kingdom or department of life. But for now, I want to try to justify the title of esoteric healing, and approach the subject from a different angle, a different paradigm, a shift away from healing as method, to *why* we want to heal—the reason we need to heal, the urgency for healing, the real purpose of living in the phenomenal world. We have so far presented the methods of healing, now we want to focus on the CAUSE.[5]

Esoteric means getting to the cause, and "The spiritual man is he who having been both a man of the world and an occult student has reached the conclusion that behind all those causes with which he has been hitherto engaged is a CAUSE; this CAUSAL UNITY then becomes the goal of his search. This is the mystery lying behind all the mysteries; this is the secret of which all that has hitherto been known and conceived is but the veil; this is the heart of the Unknown which holds hid the purpose and the key to all that IS" (Bailey, 1962, pp. 1237–38). Further on the same page these pivotal words are said: "Three times the cry goes out to all the Pilgrims upon the Path of Life: 'Know thyself' is the first great injunction.... 'Know the Self' comes next and when that is achieved, man knows not only himself but all selves; THE SOUL OF THE UNIVERSE is to him no longer the sealed book of life but one with the seven seals broken. Then when the man stands adept, the cry goes forth 'Know the ONE' and the words ring in the adepts' ears: 'Search for that which is the responsible Cause, ... search for THAT which the soul reveals'" (Bailey, 1962, p. 1238).

I want to try to reveal to you a part of the mystery of evil (cf. p. 34) that primarily concerns "the latent consciousness of matter, and works under the Law of Economy. It concerns primarily the Self-consciousness of the Logos in his dense physical body, and his polarization therein" (Bailey, 1962, p. 720). This involves every grade of form (every kingdom and every plane of this cosmic universe), until the point of origin is achieved—it is the secret of cosmic incarnation: "Through every grade of form, spirit or life progresses, until the path of return has been traversed and the point of origin achieved. This is the meaning of evolution and here lies THE SECRET OF THE COSMIC INCARNATION. Eventually spirit forces itself from form, and attains liberation" (Bailey, 1961, p. 62). Form here means manifestation on any level. Indeed, let's look at the great Lord Buddha's teaching, and we need go no further than the very first statement he made after having won enlightenment. In his profound assessment of the universe as found in the Four Noble Truths, he says: "Existence in the phenomenal universe is inseparable from suffering and sorrow." OK, this is true, this is our experience, we know all about suffering in the world although we might add, we don't know much about it "in the universe"[6] as Buddha mentions—this goes beyond human sensation, and a hint here is given about something deeper, something more than we usually think and imagine.

But let us get back to a deeper cause of disease and why we are here. H.P. Blavatsky says in her epic book, *The Secret Doctrine,* "This universal strife between good and bad spirits seems to be only the reproduction of another more ancient and more terrible strife, that, according to an ancient myth, took place before the creation of the universe, between the faithful and the rebellious legions ... the 'prologue to manifestation.'"[7] Note the use of the word *universal* strife and *before* the creation of the universe—the *prologue* to manifestation. We are not interested here in discussing cosmology or the history of the universe and its amazing evolutionary development or unfoldment (traced in my book, *The Emergence of the Planetary Heart* [1994]). What we want to reveal here is WHAT happened—as we have just found out *why* it happened—and then we can discover two things: our *purpose* for living on this planet in this cosmic universe, and the *method* of living.

So we see this amazing event. Let me try to paraphrase the inner teaching. Let's try to picture it: *Before* the creation of the universe,[8] a Cosmic Being, in a cosmic space in the wider universe, who then mysteriously started to become chaotic; the ancient universal laws of the Being were abandoned; the rules of conduct, the interaction between the entities in that Universe began to conflict; the mechanism, the life force, the cosmic harmony began to get mixed up, and "terrible strife" occurred due to "rebellious legions"—we can only speak in a kind of mythological language—one day at a later initiation we will know what really happened to this Universe and why it happened. But in fact we know something of what happened. A terrible collapse resulted, a crumpling, a contracting paralysis, a "fall" that in effect meant a kind of death, in reality a cosmic coma, a vegetative state, very different from the esoteric understanding of pralaya. This gigantic Being of Universal dimensions fell, collapsed. A most terrible and terrifying scenario. "A peculiar condition of affairs was brought about through the planetary failure" (Bailey, 1962, p. 781).

We can imagine an extraordinary meeting being called of the Cosmic Beings who witnessed this disastrous event. Something had to be done. There was a call for a response. It was here within the echelons of power, within the cosmic dimensions of timelessness and spiritual being and bliss, a dimension of subtlety very different to what we can experience, that an Entity, a Cosmic Being in totality voluntarily decided to go and help. However, this help was not like we would do when helping an injured brother or child: an external "administering," a detached "healing hand" or outward expression of sympathy and compassion. This help required something much more. It demanded a total abandonment of all that was owned or achieved, a forsaking of all the harmony and bliss of cosmic living, a complete sacrifice of all. It was like moving house from one where you had all you ever needed, where you were perfectly happy, to taking a tent in the harshest desert, or worse. This Being has become known as the Lord of Sacrifice, also as the Lord of Love. This Being is us. Us, true, but not just us as we are now, but also all that exists from stones to stars to spirits, from matter to man to monads to mega-beings up to and including the One About Whom Naught May Be Said. "[This] Lord ... through meditation is carrying forward processes which He instituted in His original, creative meditation—back in the darkest night of time in which he decided to create this planet of ours for strictly redemptive purposes. The whole creation is the result of His[9] directed and controlled thought—a process of sustained thinking which sweeps all the creative energies into evolutionary and cyclic activity, in conformity to the pattern which He eternally visualizes" (Bailey, 1962, pp. 222–23).

But at the beginning God, the Being who is us as a whole universal Cosmic Entity, living and moving in gigantic harmony and perfection, had to enter into "matter," the "Imperfect God," the Fallen Entity. Remember it wasn't fallen into matter as we know it now, hard and dense   it had to be carried into "matter" from its high spiritual level so as to be restored, salvaged. To do this a massive program of differentiation was set in motion by the incoming, salvaging Cosmic Being, with a time plan of billions of trillions of years, symbolized by the separation of the sexes in the Adam and Eve story. This cosmological evolution has progressed starting with the so-called first Solar System (the building of the Matrix of the Universe). This is veiled by H.P. Blavatsky in the word Akasa: "it is the universal Soul, the Matrix of the Universe, the 'Mysterium Magnum' from which all that exists is born by separation of differentiation. It is the cause of existence; it fills all the infinite Space; is Space itself." It is the efforts of the seven Cosmic Rays to form a substance which could eventually be liberated and restored to its original status—which is what is meant by the ending of Maya. "The will and the breath, my brother, are occultly synonymous terms. In this statement you have the clue to the ending of Maya.... The entire science of the breath is built around the use of the Sacred Word, the OM" (Bailey, 1973, pp. 245, 254).

Our work then, as healers (and is not everyone on this Path in one way or another?), is to be full of joy as we journey towards the bliss of enlightenment. "Therefore be full of joy, O pilgrim on the Way towards enlightened Being, for gain and loss are one; darkness and light eternally reveal the True; love and desire eternally invoke the Life. Naught disappears but pain. Nothing remains but bliss" (Bailey, 1951–70, v. 2, pp. 33–34). This "bliss" is the one thing we have brought with us as Eternal Monadic Beings of Light—this Bliss is our Life: "Sacrifice is, technically speaking, the achievement of a state of bliss and of ecstasy because it is the realization of another divine aspect, hidden hitherto by both the soul and the personality. It is understanding and recognition of the will-to-good which made creation possible and inevitable and which was the true cause of manifestation" (Bailey, 1951–70, v. 5, p. 492). Please note that it was our sacrifice which made creation possible and which was the true cause of manifestation. Amazing, isn't it?, that the Tibetan Master Djwhal Khul, throughout his books, never mentions, elaborates, or deepens our understanding of these fundamental esoteric causes, the purpose for the beginning, yet we can find scattered specific references to the fact. There is only one reference in the New Testament about this (by Paul) whereby we can extract an esoteric connection to this original cause: "I beseech you therefore, brethren, by the mercies of God, that ye present your bodies a living sacrifice, holy, acceptable unto God, which is your reasonable service" (Romans 12: 1). Ponder these words in the light of what I have said; they hold revelations for the sincere seeker. And it's interesting to note what DK says in the book, *Esoteric Healing,* that we must heal with the "life aspect" and not with the "consciousness aspect." This is because the life aspect is the "jewel" at the center of all things, from atoms to cells to centers to systems. In healing, if we work into the life or from the life aspect, the consciousness "petals" automatically respond and so healing is effected (more on p. 78 and p. 80—the seven glands are the replica of the universe).

We were talking about the Beings who have incarnated into Matter, ourselves included, to salvage the Imperfect God, and work towards making this planet Sacred as our service part in this gigantic process or Plan of salvation and redemption of this Universe. We have been taking Matter into ourselves ever since the beginning of our entry into time and creation—by so doing we imbue it with Light; it is this substance of our original, untainted Life that will bring about restoration of the Cosmic Plan for this Being—echoed as "Restore the Plan on Earth."

Djwhal Khul speaks of a "Way of Release" in which "all drops from our hands; everything is taken away, and detachment from the world of phenomenal life and of individuality is inevitably forced upon us. We are treading the Way of Loneliness, and must learn eventually that we are essentially neither ego nor non-ego" (Bailey, 1951–70, v. 2, pp. 33–34). And this is true, we are neither ego nor non-ego because all that we are, all our bodies or vehicles, are from the Entity we have come to save— what we are is LIFE itself, nothing else.

Allow me to quote again from H.P. Blavatsky, "in occult metaphysics there are, properly speaking, two 'ONES'—the one on the unreachable plane of Absoluteness and Infinity, on which no speculation is possible, and the Second 'One' on the plane of Emanations. The former can neither emanate nor be divided, as it is eternal, absolute, and immutable. The Second, being, so to speak, the reflection of the first One (for it is the Logos ... in the Universe of Illusion), can do all this. It emanates from itself ... the seven Rays or Dhyan-Chohans; in other words, the Homogeneous becomes the Heterogeneous, the 'Protyle' differentiates into the Elements, i.e. the (saving) Life takes on or identifies with the 'many' as the differentiating 'fractors' of the fallen Universal Being and evolves with the form until restoration (zero point) is achieved. But these, unless they return into their primal Element, can never cross beyond the

Laya, or zero-point.... Those who 'descend and ascend'—the incarnating Monads, and men striving towards purification and 'ascending, but still not having quite reached the goal'—may cross the 'circle of the Pass-Not,' only on the day 'Be-With-Us'; that day when man, freeing himself from the trammels of ignorance, and recognizing fully the non-separateness of the Ego within his personality—erroneously regarded as his own—from the UNIVERSAL EGO ... merges thereby into the One Essence to become not only one 'with us' (the manifested universal lives which are 'ONE' LIFE), but that very LIFE ITSELF" (Blavatsky, 1977). Another pivotal reference from *The Secret Doctrine.* Please let me try to explain.

So what are we doing in Healing? What are we really doing? Before I answer your question may I just say this. That all healing is purificatory but only because it is the substance itself that has been contaminated. This is the misunderstood esoteric tenet which the church calls "sin"; true, we are born in sin, not ours but that of the Cosmic Universal Being who "fell"—it is not our fault and nothing to do with us in reality. Its substance has been taken on by us (we have evolved within its substance, we are enduring the pain and suffering of compounded, restricted, matter, the fallen form of this failed Cosmic Entity); we are giving our life daily to this substance to regenerate it and bring it back to its original state—it is during this process of transformation and transmutation that diseases occur requiring special healing methods to safely defuse their toxicity, their stickiness, their "evil" quality (their fallen chaotic pattern).

In the very first law of healing it states that "all disease is the result of inhibited soul LIFE and this is true of *all forms* in *all* kingdoms" (Bailey, 1951–70, v. 4, p. 532, my emphasis). So soul life or monadic being or the Extra-Dimensional Light of who we really are, is being inhibited, fragmented, caused to frictionize—these I call fractors (see p. 272)—everything in our own multi-leveled consciousness that causes deviation, preventing our experience of our own continuous Beginningless Enlightenment. Only higher mystics and babies experience this oceanic quality. Babies, says one Tibetan Master, are reflections of Enlightenment, "... only mystics and very young children experience in this oceanic manner. Freud also uses the term 'oceanic experience' to describe the way in which young children do not divide themselves from their surroundings. Babies are reflections of Enlightenment. From the Tantric viewpoint, every experience is dynamically linked to an aspect of Liberated Energy—of Enlightenment. This oceanic experience is distorted into various perverse variants of group consciousness such as nationalism, racism, elitism and sectarianism, but we always retain some means of access to oceanic experience, although society encourages individuation. The nature of the fight between individuation and oceanic experience manifests as our attachment to distorted reflections of our own Enlightenment." However, "The Experience of Enlightenment goes beyond both oceanic and individuated experience, and enters into Limitlessness in which such distinctions are meaningless.... The Experience of Enlightenment transcends both.... The Intrinsic Spaciousness of our Being is continuously reminding us of our Enlightenment" (Nga-kpa Chögyam, 1988, pp. 151–52).

This then is the true work of healing, indeed of living. Healing is a practical science and art. There are many approaches but all with the same purpose and end: to help or serve others to transmute their fractors, the deviant crystals of distorted matter, so that the matter itself on whatever plane of our cosmic physical plane or higher can receive correct elimination to effect right restoration and salvation of matter, the many vehicles of the fallen Cosmic Universal Being. "The right use of physical energy by the initiate gives him the 'freedom' of the cosmic physical plane. The right use of astral energy gives him power on the cosmic astral, and the correct use of mental energy gives him entrance on the cosmic mental" (Bailey, 1979, p. 362). The result is initiation, revelation, enlightenment, leading to, "...'the whole creation groaneth and travaileth together in pain until now, waiting for the manifestation of the Sons of God.' St. Paul is there referring to planetary purpose and to the determined insistence of the Sons of God that eventually—as they bring about the redemption of substance, of matter and form, and thus prove the possibility of that redemption through their (our) own transfigured personalities—their (our) reward should be eventual manifestation as expressions of divinity. For this purpose and with this goal in view, the first of us who attained enlightenment (called by us Masters and Avatars), instituted the great evolutionary process of initiation, thus producing a continuity of revelation and of enlightenment. In reality, the period of time at which the final initiation is undergone is simply a climaxing, triumphant demonstration of the realization and purpose of all past experiences; it is fulfillment (by the One Initiator) of the first promise ever made to the sons of mind' which marks the time when they originally started their redemptive work: it is this merging stage when the bodies are transmuted by the individual's LIFE, that 'a sudden blazing forth of the individual glory and its merging at initiation with the glory of the whole [becomes] the true 'promised land'" (Bailey, 1944, v. 2, pp. 385–86). This "true promised land" is the rod of healing, the *sine qua non* that sends us back to our original home, an escape back into reality—our bridges are burned, we have completed our work, freedom has been earned.

This then is the real purpose of healing. The methods of healing are specific and powerful—some are simple to do, others are complex. Some are for curing disease, others are for raising consciousness and instantly transmuting fractors of illusion, glamor, and maya into an experience of the Self as THAT. All healing work is designed to evoke change, alignment, and acceptance leading to the gradual increase of the sparkling through of our Beginningless Enlightened Nature and an understanding of the Vastness of what we really are.

PART II. STANZAS AND COMMENTARY
THE INNER PURPOSE OF HEALING

As a kind of glossary, and as an aid to fuller understanding and a deepening consciousness of this perspective of the INNER OR ESOTERIC PURPOSE, the revelation or theory will be systematized simply, as stanzas, and then a tentative commentary will be made for students so as to lead thought into an amplification. The commentary will involve viewing the question from different angles; something more is visible with each repetition. The simple inscriptions can act as a password for group discussion, thoughtful reflection and meditation, and deep still contemplation.

A. Stanzas

1. This Cosmic Universe was perfect. It lost its perfection due to a cosmic disaster.
2. All that exists in this Cosmic Universe (CU) is an imposition from another Cosmic Universe.
3. There are many Cosmic Universes in this system called Dimensional Systemic Reality (DSR), the full name for this is the Ring-Pass-Not of a Dimensional Systemic Reality. There are many DSRs but we have absolutely no access to them in our present position/condition.

4. Entry into this CU involved total cosmic sacrifice by another CU within DSR.

5. Without correction of the corrupted CU, DSR could possibly be corrupted.

6. The cosmic disaster caused such total collapse of the underlying structure that repair required a total abandonment of previous achievement by one CU, and entry into such elementary life forms by the sacrificing CU, that it could be called the beginning of creation.

7. At the time of sacrifice the event of creation occurred and with it the beginning of evolution.

8. All that remained of the sacrifice by the kingdoms coming into the collapsed CU is their Life Principle. All else is tainted by the CU's misshapen patterns. These are known as Fractors.

9. This Life Principle will enable an escape or return back to the original CU.

10. All that exists in this CU is the result of the activities of the saving CU.

11. The saving CU is so totally identified with the collapsed, chaotic CU that many or most in this CU believe they belong here. This refers to all the kingdoms to be found here—from atoms to the great beings whose bodies are the galaxies of this CU.

12. It has taken literally trillions of years for this CU to have reached this stage of development on the way to its restoration.

13. The purpose of the coming of the saving CU to the CU to be saved is to restore it to its former glory and so protect the DSR of which we are all a part.

14. All that exists in this CU are brothers in the saving CU. We came together and we work with the same common aim.

15. To save/heal this CU is enormously complex. It requires the Life Principle to be an impregnating force within the matter or substance of the whole of this CU.

16. The first step was just to "get into" this CU, the nature of which is so totally different from that of the saving CU.

17. The second step is to "live out a life" within the CU.

18. The third step is to actively promote advanced change within substance/consciousness. This is the specific work of advanced or esoteric healing.

19. The fourth step is to live within that pure state of LIFE without being deflected into the fractors of that life.

20. Completion of the work for this CU is for the life of the saving/ healing CU to return back to its original home. This can only be achieved when the fourth step is continuous in the life and on all levels of being within the consciousness of this CU.

B. Commentary

1. *This Cosmic Universe was perfect. It lost its perfection due to a cosmic disaster.*

2. *All that exists in this Cosmic Universe (CU) is an imposition from another Cosmic Universe.*

3. *There are many Cosmic Universes in this system called Dimensional Systemic Reality (DSR), the full name for this is the Ring-Pass-Not of a DSR. There are many DSRs but we have absolutely no access to them in our present position/condition.*

4. *Entry into this CU involved total cosmic sacrifice by another CU within DSR.*

5. *Without correction of the corrupted CU, DSR could possibly be corrupted.*

In the clearest and briefest way possible an explanation will be offered on the first five of the esoteric stanzas, as they are best handled together.

In the cosmic sphere in which the many Cosmic Universes (CUs) live, the integrity and activity is full. It cannot be described adequately in words due to the state of existence we are in at this time. All that needs to be known is that a CU is complete in itself, is in harmony and has a purpose for its existence. Each CU is totally different to any other. Each CU exists in a dimension that is inaccessible to any other.

So what happened to this CU in which we find ourselves and in which we see such disharmony and imperfection? The details are not available to us at this time, but what we can convey will be laid out openly. This CU was perfect in every respect. We know it was (is) a dualistic system where the two elements are the ramifications for their own integrity. For example, the light depends on its lightness being revealed due to the darkness; the darkness could not be experienced as such were there not light. To illustrate what happened which led to this chaos or collapse or paralysis of the CU, we can continue with the example of the light and dark, rather like the ancient symbol of the yin and yang, where the yin is dark and the yang is light like a "69."

At some point of its eternal life (and we have an idea this must have been something in the order of 15 billion of our years ago [Hawking, 2001, p. 169], the reason for this will be made clear later), the support structure of dark and light began to break down and the dark began to infiltrate into the light and vice versa. We cannot reveal why this occurred, as it is not known and not understood unless you have reached a certain high level of realization (and you certainly would not be on this plane with such knowledge!). All that has been told us is that there was a kind of "rebellion," which is obvious and tells us nothing! But what is clear and true is that something happened which led to a complete deterioration of the former balance and stability, resulting in a kind of coma: life was preserved but it was as if death had come. Remember, all this occurred on a very high plane of expression and nothing like we think at this time in the material sphere.

So we have the scenario. A Cosmic Universe within this system (called a Dimensional Systemic Reality [DSR]) in a state of utter confusion and inoperative hopelessness throughout its entire structure of Cosmic Being, from highest to lowest, and completely unable to get out of its desperate imbroglio. Picture the scene. It is rather like a bowl of fish containing say 100 small fish and one suddenly and almost inexplicably loses all capacity to swim; it lives and can just feed to stay alive, but it sinks to the bottom of the bowl incapacitated. The other fish can do nothing to revive it or save it. That's where the analogy ends. What does happen in this cosmic "fish bowl" or DSR, we can rightly suppose, is that an emergency extraordinary cosmic conference is held at the highest level between all the CUs of the DSR. Nothing like this has ever happened in the eternal existence of the DSR. Something must be done. What can be done? Can something be actioned? If so, how and at what risk? It was also clear that such corruption in the "pool" of the DSR might lead to further "rebellion," or contamination, or corruption. Immediate action was required to avoid this possibility, quite apart from the fact that one of their "brothers" was crippled and needed help. After much deliberation and deep consultation it was seen that there was only one thing that could be done to save and restore this "comatose" CU. It meant that one of the DSR's CUs would have to sacrifice itself, or all it was, so as to enter the fallen CU with such complete identification that restoration of its energies, organization, structures and patterns of being could gradually be regained. This sacrifice was very real. Each CU is totally different to any other. Each lived in a different dimension and the structure was completely different to any other CU. Were this not so it would have been much easier, rather like one human being, a physician, acting on behalf of a sick brother, but still keeping himself separate. This is not so in the cosmic world of CUs. The difference was even greater than, say, a human being is to a praying mantis. To restore this being the sacrificing CU would have to forgo all that it was and actually become the other CU. Sacrifice had to be total abandonment. However, to perform the great healing, this total denial of itself also meant that its life would be maintained outside, external to this CU, i.e., in the saving CU. The key to its being, the central essence of its identity must remain. However, this was not a lifeline for those of the sacrificing CU. They couldn't just suddenly and at any time simply pull the rip cord if things weren't going right. No. The risk and danger was that the life of the incoming CU could actually be so identified with the paralyzed CU that it too could be lost. The purpose of this was that the saving CU, by so sacrificing itself totally to the collapsed CU, and by re-seeking its own life and true essence of being, it would do two things at the same time: first, it would restore the collapsed one to life and health, and second, it would maintain its own life and being and so enable it to return to its original home in its own space and dimension. This was the challenge. It is still not known whether it will be successful. It is still in the process of working. Hence we can to some extent understand the esoteric stanza: All that exists in this Cosmic Universe (CU) is an imposition from another Cosmic Universe; and explains the fourth step as found in stanza 19.

There is a truth in the understanding that this is the esoteric explanation of that statement found in the Bible which says, "In the beginning was the Word, and the Word was with God, and the Word was God. He was with God in the beginning. Through him all things were made, without him nothing was made that has been made. In him was life, and that life was the light (of men). The light shines in the darkness, but the darkness has not understood it." Briefly, let it be recapitulated:

"In the beginning was the Word"—this is the saving, sacrificing CU.

"and the Word was with God"—this is the saving CU in the DSR.

"and the Word was God"—all CUs are unique in themselves and are truly Enlightened, God.

"He was with God in the beginning"—a reemphasis that a CU is the Cosmic Substance and is one with the DSR.

"Through him all things were made; without him nothing was made that has been made"—here we have the clear statement that, as a result of the incoming CU to the collapsed CU, all things in this CU have been made or generated or created (by the saving CU, as will be explained in the next esoteric stanzas).

"In him was life, and that life was the light of men"—LIFE is the special quality of being which the saving CU has brought into this ailing CU, and it is the same life quality as originally held in the saving CU before it sacrificed itself into this paralyzed CU that is also in human beings (and all life forms). The distinction made that the "life was the light of men" illustrated the purposes and aspiration of men (i.e., all beings), that the purpose is to seek the light, i.e., Enlightenment.

"The light shines in the darkness, but the darkness has not understood it"—the new CU's light is now in the substance (darkness) of the collapsed CU; it will never understand it, just as the saving CU's life and light will never totally comprehend the "darkness" or essential being of the CU which it has come to restore. (This piece of information is liable of misinterpretation.) The reader who is interested in how this links with Jesus the Christ is asked to refer to the author's book, *The Emergence of the Planetary Heart*.

Let us end this part of the commentary with the following New Testament verses for consideration as they can be helpful to some. I haven't the space to offer an interpretation, but in the light of the information given, these quotations will reveal new perspectives; they hold hidden secrets:

John 3:16. For God [our DSR] so loved the world [the CU to be saved], that he gave his only begotten Son [our CU], that whosoever believeth in him should not perish, but have everlasting life.

Mark 4:22. For there is nothing hid, which shall not be manifested; neither was any thing kept secret, but that it should come abroad.

1 John 4:9. In this was manifested the love of God [our DSR] toward us [our CU in this fallen CU], because that God [our DSR] sent his only begotten Son [our CU] into the world [this fallen CU], that we might live through him. (We must hold fast to our CU's LIFE [the Son] while we life in this CU [the world].)

2 Timothy 1:9. Who hath saved us [this CU], and called us with an holy calling, not according to our works, but according to his own purpose and grace [our CU], which was given us in Christ Jesus before the world began [our CU].

1 John 3:8. He that committeth sin is of the devil; for the devil [this fallen CU] sinneth from the beginning. For this purpose the Son of God [our saving CU] was manifested, that he might destroy the works of the devil [fractors of this fallen CU].

We now turn to the next two stanzas.

6. *The cosmic disaster caused such total collapse of the underlying structure that repair required a total abandonment of previous achievement by one CU, and entry into such elementary life forms by the sacrificing CU, that it could be called the beginning of creation.*

7. *At the time of sacrifice the event of creation occurred and with it the beginning of evolution.* [Evolution means a beginning as a most elementary form and ending in a perfected state where progress in time is no longer of any use.]

The importance of these two stanzas is the link they make with two considerations regarding the condition at the beginning of time and that of its progress—the one of creation and the other of evolution. And with one simple statement the two problems are resolved. After the collapse of the CU the saving CU made a sacrificial entry into the collapsed CU's space and dimension. At this point a new "creation" began, considered to be some 3.5 billion years ago by biologists (I refer to the estimated beginning of physical life on our planet, but manifestation on the physical plane was some 15 billion years ago). Esoterically this is a misinterpretation due to a certain negligence or ignorance. The time is correct in as much as it addresses manifestation on this level or plane of expression—the physical. But it is totally incorrect to think that the beginning of the salvation process began just 15 billion years ago. No! The process of salvation began on the spiritual level the "fall" originated on. It has taken billions of eons to get it to this juncture on the physical plane. This is the juncture that took place 15 billion years ago (cf. Hawking, p. 266).

To reiterate the beginning of creation has not been as simple as just creating the cell and coccoid cyanobacteria (cf. p. 340 #10) which has led to the formation of homo erectus. Entry into this CU took place billions of eons ago, and this was the real beginning of time (for time by esoteric definition is really the first touch of the saving CU with the one who was to be saved) and gradually the "descent" of this to the present plane, whereupon the so-called "Big Bang." The CU into which the saving CU entered was, as can be imagined, multi-planar, meaning a being with many planes to its expression. At the collapse, all the planes fell into disarray. As has been stated earlier, this CU is based on a dualistic system. At the collapse, the whole system went awry. The process of correcting this mishap was not so much a putting in of hands and replacing the circuit-board. It was much more complex than that. The entering CU had to become the circuitry, had to become the force of life that ran the circuitry, had to become the picture it produced, had to become the effects it caused—had to become all that it was not, so that it could become what it originally was.

The process is in motion now. All that we can see and know on earth, on other planets, in the sun, the stars, the constellations, the galaxies and the many levels or planes of its expression are the several restoration phases that are taking place at this very moment. All the human beings, animals, birds, insects, reptiles, plant life, rocks and all, including elemental beings, angelic beings, and other nonphysical beings from the highest to the lowest, all can be seen to be the incoming, saving, CU. We are all brothers! We were that saving CU! We have all got an important part to play in this saving process. We all depend on each other for its ultimate success. Success is not guaranteed, as DK frequently emphasized. This is because there are hosts of inimical beings and forces messed up and interacting falsely with each other—the interacting fractors, the so-called latent seeds of evil (cf. p. 34). It is our task to put them right whether we are a rock in the desert, a flower on a remote hill, a bird in the Andes, an animal in a field, a human in Barbados, an angel in the fifth sphere, a Kumara or Bodhisattva—we all have a place, and we all have a function and purpose in this dramatic saving act. Devils and the black forces are as much an important part in this process as are the white forces. Our work is to put them in the right place so that harmony abounds and progress and joy result, and thus we restore the plan on earth and seal the door where evil dwelt.

What happened for evolution to have reached our present manifested state is that our CU entered the fallen CU on all its fallen levels, but in order for it to begin to regain its former glory, the process had to be reduced to a common denominator so that evolutionary development could then be instituted. On all the spheres this took place. The various writings on cosmology have not been accurate in the wider sense. They have just clarified what had to be done to achieve physical preparation—the descent of matter, the involutionary activities of all the kingdoms, and so on, without chronicling the other planar activities. But be that as it may, the descriptions of all this would have been well nigh impossible, and what we have in cosmological understanding is extremely sketchy. While acceptable for general purposes, we do need to remember that this is just a pinch of what really happened.

At the moment of entry by our CU into the fallen CU, time and creation and evolution all began. It will all end, providing it is success-ful, when we have given it all back and we depart via the "Way of Final Return" to our own Home. When will this be? As soon as it is achieved! The speed or time taken can be hastened by dedicated work, or it can be hindered and slowed down by loss of focus and misinterpretation and wrongful identification. This can occur at any time of the day and night, called "being fractored." That is, identifying with thoughts, feelings, or acting in such a way that is not in line with or losing the awareness and Presence of one's true inner purpose—the Life Purpose of our original intention. These fractors can be tiny and huge. They can be known or unknown. They affect all who work on all planes. Fractors are the means of developing and progressing evolutionary change and achievement—because they inform us of choices: the right (rather than the wrong). They are the other side of the dualistic aspect of this CU. Any recogni-tion and overcoming of fractors is a significant step in the re-patterning of this CU—another light comes on in the "rewiring" of this burnt-out mega-cosmic Being. Fractors are the memory of the fall; a loop that pre-vents liberation, right relations, the sense of beauty, and the will to good (love). Fractors are the latent seeds of evil (see p. 34) in every atom and in every level of the CU—these latent seeds are transformed to normal, right function by healing and PASE (cf. p. 278). The fractors themselves "enjoy" being overcome, because to them they can then enter their own world, as much as the light forces which overcame the fractor enters the light-world of freedom. It is a dual bonus each time. We do it in our own lives from minute to minute, indeed from second to second. It hinges on our WILL—the blissful sacrifice to our Cosmic Light Self, supported by our love and intelligence. This is the way of evolution, transformation, revelation and enlightenment.

8. *All that remained of this sacrifice by the kingdoms coming into the collapsed CU is their Life Principle. All else is tainted by this CU's misshapen patterns. These are known as Fractors.*

We need to realize that we abandoned all that we were in our CU to enter into the fallen "calling" CU. That too was imperative. All we have is our Life Principle. We were stripped of all other achievements. They were unnecessary to us in this work. We came as Life to give life. Our work therefore is to maintain connection with this Life, and not to betray it in the search of pleasure (fractors), whatever that may mean in your individual understanding. This refers to all beings in our CU, whether they came down before us and are now so-called Deities, or after us and are rocks, plants, and animals. Our work is to be here, to sojourn here without expectations unconditioned by the events of our long and extended past progress, de-fractoring our lives and so allowing the lights to be turned on. We only have ourselves to work on; that is our assignment and that is enough. This goes for all who are in our CU.

9. *This Life Principle (LP) will enable an escape or return back to the original CU.*

As has been explained above, the purpose for our work in this CU is to restore it to its original expression. It involves the whole of our CU, and working on multi-levels of this CU, we are moving forward with great strides. The initial work has taken a long time due to its tediously intricate nature of declassifying the forces with which we were to work. We came into this CU without the foggiest idea of what to do! We know nothing about this CU. Its structure and activities are totally different to ours. Its state, or dimension, is totally different to ours. Everything, in a word, was unknown to us and dissimilar to our CU. What was worse, or more difficult, it was in chaos, collapsed, comatose, but still alive. Life, of course, cannot be killed or done away with; it simply goes into a different expression. What would have happened if our CU did not come to the rescue? Would the fallen CU eventually have dug itself out of its own grave? The answer is hypothetical, but it is clear that the decision to set out to rescue the languishing CU was not a small one, and that had some other course of action been implemented that would have been the right thing to do, we must suppose.

We have nothing but our original Life Principle (LP) to keep us from falling among the thieves, liars, murderers, and muggers. Nothing in this CU belongs to us or can be taken with us back home to our CU when the time comes. The life in our CU far outweighs the life in this CU simply because we belong there and wouldn't wish to be anywhere else. An ice cream here tastes like the cream of nectar at home in our CU! There are actually no comparisons to be drawn. It is just so totally different, we cannot even think of a simile to describe an experience; even memory of our CU has gone. This is because when we originally came to this CU, we had to arrive stripped of all we were so that we could work within this CU simply as Beings of Life. Time and time again we return to earth—we are talking about human beings now—and all our LPs are brought to influence and change and transform substance—the matter of our bodies—on all levels of our being. We reincarnate and gather experiences, and so we live. The importance of who we are, where we are, who we meet, what we do, what we own, is of no value at all save to bring us through our fractors to the constant awareness of our LP. Once the LP is held in constant awareness by any one being, we enter a higher level of help. As this area is filled and strengthened, the work of progress will correspondingly be empowered and evolution will hasten much more quickly. Once the LP is held in constant awareness by all our CU, we will leave to return to our own CU. It is like a race to get on a boat, where the more "people" who manage to get on, the lighter it becomes, and the more easily it makes it for others to board, and the sooner it will depart.

10. All that exists in this CU is the result of the activities of the saving CU.

Everything that is happening in this CU, the galaxies moving and spiralling, the constellations, the stars and planets and suns; everything on the earth planet, all the human activities, animal movements, plants growing, crystals, metals and soils and rocks, all that is happening, all that these things are, is the result of the work of our CU as it reprograms, re-patterns, transforms, and restores the life of the ailing CU. The more we do, the more we work, the more we think, the more we feel within our Life Principle (LP), the more the progress towards fulfillment is achieved. We are all brethren. All the kingdoms of this planet and all the beings in the cosmos are of the same CU, as one giant family. It is a family affair. A family business. We have the family's interest at heart. As we work for the family, we improve ourselves and so the whole is helped.

11. *The saving CU is so totally identified with the collapsed, chaotic CU that many or most in this CU believe they belong here. This refers to all the kingdoms to be found here—from atoms to the great beings whose bodies are the galaxies of this CU.*

   The problem facing our CU as we work within this fallen CU is that we have been here so long that we are beginning to believe that we belong here, that what we see is what we are, and that what we see belongs to us. This can be a problem on any level from the great to the small. It is not without reason that this should be so. After all, we came into this CU having left all and everything behind. We entered this CU with nothing but our LP (Life Principle, or Principle of Life). And in order to enter completely we had to become the CU. This means that we had to enter the actual mechanics of the Cosmic Universe in its fallen, chaotic state of existence; it means that we had to bow down to the totally different structure of this CU, totally different interaction and purpose of this CU. To do this we had to mutate and develop according to the opportunities around us. It was a spiritual happening. This means that this took place on a higher level of expression at first, gradually incarnating downward into manifestation on the physical level. This took a very long time. But once it was on the physical level, the diversity had been accomplished and the development of structure and foundation (a good solid form) was secured for the next phase of the work of salvation. In a way, a circle had to be drawn: first the downward, in-drawing activity to stabilize the form, then the gradual elevation of the form, so that it became once more what it was before. In other words, the entry into this CU was on all levels, but in a higher dimension, and to secure its patterns in substance there had to be a period of materializing and manifesting; only then could the third and fourth phases be started. The phases are as follows:

   a. Entry into the fallen structure of the CU.
   b. Identifying with the structure and patterns of the CU by bringing it down into matter on the physical plane.

c. The gradual elevating of the form back into the higher expressions of its being.

d. Once complete, the leaving of this CU to its own life and livelihood.

The third phase is where we are in the work of salvation of this CU. It is the phase which entails great determination and moral endeavor, whether a tree, a man, or a god. The reason for this is that there can be too much identification with the form of this CU. Remember all that is seen is ourselves, our own CU encapsulated in the forms of this CU. This is a most important recognition. All who we see, be it sea, sky, stone, herb, flower, bush, mushroom, dog, cat, horse, elephant, fish, insect, bird, reptile, human being, angel forms, elemental forms, masters, gods, all and everything is of our own CU. They are our brethren. They are representing the forms of this CU for its own salvation. That is their sacrifice be it a wombat, whale, worm, witch-hazel, or woman. Of course it is no problem at this point in time. And mostly people and animals, plants and minerals are rightly identifying with their own ways: one into matter as one with themselves, and the other into self as separate from matter. It has taken literally trillions of years for this CU to have reached this stage of development on the way to its restoration.

As we have seen, all is timeless and eternal. Time and finitude began at the moment, the Flash, the original "big bang," when our CU entered the fallen CU.[10] We therefore can experience the duality of time and timelessness, the form and the spirit. The former is of this CU in its fallen state; the latter is of the original Life which we know is Enlightenment. Progress in the restoration of the patterns of the fallen CU have gone on ever since the Flash entry. What we see in ourselves, and the planet, and the cosmos, with all its achievements, adaptations, troubles, disasters, mistakes, and marvels is where we have got, where we have evolved to, where the re-patterning has reached. How long this has really been in terms of years is impossible to say. To say a million years is hard enough to conceive, to say a billion years impossible, to say trillions of years is meaningless to the intellect. Everything is working towards restoration, no matter what is happening. This is sometimes difficult to understand. If we don't understand, and also if we do, we can hold no judgment over what is happening and why. Everything is part of the great unwinding. In the Eternal Now whatever is being said, whatever is being done, thought, caused, is exactly right. The expelling, the elimination, the disease and healing process may look to the unenlightened eye to be recipes for di-saster. There may appear some paradoxes, but it is just the lower mind, the unenlightened matter of self, that cannot see or reconcile. The course or curse we have taken could well have developed in a different way. How the international borders came to be, how capitalism, communism, and totalitarianism came to be, how the various religious faiths came to be, how business came to be, how the innumerable artifacts of our world have come to be, etc., and all the results thereof, is entirely based on conditioning factors and the interacting fractors. It could have been very different—either better or worse. The salvaging efforts of many individuals down the centuries have endeavored to steer us clear of cliff-top danger. And still we kill, maim, rape, torture, hurt our brethren—be this in our own kingdom or in other kingdoms. History is truly written in blood. All due to mis-identification.

The purpose of the coming of the saving CU to the CU to be saved is to restore it to its former glory and so protect the DSR of which we are all a part. Significantly, the work that we are doing, that is being done by all kingdoms throughout this Cosmic Being, can, and eventually will be seen to be an act of continuous bliss, of supreme beauty. It is only drudge and hell if we allow the fractors with which we are dealing in ourselves to get the better of us. This experience is of the Great Illusion, Maya. Once this glamor is dismantled, we enter the Pathless Path which restores the few grains of matter to their former glory; at which time we also achieve Illumination. As each Life within substance (in incarnation), be it hu-man, hornet, heavenly hosts, hedge in a field, or heliocentric organism in the outer limits of cosmos, or whoever, achieves this non-dualistic realization of Oneness as Self, so the changes required throughout this CU will be gained. When all have done their bit, having transformed matter by their own transformed consciousness, or in other words, their recognition of their own Absoluteness and Allness, a Vast Knowing, identified not with this CU but with its own Self, as the saving CU, not as something other, but as SELF, then the restoration is complete. Then Lucifer, this CU, is set back on its own two feet, and it can then begin to function as it did before, with everything working, in their rightful place. Then the "big bang" will flash again, like an implosion, a coming into itself, and in an instant the saving CU leaves. Time then is not. Dualism is ended. The work is completed. The purpose is achieved.

14. All that exists in this CU are brothers in the saving CU. We came together and we work with the same common aim.

All that is sensed, everything that is in the realm of the sensory, can be seen to be the workings of the Brothers of Light. Everything on earth, in the planetary system, in the constellations, and cosmoses, are workers from our CU. Incredibly, at first thought, everything that exists is of our CU. We might even put it more esoterically: everything is the SELF, you, me, it. THAT. This even includes our matter, form-selves. The duality is lost when we achieve enlightenment, or put more accurately, when we realize that WE ARE ALREADY COSMICALLY ENLIGHTENED. During our progress towards this state, we call it evolution. We work together with our brothers—be they pebbles, plants, platypuses, people, planetary beings, etc. We have one purpose and goal: to realize that WE ARE ALREADY COSMICALLY ENLIGHTENED. Our work here will then be finished. The way to this complexly simple state of being is to recognize all as brothers working towards the same end and to maintain the presence of awareness of the Life, or Monad Self, which is the Real You (cf. PASE, see p. 279).

15. To save/heal this CU is enormously complex. It requires the Life Principle to be an impregnating force within the matter or substance of the whole of this CU.

The Life Principle is the Cosmically Enlightened Self. We need to allow it to flower through our form. We need to accept it as the non-duality, all-encompassing state of peace, beauty, bliss, ultimate reality of who we are. Never mind the others. Never mind the plants, the minerals, the animals, the higher and lower beings on all the different levels. We all work under strict guidelines and cosmic rules and laws according to our nature and individual purpose. At all levels this work is being carried forward. The transformation is succeeding. The Life Principle of every entity that originally came into this CU at the time of the Flash, has been gathering matter and substance into itself and via life and death and rebirth as an endless chain reaction, so the fallen entity is being re-engineered; the machinery of its expression is being re-harnessed to its original energy, and everything is being restored to its rightful place. We don't need to do anything. The Cosmic Being in us, the Cosmic Being who is you, will achieve the result desired; you need do nothing at all. Says the poem: "Just live, simply live."[11]

16. The first step was just to "get into" this CU, the nature of which is so totally different from that of the saving CU.

That is, the acceptance of "form" and "other" self, and many intermediaries to the true self, ranging from the actual physical form to the emotional and mental, abstract mind and intuitive self, up to atmic self, and this both on the cosmic physical plane and on the cosmic levels themselves (for other higher conscious identities). Only the Life Self, the Zero Point, the Beginningless Being of Light is not of form. It is ONE. It needs nothing and no one. It is Life; it is Purpose; it is Fulfilled; it is Bliss. It is a vague hint of what religions call God. But it is not "out there," rather it is our True Self on a Cosmic Scale. We entered the collapsed CU and sacrificed all except this Perfect and Enlightened Self. But this too was "covered," or "veiled" so that we would forget it in our identifying work of salvation of substance. But the irony is that only by finding ourselves as the Enlightened Self, that has always been since the Beginningless Reality, could and can we complete this saving healing work.

17. The second step is to "live out a life" within the CU.

Having realized the truth of the Enlightened Self that has Always Been, we can accept that life within this fallen, wounded, comatose, paralyzed Cosmic Being means just that, viz., living out one's life. This involves releasing transforming fractors and the illusions of this CU, and reconnecting with the truth of who we really are. Then there is no glamor attached as to who we are in the personality, what achievements we gain or have in the personality life, even what consciousness we claim to have. All we need to do is to live out a life of detachment, love, and service. There is nothing to gain, there is nothing to lose (see #15, p. 277). The Self is all there is. The Absolute is in all, transforming all. There can be no judgment about anything, anyone, ideas, ideals, hopes, fears, strengths, weaknesses, etc., for each is complete and whole in itself. There is One. This is the Beauty, the Bliss. It is a Continuous PRESENCE.

18. The third step is to actively promote advanced change within substance/consciousness. This is the specific work of advanced or esoteric healing.

The transformation of substance in forms, on whatever level, from the lowest subplane to the highest cosmic dimension of this Cosmic Being is the esoteric work of the true esoteric healer. This is done by the

one who holds the ***Presence of Awareness of the Self as Enlightened***
(PASE), by living. Simply living. PETA.[12] This is the so-called **Secret
of the Lost Word.** It doesn't matter if the person is a taxi driver, a doctor, a professor, a cook, a statesman, housewife, a surfer, or whatever—
they are all just labels and of absolutely no significance in this context.
Holding the PASE (or SLW), the emphasis of the life changes. Such a
person, holding this alignment, works the wondrous work of healing. If
the person knows the art of esoteric healing as taught by teachers of the
INEH and GAEH and others, the work takes on a specific form of help
to the one being healed. It has no influence, ultimately, to the one healing and is no greater or less than a gardener or priest who has reached
the stage of PASE. But approaching the state of PASE during the act
of esoteric healing has significant healing help to the one healing, as to
the one receiving the healing. In both cases the "fractors" are being re-
patterned and transformed for the great expression of PASE.

19. *The fourth step is to live within that pure state of* LIFE *without being
    deflected into the fractors of that life.*

How is PASE achieved? In esoteric healing, or in esotericism in
general, we have learned two major truths.

A) That Energy follows Thought (and that Effects follow Thought).

B) That the principle of "As If" becomes real the more it is practiced.

These two occult truths can help us who are in the uninspired,
unenlightened state—the more we recognize that our true nature is
Absolute Enlightenment, the Monadic Being of Light, Life Itself, and
that everyone else is also, and that all kingdoms are going through the
phases of restoring this to their consciousness, and that the very business
of restoration is the reality of healing the patterns of the distressed CU
on whatever level we operate (whether we may be operating as an atom,
an asteroid, an ape, an aster in the field, or as an archangel of cosmic
consciousness). So using these two truisms, as we work with PASE, is
the journey, the Path, healing. We all have the same work or purpose
according to the domain we have been attributed from the beginning.
Every time we deviate into the senses, the desires, the wants, and hates,
loves and fears, lusts, hopes, wishes, etc., we stumble into the fractors
of our lives. The fractors of our life are the very patterns of substance
on all levels we are trying to repair—the illusions and glamors of our

lives which need transforming. The more we recognize this at the time of stumbling, the more we are imbuing these threads of fallen matter with the light of our PASE. Transformation, transmutation, and transfer are progressed within us (within the CU of whom we have temporarily become a part).

20. *Completion of the work for this CU is for the life of the saving/healing CU to return back to its original home. This can only be achieved when the fourth step is continuous in the life and on all levels of being within the consciousness of this CU.*

When PASE is continuous, the work and purpose has been achieved by us in our own realm. The pattern (mechanism) of the CU is restored. We, as individuals, stand ready to return to our own "Home." When all beings of the saving CU have done their destined work, we will abandon the saved CU and leave It to continue Its own Life. We will leave with love and understanding. We will have achieved for the CU the consciousness It fell from. We will leave (the "Way of Escape") all we have achieved to the saved CU. We will take nothing back. We will return as we came.

9.

HEALING YOURSELF

To treat yourself using esoteric healing is very easy. There are two methods of self-healing. In the first method, treat yourself as a stranger. In this way you can keep detached from the therapy you apply to yourself intuitively and from the results that will start working through your bodies and consciousness. With your eyes closed, visualize yourself as being in front of you, and as though you were a patient you had not met before. Then make your alignment and attunement as usual. Next, assess the balance of the centers (diagnose the centers in the ajna); do the four energy triangles, the synchronizing triangle and then start working through the triangles as necessary for your condition and as the intuition dictates. This should last for about 15-30 minutes. You conclude by balancing the centers against their opposites by closing the Healing Triangle just as you would for consulting patients.

The second method is very similar to the first, but here you actually work on the centers in your body. Do not visualize the etheric outside but reach each center either directly or in visualization. For example, point a finger at yourself and visualize the energy flowing to the center or triangle, thus avoiding getting the arms in a knot! Then do the healing on yourself as you would on another patient, pointing and directing energy into yourself (rather than into your projected self). Both these methods are effective. Try them both, and use the one suited to your needs. You may even combine the methods in a sitting.

10.

SEVEN ADVANCED "MAGICAL" HEALING TECHNIQUES

This information is given only because I know there are some advanced healers who will benefit from it. Since space is limited, I am presenting the ray technique as written by Alice Bailey in the final section of her book, *Esoteric Healing*, and providing a very brief interpretation.

The ray techniques are given in the form of seven ancient symbolic statements or formulas, gathered out of the Book of Rules for Initiated Disciples. I quote from DK: "I dare not yet give the simple physical application of these ray techniques, as it would be too dangerous. When rightly used and understood they carry terrific force and—in the wrong hands—could work real damage ... the lowest significance the modern student may succeed in interpreting for himself if he reflects adequately and lives spiritually" (Bailey, 1951–70, v. 4, pp. 705–6). This lowest or most general interpretation I offer simply to make these techniques more accessible to a wider group of healers interested in the rays, and also to stimulate a deeper understanding from those already well-versed in the ray philosophy. Read also the hints and indications given in *Esoteric Healing*. The earnest esoteric healer, by following the indications I have given for each technique, could apply the specific ray rulers given in Chapter 5 for each of the centers to develop a ray technique for each of the three stages of human development, viz., for undeveloped or average people, for developed people or disciples, and for advanced people or initiates (see pp. 74–77). This is an important hint for the one who would take it up, and refers directly to the words of the Master: "These seven techniques or magical statements are susceptible of three significances" (p. 706).

I am also listing the major group of diseases and illnesses related to each ray. These are associated with the seven ray causes of disease, which can in turn be used in connection with the specific technique (pp. 292, 298–305). (Regarding these techniques, I acknowledge the input given by the students of the University of the Seven Rays in UK and USA.)

Ray I technique

(Aries; lesser influence on Leo and Capricorn)

Let the dynamic force which rules the hearts of all within Shamballa come to my aid, for I am worthy of that aid. Let it descend unto the third, pass to the fifth and focus on the seventh. These words mean not what doth at [first] sight appear. The third, the fifth, the seventh lie within the first and come from out the Central Sun of spiritual livingness. The highest then awakens within the one who knows and within the one who must be healed and thus the two are one. This is mystery deep. The blending of the healing force effects the work desired; it may bring death, that great release, and re-establish thus the fifth, the third, the first, but not the seventh (Bailey, 1951–70, v. 4, p. 707).

INTERPRETATION

"Let the dynamic force which rules the hearts of all within Shamballa come to my aid, for I am worthy of that aid." This is the heart element of the first ray force of will and power, both destructive and constructive. The healer works from the heart-in-the-head center.

"Let it descend unto the third, pass to the fifth and focus on the seventh. These words mean not what doth at [first] sight appear." At first we may think this refers to the centers, but actually the numbers refer to the planes. The will force must be allowed to descend to the third (atmic) plane, pass to the fifth (mind) plane and focus on the seventh (physical) plane.

"The third, the fifth, the seventh lie within the first and come from out the Central Sun of spiritual livingness." The Central Spiritual Sun is first ray, related to the place where the will of God is known, Shamballa. Three, five and seven are in the same line (the so-called "hard" rays or "will" line of energy progression).

"The highest then awakens within the one who knows and within the one who must be healed and thus the two are one. This is mystery deep. The blending of the healing force effects the work desired; it may bring death, that great release, and re-establish thus the fifth, the third, the first, but not the seventh." This is the healing treatment. The highest spiritual energy vibrates in unison or harmony with the one to be healed. The two synchronize. The result is destruction leading to healing, or destruction leading to death of the physical body ("... not the seventh").

This is the triangle you hold if the patient has a first ray soul: Head center (healer) to head center (patient) to the center governing the threatening disease.

Here are the triangles to hold if the patient has a first-ray personality but does not have a first-ray soul:

1. If the seat of the trouble is the base center: sacral (healer) to sacral (patient) to base.
2. If the seat of the trouble is the sacral center: throat (healer) to throat (patient) to sacral.
3. If the seat of the trouble is the solar plexus center: throat (healer) to throat (patient) to solar plexus.
4. If the seat of the trouble is the heart center: throat (healer) to throat (patient) to heart.
5. If the seat of the trouble is the throat center: ajna (healer) to ajna (patient) to throat.
6. If the seat of the trouble is the ajna center: head (healer) to head (patient) to ajna.
7. If the seat of the trouble is the head center: soul (healer) to soul (patient) to head center.

You will note that we use the "hard" ray closest to the center in trouble.

If death is indicated, allow the patient's soul and personality to awaken and blend, and then release the physical body.

Ray I causes of disease:

Key: Pain and Sorrow; the Destroyer.

Soul calling for: Synthesis (Bailey, 1951–70, v. 2, p. 220); Inclusion; Isolated Unity.

Other connections: Touch; the Occultist; the Law of Vibration (Bailey, 1962, p. 574); the Law of Repulse; Sense of Time; Singleness of Purpose.

Indications of first ray activity suggesting use of the first ray technique:

Crystallization, gall stones, kidney stones, gout, autoimmune diseases, including certain types of arthritis, ankylosing spondelitis, atherosclerosis, TMJ (jaw) clenching, calcification of the pineal gland, some kinds of cancer (Bailey, 1951–70, v. 4, p. 383), hard tumors, keratosis, anorexia, autism (blocked frontal brain), tightness, tension, retention (e.g., chronic constipation), ideé fixe (obsessions from the mental plane), breaking bones, death, Parkinson's disease, rigidity in body, denial, egotism, arrogance, destructiveness, suicide (the will to die), killers, murderers, hardness, suppression, relentless control, inhibition, love of power, solitariness, foot binding (as in China, which has a Ray I soul).

Initiation: the Fifth: Revelation (a glimpse of the Seven Paths in Shamballa).

Statement: I still persist.

Ray Word of Power: I assert the fact.

Ray II technique

(Gemini; lesser influence on Virgo and Pisces)

> Let the healing energy descend, carrying its dual lines of life and its magnetic force. Let that magnetic living force withdraw and supplement that which is present in the seventh, opposing four and six to three and seven, but dealing not with five. The circular, inclusive vortex—descending to the point—disturbs, removes and then supplies and thus the work is done.

> The heart revolves; two hearts revolve as one; the twelve within the vehicle, the twelve within the head and the twelve upon the plane of soul endeavor, cooperate as one and thus the work is done. Two energies achieve this consummation and the three whose number is a twelve respond to the greater twelve. The life is known and the years prolonged (Bailey, 1951–70, v. 4, pp. 707–8).

INTERPRETATION

The use of this technique is as follows: hold the heart center in a triangle with the base (four) and solar plexus (six) and then with the adaptive mind allow these centers to oppose the sacral (three) and ajna (seven). This forms two tetrahedrons with the one triangle of heart, base and solar plexus (one to the sacral; the other to the ajna). Once this is held, open the heart to the linking twelves (the heart itself with its four valves, four chambers and four vessels, the heart lotuses on higher levels, the causal body and the Hierarchy, connecting with the second ray energy itself), hence, healing will occur, "the life is known and the years prolonged."

Another suggestion for this technique: the seventh is the physical plane where you are working with the magnetic, disturbing *force* of the life energy. You hold the buddhic and astral energies together in balance—four and six—and the spiritual will with the physical will-to-be in incarnation—atmic with physical—but do not activate the mind or manasic principle. This is what you do: as the healer make a triangle with your heart center, heart-in-the-head center, and heart of the soul (the twelve petals of the egoic lotus). Now allow this triangle to act as an interactive transmitter between the heart center of your patient and the greater twelve of the Maitreya and the Life Energy of the Monad (2nd Ray).

Try both possibilities to see which suits your patient better.

Ray II causes of disease:

Key: Suffocation; Centralization.

Soul calling for: Illumination, e.g., physical sight due to astral illusion and concrete knowledge; Occult Vision; Love and Wisdom; Radiance.

Other connections: Intuition; the True Psychic; the Law of Cohesion; the Law of Magnetic Impulse; Power to Save.

Indications of second-ray activity suggesting use of the second-ray technique:

Cancer (the majority), soft tumors, pericarditis, hydrocephalus, cysts, endometriosis, hyperglandular conditions, fungal diseases, leukemia, high blood pressure, asthma (allergic type), emphysema, diseases of the immune system, heart attack, hyperactivity (restlessness), bronchitis, pneumonia, lymphomas, circulatory problems, tuberculosis, extra organs, fear, self-pity, over-sensitivity, attachment, psychic excesses, love of being loved, over-study, gluttony, coldness, indifference, contempt for mental limitations in others, over-accumulation of things.

Initiation: The Seventh: Resurrection.

Statement: Naught is but Me.

Ray Word of Power: I see the greater light.

Ray III technique

(Libra; lesser influence on Cancer and Capricorn)

> The healer stands and weaves. He gathers from the three, the five, the seven that which is needed for the heart of life. He brings the energies together and makes them serve the third; he thus creates a vortex into which the one distressed must descend and with him goes the healer. And yet they both remain in peace and calm. Thus must the angel of the Lord descend into the pool and bring the healing life (Bailey, 1951–70, v. 4, p. 708).

INTERPRETATION

Make a triangle from the sacral center to throat center to base center, since these are the centers governed by the astral ray influences. Place the heart center in the middle of the triangle and visualize the third ray energy descending to it, dispelling the astral force flowing into the solar plexus center.

Next, make a triangle between the three head centers (as one), the five centers up the spine (as one), and the solar plexus center. In the center of this triangle visualize the heart (the healing life). Allow the third ray force to "descend into the pool" and thus resist the astral glamor in which the patient is engulfed (see below for the diseases and conditions which indicate this).

Ray III causes of disease:

Key: Manipulation.

Soul symptom: Separative and selfish behavior.

Soul calling for: Cooperation.

Other connections: Sight; the Magician; Law of Economy; Spheroidal Forms; Rotary Movement (Bailey, 1962, pp. 40, 48); Law of Disintegration (p. 580); Stillness. Law of Expansive Response; Power to Manifest; Power to Evolve; the Weaver.

Indications of third-ray activity requiring the third-ray technique:

Solar plexus related diseases, astral-plane related diseases, gastrointestinal (GI) tract problems, GI sphincter spasm, stomach ulcers, ulcerative colitis, irritable bowel syndrome, colitis, gastritis, spastic colon, liver problems, pancreas problems, gall bladder problems, spleen problems, anorexia, bulemia, ulcers, hyperthyroidism, hypoglycemia, esophageal problems, arrhythmia, obesity, diabetes mellitus, anxiety or panic attacks, low vitality, brain disorders, syphilitic diseases, manic depressive, epilepsy, mental pride, criticism, obsessive/compulsive behavior, schizophrenia, over-complex thoughts, carelessness, manipulation, opportunism, deviousness, lying, indecisiveness, overadaptablility.

Initiation: The Sixth: Ascension or Decision.

Statement: I am the Worker and the Work, the One that Is.

Ray Word of Power: Purpose itself am I.

Ray IV technique

(Scorpio; lesser influence on Taurus and Sagittarius)

The healer knows the place where dissonance is found. He also knows the power of sound and the sound which must be heard. Knowing the note to which the fourth great group reacts and linking it to the great Creative Nine, he sounds the note which brings release, the note which will bring absorption into one. He educates the listening ear of him who must be healed; he likewise trains the listening ear of him who must go forth. He knows the manner of the sound which brings the healing touch; and also that which says: Depart. And thus the work is done (Bailey, 1951–70, v. 4, p 709).

INTERPRETATION

There are two uses for this technique: one for death, the other for life.

If the person to be healed is dying, form a triangle from the Soul (linked to the base center), to the throat center, to the heart center. Then play continuously the pure E note. This sound will bring release of the life thread.

For life, use the same triangle as above, and as you hold the triangle and visualize the energy flow, play music, especially that which is keyed or composed in E. But any creative, beautiful music will do the work required, particularly music the patient prefers.

Ray IV causes of disease:

Key: Diffusion.

Soul symptom: Warfare and Struggle.

Soul calling for: A Search for Meaning and its Revelation; Harmony; Rest; Peace; Synthesis of True Beauty.

Other connections: Smell; the Artist; Law of Magnetic Control; the Law of Sacrifice; Power to Reveal the Path; Power to Reveal the Past; the Harmony of the Spheres.

Indications of fourth-ray activity indicating the fourth-ray technique:

Acute viral infectious diseases, epidemics, influenza, diseases due to debility and devitalization, insanities, asthma (viral), ME (postviral syndrome, chronic fatigue syndrome—see also Ray VII), AIDS, kidney diseases, temperamental problems, lack of stability, unpredictability, unreliability, confusion, vacillation, despair, self-abuse, addiction, suicidal tendencies, depression, psychosis, narcissism, over-eagerness for compromise, inertia, turmoil, self-absorption in suffering, lack of confidence, worry, moodiness, exaggeration, dramatic type, the artist.

Initiation: The Fourth, Crucifixion/Renunciation.

Statement: Beauty and Glory veil me not. I stand revealed. I am.

Ray Word of Power: Two merge in one.

Ray V technique

(Leo; lesser influence on Sagittarius and Aquarius)

That which has been given must be used; that which emerges from within the given mode will find its place within the healer's plan. That which is hidden must be seen and from the three, great knowledge will emerge. For these the healer seeks. To these the healer adds the two which are as one, play its part and the five must function as if one. The energies descend, pass through and disappear, leaving the one who could respond with karma yet to dissipate and taking with them him who may not thus respond and so must likewise disappear (Bailey, 1951–70, v. 4, p. 710).

INTERPRETATION

The person who is indicated for this technique (see below) must also be taking appropriate physical care as applied by the medical therapist of the patient's choice or the healer's recommendation. The healer should hold the following triangle: ajna, which is receptive to fifth-ray energy, throat center and alta major center (the five centers in one) or heart center, as this is the last center of transference to ajna. The healer is to feel which of these two centers is right for the particular patient. Group therapy and social involvement is important for right healing.

Ray V causes of disease:

Keynote: Cleavage.
Soul symptom: Over-Analytical and Critical; Detachment.
Soul calling for: Understanding Leading to Identification; Revelation of the Way; Manifestation of the Great White Light.
Other connections: Mind; the Scientist; Law of Fixation; Law of the Lower Four; Power to make the Voice of the Silence Heard.
Indications of fifth-ray activity requiring the fifth-ray technique:

Cleavages (psychological), mental disorders, dyslexia/catatonia, insanities, brain lesions, migraine, metabolic diseases (blockages), cancers (types), imbecilities, retardation, senility, antisocial behavior, psychopaths, over-analysis, excessive doubt, rigid atheism, classism, separativeness (eg. racists), irreverence, excess objectivity, rigidity, narrowness, harsh criticism, social awkwardness, associative disassociation states (i.e. believing themselves to be someone else, e.g. as a child).
Initiation: The Third, Transfiguration.
Statement: I mastered energy for I am energy itself. The Master and the mastered are but One.
Ray Word of Power: Three minds unite.

Ray VI technique

(Sagittarius; lesser influence on Virgo and Pisces)

Cleaving the waters, let the power descend, the healer cries. He minds not how the waters may respond; they oft bring stormy waves and dire and dreadful happenings. The end is good. The trouble will be ended when the storm subsides and energy has fulfilled its charted destiny. Straight to the heart the power is forced to penetrate, and into every channel, nadi, nerve and spleen the power must seek a passage and a way and thus confront the enemy who has effected entrance and settled down to live. Ejection—ruthless, sudden and complete—is undertaken by the one who sees naught else but perfect functioning and brooks no interference. This perfect functioning opens thus the door to life eternal or to life on earth for yet a little while (Bailey, 1951–70, v. 4, p. 711).

INTERPRETATION

This technique is also for healing (life) or to help the dying. This technique also may be employed alongside the Fertility Triangles, for it can "open the door... to life on earth" (p. 711). DK recommends that people who have a sixth-ray soul do not use this technique, for it is too drastic and potent. The healer is called on to build the following triangle: head center (open to the sixth-ray energy, "let the power descend"), down to the solar plexus center ("cleaving the waters" of the astral glamors and perversions), to the heart center (from which the energies will be distributed to affect the whole body, channel, nadi, nerve and spleen).

The therapy should include the Taste Triangle, for help towards right discrimination and creativity; heart activities (to evoke compassion); and singing.

Ray VI causes of disease:

Keynote: Perversion.

Soul symptom: Cruelty and Sadism.

Soul calling for: One-pointed Purpose and Devotion to the Ideal; Restraint.

Other connections: Taste; the Devotee; Law of Love; Law of Service; Power to Kill Out Desire.

Indications of sixth-ray activity requiring the sixth-ray technique:

Sexual diseases, sexual perversions and misuse, sexually transmitted diseases, sadistic cruelty, impulsive rape, violent sex, sexual abuse, rigid idealism, emotionalism, selfish love, jealous love, dependency, unreasoning devotion, masochism, excesses in all things, mania, sex cults, cannibalism, genetic engineering leading to perversion, self-immolation.

Initiation: The Second, Baptism.
Statement: I am the seeker and the sought. I rest.
Ray Word of Power: The highest light controls.

Ray VII technique

(Capricorn; lesser influence on Aries and Cancer)

Energy and force must meet each other and thus the work is done.
Color and sound in ordered sequence must meet and blend and thus the
work of magic can proceed. Substance and spirit must evoke each other
and, passing through the center of the one who seeks to aid, produce the
new and good. The healer energizes thus with life the failing life, driving it forth or anchoring it yet more deeply in the place of destiny. All
seven must be used and through the seven there must pass the energies
the need requires, creating the new man who has for ever been and will
for ever be, and either here or there (Bailey, 1951–70, v. 4, p. 712).

INTERRPRETATION

The interpretation and use of this technique involves holding the
following triangle: the center in the healer corresponding to the patient's
soul ray. For example, if the patient is soul ray two, the healer holds their
own heart center, which also must be opened up to the energy of the Lord
of the Seventh Ray. This center then radiates out in two directions to the
other points in the triangle: to the heart center in the head (life thread,
energy-spirit); and to the base center (force, personality, substance).
These two latter points link all the seven centers producing the new and
good—the new man.

The therapy should include work with rhythms (dancing, music,
drumming), and sequential activities.

Ray VII causes of disease:

Keynote: Promiscuity.
Soul symptom: Stickler for Time; Haste; Frustration.
Soul calling for: Rhythmic Living; Orientation.

Other connections: Hearing; the Ritualist; Law of Sacrifice and Death; Law of Group Progress; Power to Create and to Cooperate; Power to Vivify.

Indications of seventh ray activity requiring the seventh ray technique:

Infectious diseases (slow as well as bacterial or fungal), autoimmune deficiency syndrome (AIDS), chronic fatigue syndrome (see also Ray IV), parasites, candida (fungus), bacterial conditions (e.g., vaginitis), heart disorders (astral only), tumors (astral only), cysts, fibrocystic diseases, various types of hypertrophy, leprosy, rigid order, overconcern with rules, subservience to habits, bigotry, perfection, sex magic, addictions to occult phenomena, perversions of magical processes and rituals, lack of originality, dishonor of other life-forms (genetic work on plants and animals), SIDS (sudden infant death syndrome), exclusive cults, electromagnetic pollution.

Initiation: The First, Birth.

Statement: The creative work is over. I, the Creator, am. Naught else remains but Me.

Ray Word of Power: The highest and the lowest meet.

The two highest initiations have not been included in the seven ray qualities as they involve groups of rays, as follows: the Eighth Initiation of Transition involves all the Rays of Attribute. The Ninth Initiation of Refusal (Choosing a Path) involves all the Rays of Aspect.

"The healer in the New Age does not and will not work directly with the physical body at all; being an occultist, he will regard that body as not a principle. He works practically entirely with the etheric body and with the vital energies, leaving those energies to make their impact on the automaton of the physical body according to directed intent; they will then produce their effect according to the response of that body, conditioned as it will be by many factors. The healer has to think clearly before he can bring about the desired results, but the energy poured into the patient's vehicle is not mental energy, but one of the seven forms of pranic or life energy. This travels along the line of force or the channel which relates and links all the centers and connects those centers with the glands." —Djwhal Khul (Bailey, 1951–70, v. 4, p. 538).

11.

CASE HISTORIES

The case histories here presented are random examples of what an esoteric healer does. Each case included, by the Esoteric Healing Group Clinic in the U.K., a full treatment which may have lasted for many weeks. The points here shown have been deliberately kept simple and are merely for interest in the hope they will be of some help and encouragement to the new healer. These indications and methods do not mean they should be used for other patients with similar symptoms. Each person is unique and requires individual treatment, allowing the soul and intuition to inform and direct the therapy.

Clinical sketch 1: A woman says she is constantly irritable and angry, and frequently has nightmares. She complains of occasional dizziness, but otherwise feels in good health. Her general practitioner has found she has slightly high blood pressure, but no other problem. He suggests that the patient see a psychiatrist to deal with her mental state. The esoteric healing group finds she has an overstimulated Liver Triangle of Force with a strong involvement of the throat center. The major triangles the group works with are: the Liver Triangle of Force, the Gall Bladder Triangle, the PSL Triangle, the Stomach Triangle, and the GIT (gastrointestinal tract) Triangle (throat center, solar plexus center, and the etheric gastrointestinal system as a whole), and the triangle for irritation (the Triangle for Imperil). The Blood Pressure Triangle is also included at first. We work primarily in the astral/emotional body. Such treatment cools and disperses excess energy being deflected to the liver from the solar plexus center, markedly improving her condition.

Clinical sketch 2: A male patient complains of difficulty in urinating, a problem that gradually has become more frequent over the last few years. He tells us his GP diagnosed a prostate condition. We notice he is very pale and wearing a lot of sweaters. He tells us he has always disliked the cold. The esoteric healing group finds he has a very weak Kidney Triangle (base center and the two etheric kidney organs) and that the Prostate Triangle (sacral center, etheric gonad glands and etheric prostate gland) is unbalanced and overactive. The major triangles the group works with are: the Basic Triangle, the sacral triangles, the Prostate Triangle, the Fear Triangle and the Heart Triangle. We work primarily in the etheric body to stimulate the circulation of vital force through these triangles together, thereby reducing the overactive condition of the prostate. The patient speaks with interest of new contacts and relationships, and that the urinary problem has become less of a bother.

Clinical sketch 3: A man with an upper respiratory infection comes to the clinic. He feels chilled and has a stuffed nose, a slight fever, and a pounding headache. The esoteric healing group finds that the lung minors are in a poor condition due to a deficient throat center. The major triangles the group works with are the Respiratory Triangle, and the Immune Triangle. The next day the patient reported his headache had gone by the time he had reached home and that he felt a lot better. He had taken no external treatment. I suggested he come again in a week for further preventive treatment. He did and the major triangles the group worked with were: the Service Triangles, the Diaphragm Triangle, the Immune Triangle, the Touch Triangle (from the heart center in this case) and the Ear Triangle. This man was interested in dowsing and the group found it necessary to work on the higher and wider aspects of hearing and sound as well as of touch and contacts (the hand minors were indicated here).

Clinical sketch 4: A young woman comes to us who is unable to sit for very long due to an acute back problem. She has seen over the years an osteopath, a chiropractor, and a medical herbalist, and, finally, since nothing else helped for very long, she asked for our help. We looked at her X-rays and saw where the problem lay: in the second and third lumbar vertebral disks of her spine. The disks were practically nonexistent. The esoteric healing group finds that her base center, sacral center and throat center are particularly low in energy. The major triangles the group works with are: the Service Triangles, the Lower Clearing Triangle, the Sacral Triangles, the Basic Triangles, the Fear Triangle, and the Eye Triangles (she is a person on the spiritual path, so we use the appropriate triangles for this state of consciousness). The group finds she is in need of more focussed vision and a personality-will to grasp that vision. She finds almost immediate relief from the pain and she decides to pursue her interest in art. She returns to the clinic weekly for many months. Although she is not cured in the ordinary sense, her sense of confidence and direction have given her a new sense of purpose. She is able to live almost normally now.

Clinical sketch 5: A woman with stomach cancer comes to us and expresses a deep fear of dying. She was given six months to live. We find that the solar plexus center is the major cause of this condition. The major triangles the group works with are: the Cancer Triangles, the Stomach Triangle, the PSL Triangle, the Fear Triangle, the Force Triangles and the Lower Clearing Triangle. There was no evident improvement of the cancer, although we were able to speak with her on many occasions about death as a phase of transition. This brought her comfort.

Clinical sketch 6: A woman with arthritis in her fingers and hips comes to us saying that the condition had significantly worsened since she had moved from another part of the country. She had lost all incentive to get involved in anything. We find her throat center is hardly active at all and her base center is difficult to balance. The major triangles the group works with are: the Service Triangles, the Basic Triangles, the Parathyroid Triangle and the Lymphatic Triangles. This is a very chronic case and the progress forward was very slow. She came to us for years, which suggested that the soul was definitely keen to work out the problem despite the rigid personality. She did show she had moved somewhat. The astral condition had fixed itself in the etheric body, using the minute centers as anchors and excuses for inaction.

Clinical sketch 7: A child with a squint was brought to us by his mother. He had been born with this condition in both his eyes, and had been going to the local eye hospital for regular check-ups. He was short-sighted in one eye and long-sighted in the other. He was a very shy boy who lacked confidence and who tended to be short-tempered and rude, but who could be very gentle and responsive at times. We find that his sacral center needs the most work. The major triangles the group works with are: the sacral triangles on the etheric and astral levels, the Basic Triangle, since this was very arrhythmical in its energy, the eye triangles (we used the disciple triangles, since he was still very much in the higher world, as children are), and the Fear Triangle. After the first treatment the boy responds in a way that was quite beyond belief, becoming calmer, more sensitive to the family, and generally much more integrated in his behavior. The eyes, however, show no improvement and he is to have an operation to improve the squint. Remarkably, subsequent to the operation, he does not need to wear glasses.

Clinical sketch 8: A man with muscular dystrophy comes for healing; he has a keen intellect and a wide range of interests, a teacher by profession. The esoteric healing group finds his head center overactive and his alta major center unresponsive. The major triangles the group works with are: the Immune Triangle, the Base Triangles (especially relating to the spine), the Head Triangle and the Taste Triangle. After some treatments he becomes even more intent on overcoming this muscular wasting by doing exercises and dietary cleansing. Physical improvement is not noticeable, although he appears much better in himself and is determined to succeed. He is thankful for the healing and believes it to be very helpful. He discontinues his treatments after the ninth visit.

Clinical sketch 9: A woman with angina comes to see us who suffers periodically from pain in the chest when walking or over-working. She has her own successful business, but it is taking its toll on her heart. She is taking orthodox medicine for the pain. We find she is well balanced in the solar plexus center, but the vagus nerve center and heart center are both over-fired. The major triangles the group works with are: the

Pranic Triangle, the Blood Pressure Triangle, the Diaphragm Triangle, Eye Triangle, the Triangle of Being and the Synchronizing Triangle. We use these triangles because she is quite an advanced person on the path of spiritual development. However, she has not been able, due to the pressure of work, to bridge the gap securely between her personality work and her soul work, hence the strain on the heart. The therapy causes her to regulate her diet more strictly than before, and she joins an environmental group to give her a change of focus. She also assigns herself more time for meditation and relaxation. After some months she reported that the angina had not troubled her for some time.

Clinical sketch 10: On a different note, I would like to indicate another healing activity that our healing group has performed. These concern the wider aspects of healing. Here are a few examples. Esoteric healing can also be helpful to sick animals, but it is not a practice that is easily performed. It is usually done for the healer's own pets or for friends' pets (in "person" or as distant healing). A healing group can be formed to work at healing "planetary illnesses" (international fear, greed, superiority, power, materialism, evil separatism, terrorism, exploitation, and so on), which may include the relationship between animals and humans. This can be helpful in the long term especially considering factory farming, vivisection and animal sports, not to speak of the cruelty and greed of certain groups of people working under the banner of supplying industry or manufacturers with natural animal products. The major triangles the group works with are: the human kingdom as a whole (this can be visualized as a planetary throat center), the particular human group perpetrating the crime (visualize this as a minor center closely linked with the planetary solar plexus center), and the animal species involved, or simply with the human kingdom, the animal kingdom and the Earth (as a vital living energy).

Note: This healing group has disbanded due to circumstances beyond their control. However, the individual members continue healing. Due to our long association (15 years), we remain deeply connected on the soul level.

12.

QUICK REFERENCE SUMMARY

Summary of opening the healing treatment

Note: When opening triangles, the intuition will direct the healer where to place the hands. But as a general principle, the Ajna usually connects with the highest of the centers being worked with and the hands connect with the centers nearest to them.

A. ALIGNMENT AND ATTUNEMENT (P. 147)

1. Alignment
2. Higher Triangle (Healer's Soul—Patient's Soul—Source of Power, Love and Light)
3. Opening the Triangles of Healing:
   i)   Radiatory (Soul—Brain—Heart Center, and to the aura)
   ii) Magnetic (Soul—Heart Center—Brain)
   (For working with the Rays, open the Greater then the Lesser Triangles) (pp. 149–151, or see p. 306)
4. Protecting Triangle (Heart Center—Head Center—Patient)
5. Activating Triangles:
   i)   Placing Triangle (Head Center—Alta Major Center—Ajna Center)
   ii) Vitalizing Triangle (Pineal gland—Carotid gland—Pituitary body)
   iii) Directing Triangle (Right Eye—Left Eye—Ajna Center)
6. Triangle of Transfer (Ajna Center—Hand Minor Centers)

B. Diagnosis (p. 155)

Diagnosing the center "of greatest need" in the aura and the ajna center

The triangles of esoteric healing

What follows is a complete summary of all the esoteric healing triangles in this book. The number of each triangle (e.g. 6. Stomach Triangle) is the same numeral as in Chapter 7.

C. Vitalization of the Bodies of the Patient (p. 157)

Vitality triangles

1. Pranic Triangle (Vagus Nerve Center—Center Below Heart Center—Spleen minor)
2. Spleen Triangle of Force (Spleen minor—Sacral Center—Base Center)
2. Spleen Triangle (Solar Plexus Center—Spleen minor—Spleen)
3. Immortality Triangle (Throat Center—Pituitary gland—Pineal gland, transmuted from Spleen Triangle of Force)
4. Lower Prana Triangle (Spleen minor—Base Center—Throat Center)

D. Esoteric Healing Treatment (p. 163)

[At this point the Synchronizing Triangle is done, following the indication given during the assessment of the major centers in the ajna center.]

Triangles for the gastrointestinal tract

5. Liver Triangle of Force (Solar Plexus Center—Stomach minor—Liver minor)
5. Liver Triangle (Solar Plexus Center—Liver minor—Liver)
5. Gall Bladder Triangle (Solar Plexus Center—Stomach minor—Gall Bladder point)
6. Stomach Triangle (Solar Plexus Center—Stomach minor—Stomach)

7. Astral Preparation Triangle (Head Center of Healer—Solar Plexus Center of Healer—Astral Body of Patient)

8. Mental Congestion Triangle (Head Center of Healer—Head Center of Patient—Centers below diaphragm of Patient)

9. GIT Triangles (Throat Center—Solar Plexus Center—Intestinal Point)

10. Triangle for Imperil (Solar Plexus Center—Head Center—Heart Center)

11. PSL Triangle (Pancreas—Stomach—Liver)

12. Diabetes Triangle (Solar Plexus Center—Stomach Minor—Base Center)

13. Lower Clearing Triangle (Solar Plexus Center—Heart Center—Ajna Center)

13. Triangle for Spiritual Facilitation (Ajna Center—Heart Center—Heart-in-the-Head, with Solar Plexus Center) (see #66)

14. Responsive Triangle (Soul of Patient—Ajna Center—Heart Center)

14. Triangles of Stability and Right Group Relation (Solar Plexus Center—Heart Center—Throat Center; then Solar Plexus Center—Sacral Center—Base Center)

15. Triangle for Dispelling Astral Glamor (Soul: Astral Body—Solar Plexus Center—Heart Center)

16. Consciousness Stream Triangle (Head Center—Astral Body—Solar Plexus Center)

Triangles for the spine and renal system

17. Basic Triangle (Base Center—Adrenal points)

18. Spinal Triangles (Base Center—Alta Major Center—Spinal Cord; see variations)

19. Triangle for Addictions or Obsessions (Base Center—Sacral Center—Throat Center)

20. Fear Triangle (Base Center—Kidney points)

21. Fear Transformation Triangle (Base Center—Solar Plexus Center—Ajna Center)

22. First Initiation Triangle (Base Center—Solar Plexus Center—Heart Center)

22. Second Initiation Triangle (Base Center—Heart Center—Throat Center)

23. Third Initiation Triangle (Heart Center—Throat Center—Seven Head Centers)

Triangles for the reproductive system

24. Sacral Triangle (Sacral Center—Gonad minors; see variations)
24. Feet Triangle (Sacral Center—Feet minors) (for use see #42)
24. Prostate Triangle (Sacral Center—Gonad minor—Prostate point)
25. Triangles of Force (Breastbone minor—Breast minors, and Sacral Center—Solar Plexus minor—Base Center)
25. Shock Triangle (Solar Plexus minor—Ileocaecal Valve point—Sigmoid point)
25. Life Stream Triangle (Head Center—Heart Center—Spleen Minor Center)
26. Triangle for Sexual Problems (Head Center—Throat Center—Sacral Center)
27. Fertility Triangles (a progression of five triangles)
27. Advanced Fertility Triangles (Sacral Center ... Adrenal points—Male gonads—Female gonads; then Sacral Center ... Adrenal points—Gonads (as one)—Base Center)
28. Triangle of Creative Energy (Throat Center—Sacral Center—Physical Body)
29. Triangle of the Practical Mystic (Sacral Center—Throat Center—Ajna Center)
30. Triangle for Creative Energy Distribution (Sacral Center—Throat Center—Ajna Center)
31. Triangle of Yoga (Buddhic—Astral—Monad)

Triangles for the cardiovascular system

32. Heart Triangle (Heart Center—two Lung minors)
33. Triangles at Death:
33. Desire Triangle (Soul—Astral Body—Solar Plexus Center)
33. Withdrawing Triangle (Soul—Head Center—Ajna Center)
33. Triangle for the Dying (Spleen Minor Center—Lung Minors—Heart Center)
33. Triangles of Force (see #25)
33. Immortality Triangle (#3)
33. Samadhi Triangles (see #39)

33. First and Fourth Ray Technique (see Chapter 9)
34. Immune Triangle (Heart Center—Spleen Center—Thigh Bone Marrow Point, Heart Center—Thymus Point—Spleen Point, Heart Center—Spleen Center—Heart in the Head Center)
35. Lymphatic Triangle (Heart Center—Lymph duct points)
36. Allergy Triangle (Vagus Nerve Center—Adrenal minute points)
37. Blood Pressure Triangles (Heart Center—Ajna Center—Spleen Minor Center) (also, Alta Major Center—Vagus Nerve Center—Base Center)
38. Kundalini Triangle (Head Center—Heart Center—Base Center ... Vagus Nerve Center)
39. Samadhi Triangles (Heart Center—Spleen Minor Center—Solar Plexus Center with Head Center—Base Center—Spleen Minor Center)

Triangles for the respiratory and metabolic systems

40. Diaphragm Triangle (Vagus Nerve Center—Diaphragm points)
41. Service Triangles (Throat Center to centers on Shoulders, Elbows and Hands). Feet Triangle (Sacral Center—Feet minors)
42. Parathyroid Triangle (Throat Center—Parathyroid points)
43. Respiratory Triangle (Throat Center—Lung minors)
44. Triangle of Purpose (Brain—Mind—Soul Will via [Sacrifice Petals])
45. Sinus Triangle (Throat—Solar Plexus—Sinus points)
45. Sound Triangle (Throat—Ear Minor—Vocal apparatus)

Triangles for the nervous system

47. Triangle for the Nerves (Ajna Center—Alta Major Center—Vagus Nerve Center)
48. Cranio-Sacral Triangle (Ajna Center—Alta Major Center—Sacral Center)
49. Migraine Triangle (Throat Center—Pituitary gland—Pineal gland)
50. Creative Fusion Triangle (Throat Center—Heart Center—Ajna Center)
51. Head Triangle (Head Center—Ajna Center—Alta Major Center)
52. Triangle of Being (Head Center—Heart Center—Base Center)
52. Triangle of Becoming (Base Center—Head Center—Ajna Center)

52. Triangle for the Majority (Ajna Center—Solar Plexus Center—Sacral Center) (see #63)
53. Triangle of the White Magician (Heart in the Head Center—Heart Center—Throat Center)
54. Synchronizing Triangle (Head Center of Healer—Center of Healer—and Corresponding Center in Patient)
55. General Healing Triangles

Triangles and the senses

56. Hearing Triangle (Throat Center—Ear minors)
57. Touch Triangle (Heart Center or Solar Plexus Center—Hand minors)
57. Psoriasis Triangle: Heart Center—Base Center—Sacral Center
58. Triangle of the Third Seed Group (Head Center—Heart Center—Ajna Center)
59. Eye Triangle (Head Center—Eye minors) (four specific triangles).
60. Triangle for Dissipating Illusion (Head Center—Ajna Center—Right Eye minor)
60. Triangle of the First Thread (Throat Center—Ajna Center—Head Center)
60. Triangle for Dissipating Glamor (Ajna Center—Left Eye—Right Eye)
60. Triangle of the Second Thread (Throat Center—Solar Plexus Center—Heart Center)
60. Triangle for Dissipating Maya (joining the triangles of Illusion and Glamor)
60. Triangle of the Third Thread (Throat Center—Heart Center—Spleen minor)
61. Taste Triangle (Solar Plexus Center—Spleen minor—Tongue point or, Solar Plexus Center and Spleen minor—Brain point—Tongue point)
62. Smell Triangle (Base Center—Nose point—Ajna Center)

Advanced triangles

63. Triangle for the Majority (Ajna Center—Solar Plexus Center—Sacral Center)
64. Triangle for Average Humanity (Soul—Head Center—Solar Plexus Center)

65. Triangle for Imbeciles and Animals (Group soul—Solar Plexus Center—Spleen minor center)
66. Triangle of Spiritual Facilitation (Solar Plexus Center with the triangle: Ajna Center—Heart Center—Heart-in-the-Head Center)
67. Triangle Aiding Self-Consciousness (Solar Plexus Center—Ajna Center—Heart Center [and planetary and cosmic connections])
68. Threads Triangle (from the Base Center... to Solar Plexus Center—Heart Center—Head Center)
    Radiatory Triangle (Soul—Brain—Heart Center .... Aura)

Inherited planetary influences triangles (Chapter 8)

Triangle of Transmutation (for cancer) (Solar Plexus Center—Sacral Center—Throat Center), see Chapter 8

Tuberculosis Triangle (Throat Center—Solar Plexus Center—Heart Center), see Chapter 8

Cancer Triangle (same as Triangle of Transmutation), see Chapter 8.

Syphilis Triangle (Sacral Center—Base Center—Throat Center), see Chapter 8

Ray alignment triangles (Chapter 7, pp. 149–151)

Greater Triangle (Soul Ray—Appropriate Vehicle—Heart Center)

Lesser Triangle (Head Center—Ajna—Center Related to the Soul Ray)

Seven advanced "magical" triangles (see Chapter 10)

First Ray Technique (Head Center—Head Center—Center of distress)

Second Ray Technique (Heart Center—Base Center (opposing Sacral)—Solar Plexus Center (opposing Ajna); (Heart Center [of patient]—Heart Center [healer]—Heart-in-the Head Center)

Third Ray Technique (Sacral Center—Throat Center—Base Center)

Fourth Ray Technique (Base Center (soul)—Throat Center—Heart Center)

Fifth Ray Technique (Ajna Center—Throat Center—Alta Major Center)

Sixth Ray Technique (Head Center—Solar Plexus Center—Heart Center)

Seventh Ray Technique (Heart Center (if second ray soul)—Heart-in-the-Head Center—Base Center)

E. Closing and Sealing the Healing Triangle (p. 239)

The triangles according to their governing center

(The number refers to the number of the triangle in Chapter 7)

Base Center

17. Basic Triangle (Base Center—Adrenal points)
18. Spinal Triangles (Base Center—Alta Major Center—Spinal Cord; see variations)
19. Triangle for Addictions or Obsessions (Base Center—Sacral Center—Throat Center)
20. Fear Triangle (Base Center—Kidney points)
21. Fear Transformation Triangle (Base—Solar Plexus—Ajna Center)
22. First Initiation Triangle (Base Center—Solar Plexus Center—Heart Center)
22. Second Initiation Triangle (Base Center—Heart Center—Throat Center)
52. Triangle of Becoming (Base Center—Head Center—Ajna)
57. Psoriasis Triangle: Heart Center—Base Center—Sacral Center
62. Smell Triangle (Base Center—Nose point—Ajna Center)
68. Threads Triangle (from the Base Center to Solar Plexus Center—Heart Center—Head Center)
    Fourth Ray Technique (Base Center (soul)—Throat Center—Heart Center). See Chapter 10 for use

Sacral Center

24. Sacral Triangle (Sacral Center—Gonad minors) (see variations)
24. Feet Triangle (Sacral Center—Feet minors) (for use see #41)
24. Prostate Triangle (Sacral Center—Gonad Minor Center—Prostate point)
27. Fertility Triangles (a progression of five triangles)
27. Advanced Fertility Triangles (Sacral.... Adrenals—Male gonads—Female gonads; then Sacral... Adrenals—Gonads (as one)—Base Center)
29. Triangle for the Practical Mystic (Sacral Center—Throat Center—Ajna Center)

30. Triangle for Creative Energy Distribution (Sacral Center—Throat Center—Ajna Center)
41. Feet Triangle (Sacral Center—Feet minors)
    Syphilis Triangle (Sacral Center—Base Center—Throat Center), see Chapter 8
    Third Ray Technique (Sacral Center—Throat Center—Base Center), see Chapter 10 for use

SPLEEN CENTER

2. Spleen Triangle of Force (Spleen Minor Center—Sacral Center—Base Center)
4. Lower Prana Triangle (Spleen Minor Center—Base Center—Throat Center)
33. Triangle for the Dying (Spleen Minor Center—Lung Minor Centers—Heart Center)

SOLAR PLEXUS CENTER

2. Spleen Triangle (Solar Plexus Center—Spleen Minor Center—Spleen Center)
5. Liver Triangle (Solar Plexus Center—Liver Minor Center—Liver Center)
5. Liver Triangle of Force (Solar Plexus Center—Stomach Minor Center—Liver Minor Center)
5. Gall Bladder Triangle (Solar Plexus Center—Stomach Minor Center—Gall Bladder point)
6. Stomach Triangle (Solar Plexus Center—Stomach Minor Center—Stomach Center)
10. Triangle for Imperil (Solar Plexus Center—Head Center—Heart Center)
11. PSL Triangle (Pancreas—Stomach—Liver)
12. Diabetes Triangle (Solar Plexus Center—Stomach Minor Center—Base Center)
13. Lower Clearing Triangle (Solar Plexus Center—Heart Center—Ajna Center)
14. Triangles of Stability and Right Group Relation (Solar Plexus Center—Heart Center—Throat Center; then Solar Plexus Center—Sacral Center—Base Center)

15. Triangle for Dispelling Astral Glamor (Astral Body—Solar Plexus Center—Heart Center)

25. Shock Triangle (Solar Plexus Minor Center—Ileocaecal Valve point—Sigmoid point)

61. Taste Triangle (Solar Plexus Center—Spleen Minor Center—Tongue point, or Solar Plexus Center and Spleen Minor Center—Brain point—Tongue point)

66. Triangle of Spiritual Facilitation (Solar Plexus Center with the triangle: Ajna Center—Heart Center—Heart-in-the-Head Center)

67. Triangle Aiding Self-Consciousness (Solar Plexus Center—Ajna Center—Heart Center [and planetary and cosmic connections])
    Triangle of Transmutation (for cancer) (Solar Plexus Center—Sacral Center—Throat Center), see Chapter 8
    Sixth Ray Technique (see Chapter 10 for use)

HEART CENTER

23. Third Initiation Triangle (Heart Center—Throat Center—Seven Head Centers)

31. Triangle of Yoga (Buddhic—Astral—Monad)

32. Heart Triangle (Heart Center—two Lung Minor Centers)

34. Immune Triangle (Heart Center—Spleen Center—Thigh Bone Marrow Point, Heart Center—Thymus Point—Spleen Point, Heart Center—Spleen Center—Heart in the Head Center)

35. Lymphatic Triangle (Heart Center—Lymph duct points)

37. Blood Pressure Triangle (Heart Center—Ajna Center—Spleen Minor Center) (also, Alta Major Center—Vagus Nerve Center—Base Center)

39. Samadhi Triangles (Heart Center—Spleen Center—Solar Plexus with Head Center—Base Center—Spleen Center)

57. Touch Triangle (Heart Center or Solar Plexus Center—Hand minors)
    Second Ray Technique (Heart Center—Base Center (opposing Sacral)—Solar Plexus Center (opposing Ajna). See Chapter 10 for use
    Seventh Ray Technique (Heart Center (if second ray soul)—Heart-in-the-Head Center—Base Center), see Chapter 10 for use

57. Psoriasis Triangle: Heart Center—Base Center—Sacral Center

VAGUS NERVE CENTER

1. Pranic Triangle (Vagus Nerve Center—Center Below Heart Center—Spleen Minor Center)
36. Allergy Triangle (Vagus Nerve Center—Adrenal Minutes)
40. Diaphragm Triangle (Vagus Nerve Center—Diaphragm points)

THROAT CENTER

3. Triangle of Immortality (Throat Center—Pituitary gland—Pineal gland, transmuted from Spleen Triangle of Force)
9. GIT Triangles (Throat Center—Solar Plexus Center—Intestinal Point)
25. Triangles of Force (Breastbone minor—Breast minors, and Sacral Center—Solar Plexus minor—Base Center)
28. Triangle of Energy (Throat Center—Sacral Center—Physical Body)
41. Service Triangles (Throat Center—to centers on Shoulders, Elbows and Hands)
42. Parathyroid Triangle (Throat Center—Parathyroid points)
43. Respiratory Triangle (Throat Center—Lung minors)
45. Sinus Triangle (Throat Center—Solar Plexus Center—Sinus points)
49. Migraine Triangle (Throat Center—Pituitary gland—Pineal gland)
50. Creative Fusion Triangle (Throat Center—Heart Center—Ajna Center)
56. Hearing Triangle (Throat Center—Ear minors)
60. Triangle of the First Thread (Throat Center—Ajna—Head Center)
60. Triangle of the Second Thread (Throat Center—Solar Plexus Center—Heart Center)
60. Triangle for Dissipating Maya (joining the triangles of Illusion and Glamor)
60. Triangle of the Third Thread (Throat Center—Heart Center—Spleen minor)
Tuberculosis Triangle (Throat Center—Solar Plexus Center—Heart Center), see Chapter 8
Cancer Triangle (same as Triangle of Transmutation), see Chapter 8

AJNA CENTER

47. Triangle for the Nerves (Ajna Center—Alta Major Center—Vagus Nerve Center)

48. Cranio-Sacral Triangle (Ajna Center—Alta Major Center—Sacral Center)

60. Triangle for Dissipating Glamor (Ajna Center—Left Eye—Right Eye)

    Fifth Ray Technique (Ajna Center—Throat Center—Alta Major Center). See Chapter 10 for use

63. Triangle for the Majority (Ajna Center—Solar Plexus Center—Sacral Center)

66. Triangle for Spiritual Facilitation (Ajna Center—Heart Center—Heart-in-the-Head Center, with Solar Plexus Center)

HEAD CENTER

7. Astral Preparation Triangle (Head Center of Healer—Solar Plexus Center of Healer—Astral Body of Patient)

8. Mental Congestion Triangle (Head Center of Healer—Head Center of Patient—Centers below diaphragm of Patient)

14. Responsive Triangle (Soul of Patient—Ajna Center—Heart Center)

15. Triangle for Dispelling Astral Glamor (Soul: Astral Body—Solar Plexus Center—Heart Center)

16. Consciousness Stream Triangle (Head Center—Astral Body—Solar Plexus Center)

25. Life Stream Triangle (Head Center—Heart Center—Spleen Center)

26. Triangle for Sexual Problems (Head Center—Throat Center—Sacral)

33. Triangles for Death:

    Desire Triangle (Soul—Astral Body—Solar Plexus Center)

    Withdrawing Triangle (Soul—Head Center—Ajna Center)

38. Kundalini Triangle (Head Center—Heart Center—Base Center.... Vagus Nerve Center)

44. Triangle of Purpose (Brain—Mind—Soul Will [Sacrifice Petals])

51. Head Triangle (Head Center—Ajna Center—Alta Major Center)

52. Triangle of Being (Head Center—Heart Center—Base Center)

53. Triangle of the White Magician (Heart in the Head Center—Heart Center—Throat Center)

54. Synchronizing Triangle (Head Center of Healer—Center of Healer and Corresponding Center in Patient)

58. Triangle of the Third Seed Group (Head Center—Heart Center—Ajna Center)

59. Eye Triangle (Head Center—Eye minors), (four specific triangles).

60. Triangle for Dissipating Illusion (Head Center—Ajna Center—Right Eye minor)

64. Triangle for Average Humanity (Soul—Head Center—Solar Plexus Center)

65. Triangle for Imbeciles and Animals (Group soul—Solar Plexus Center—Spleen minor center)

    Radiatory Triangle (Soul—Brain—Heart Center.... Aura)

    Greater Triangle (Soul Ray—Appropriate Vehicle—Heart Center), see pp. 149–151

    Lesser Triangle (Head Center—Ajna Center—Center Related to the Soul Ray), see pp. 149–151

    First Ray Technique (Head Center—Head Center—Center of distress), see Chapter 10 for use

    Sixth Ray Technique (Head Center—Solar Plexus Center—Heart Center), see Chapter 10 for use

13.

CONCLUSION

I realize that, by opening up esoteric healing in this way, it could be misused. My hope is that it will not be. Esoteric Healing has its own in-built safeguard: the less one knows about its use, the less harm can be done either to oneself or to others. On the other hand, the more that is known about the philosophy, psychology, and pneumapharmacology, the more harm can be done both to oneself and to one's patients (this would require deliberate abuse of the techniques). The real safeguard as one advances in occultism and white magic is, of course, the amount and quality of one's knowledge. By the time one has explored esotericism in general and esoteric healing in particular, the probability of willfully wanting to harm another or even unwillingly seeking to harm is both extremely unlikely and extremely small. But falls are possible, even to the most advanced. So we are called on to maintain steady watchfulness, for, as the saying goes, "the price of liberation is constant vigilance."

My hope is that those of you who have bought this book will use it, first by studying it—(along with the works of the Ageless Wisdom), noting the essentials and building up confidence by applying it to yourselves and on close friends and colleagues. If you can, start an esoteric healing clinic with one or two others. Study this book with them. Practice with them. When real patients are magnetically drawn to you, the importance and power of this healing technique will be realized. The tool of esoteric healing is the power of thought as it controls and directs energy. There is a danger in this work just as there is in any science. But with the motivation for success backed up by love, harmlessness and service, safety is assured. And remember, energy follows thought.

The Master Djwhal Khul thought it necessary that esoteric healing be revealed publicly in the twentieth century. The disciple Alice A. Bailey considered it warranted. Her book was first published in 1953. It has taken over fifty years of subjective group work for a complete and practical text on esoteric healing to be written and published based on her book. I hope this greatly up-dated text book will find its place beside all earnest practicing healers of every generation. Esoteric healing has a great future—both in its own development and its partnership and bridging work with the whole field of medicine. Hold true to its roots!

This book is just a beginning. There came a time when I had to simply accept I could never complete this book! There is a wealth of material still waiting to be collated and utilized by the esoteric healer. I refer especially to that vast body of knowledge called esoteric astrology, which, when applied under the Law of Correspondence, will become a specialist facet of esoteric healing. There is also the whole issue of the use of the rays in healing which has been touched on in this book. This too has an importance beyond our reckoning. In the main, esoteric healers are not yet ready for these aspects of esotericism. There is still more than enough for us to work with and to learn. In this manner we are preparing the way for future esoteric healers. And by learning all that is in this book, we will be more than made ready to take on those "heavyweights" of the rays and esoteric astrology if and when necessary. So this book remains a "guide" and "preparation" to potential and to established esoteric healers.

I wish you well in this medicine of the future.

"MAY HEALING BE IN YOUR WINGS!"

"Brother, I do not come to offer you any dogmas and I do not ask you to believe in that which so many others believe. I only exhort you to independent enlightenment, to use your own mind, developing it instead of letting it become dull.... I implore you to be persons with right views, persons who toil untiringly for the acquisition of real knowledge which will prevail over suffering." —Lord Buddha

14.

ESOTERIC HEALING
GROUP MEDITATION

A. GROUP FUSION (ESOTERIC INHALATION).

We affirm the fact of group fusion and integration within the heart center of the world group of healers. We say together:

"I am one with my group, and all that I have is theirs. May the love which is in my soul pour forth to them. May the strength which is in me lift and aid them. May the thoughts which my soul creates reach and encourage them."

Alignment and Spiritual Penetration:

Let the group project a line of lighted energy towards the spiritual Hierarchy of our planet; and towards the Christ-Maitreya; and extend the line of light towards Shamballa, the center where the Will of God is known.

B. HIGHER INTERLUDE (ESOTERIC INHALED PAUSE).

Focussed in the group within the light of Hierarchy, hold the contemplative mind steady, perceiving this greater light, being impressed and infused by the hierarchical Plan for the Planet.

Meditation. Reflect on one of the seed thoughts: Love. Harmlessness. Sharing. Right Relationships. Energy. Planetary Healing. Group Awareness (or meditate on one of the mantrams in Chapter 15).

C. PRECIPITATION AND ENERGY GROUNDING (ESOTERIC EXHALATION).

Now, using the creative imagination, visualize these healing energies streaming into the human consciousness, directing a planned action on Earth in line with the esoteric purpose of the ONE.

D. LOWER INTERLUDE (ESOTERIC EXHALED PAUSE).

Now, re-attune and refocus the consciousness as a group, within the Second Ray Ashram of Hierarchy. Together, in the group soul, sound the affirmation:

"In the center of all Love I stand. From that center I, the soul, will outward move. From that center, I, the one who serves, will work. May the love of the divine Self be shed abroad, in my heart, through my group, and throughout the world."

Distribution.

As we sound The Mantram of Unification or The Great Invocation, visualize the energy of love pouring throughout the planet.

The mantrams can be found on the following pages.
End by sounding the sacred word, OM, three times.

15.

ANCIENT HEALING MANTRAMS

For All Disciples

These words are written for all disciples, attend you to them:
Before the eyes can see, they must be incapable of tears;
Before the ear can hear, it must have lost its sensitiveness;
Before the voice can speak in the presence of the Masters,
it must have lost its power to wound;
Before the Soul can stand in the presence of the Masters,
it must have washed its feet in the blood of the heart.

Mantram of Heart, Mind and Soul

Enter thy brother's Heart and see his woe. Then Speak.
Enter thy brother's Mind and read his thoughts,
but only when thy thoughts are pure. Then Think.
Blend with thy brother's Soul and know him as he is.
Then focus on the Plan.

Group Healing Mantram

With purity of motive, inspired by a loving heart,
we offer ourselves for this work of healing.
This offer we make as a group and to the one we seek to heal.

Radiatory Mantram

May the love of the One Soul, focussed in this group,
radiate upon you, my brother,
and permeate every part of your body—
healing, soothing, strengthening,
and dissipating all that hinders service and good health.

Mantram of Unification

The sons of men are one, and I am one with them.
I seek to love, not hate;
I seek to serve and not exact due service;
I seek to heal, not hurt.

Let pain bring due reward of light and love.
Let the soul control the outer form, and life and all events,
and bring to light the love that underlies the happenings of the time.

Let vision come and insight.
Let the future stand revealed.
Let inner union demonstrate and outer cleavages be gone.
Let love prevail. Let all people love.

Mantram of the New Group of World Servers

May the power of the One Life pour through the group of all true servers;

May the love of the One Soul characterize the lives of all who seek to aid the Great Ones;

May we fulfill our part in the One Work through self-forgetfulness, harmlessness and right speech.

Noontime Recollection

I know, O Lord of Life and Love, about the need.
Touch my heart anew with love
That I, too, may love and give.

The Affirmation of the Disciple

I am a point of light within a greater Light
I am a strand of loving energy within the stream of Love divine.
I am a point of sacrificial Fire, focused within the fiery Will of
God.
And thus I stand.

I am a way by which all people may achieve.
I am a source of strength, enabling them to stand.
I am a beam of light, shining upon their way.
And thus I stand.

And standing thus, revolve
And tread this way the ways of all people,
And know the ways of God.
And thus I stand.

The Gayatri

O Thou Who givest sustenance to the universe,
From Whom all things proceed
To Whom all things return,
Unveil to us the face of the true Spiritual Sun
Hidden by a disc of golden Light
That we may know the Truth
And do our whole duty
As we journey to Thy sacred feet.

Mantram to Destroy Glamor

Radiance we are and power.
We stand forever with our hands stretched out,
linking the heavens and the earth,
the inner world of meaning and the subtle world of glamor.
We reach into the light and bring it down to meet the need.
We reach into the silent place
and bring from thence the gift of understanding.
Thus with the light we work
and turn the darkness into day.

The Soul Mantram

I am the Soul.
I am the Light Divine.
I am Love.
I am Will.
I am Fixed Design.

The Soul Mantram (full version)

I am the Soul. And also love I am.
Above all else I am both will and fixed design.
My will is now to lift the lower self into the light divine.
This light I am.
Therefore, I must descend to where the lower self awaits my coming.
That which desires to lift and that which cries aloud for lifting are
    now at-one. Such is my will.

Affirmation of Love

In the center of all love I stand.
From that center I, the soul, will outward move.
From that center I, the one who serves, will work.
May the love of the divine Self be shed abroad,
In my heart, through my group, and throughout the world.

Mantram of Group Unity

I am one with my group, and all that I have is theirs.
May the love which is in my soul pour forth to them.
May the strength which is in me lift and aid them.
May the thoughts which my soul creates reach and encourage them.

Mantram for Money

O Thou in whom we live and move and have our being,
The Power that can make all things new,
Turn to spiritual purposes the money in the world;
Touch the hearts of people everywhere
So that they may give to the work of the Hierarchy
That which has hitherto been given to material satisfaction.
The New Group of World Servers needs money in large quantities.
I ask that the needed vast sums may be made available.
May this potent energy of Thine
Be in the hands of the Forces of Light.

Into the Light Mantram

Into the light we move, beckoned thereto by You.
Out of the dark we come, driven thereto by the soul of all.
Up from the earth we spring and into the ocean of light we plunge.
Together we come.
Together we move, guided and led by the soul we serve
And by You, the Master we know.
The master within and the Master without are One.
That One are we.
The One is all—
My soul, Your soul, the Master and the soul of all.

The Self

More radiant than the Sun,
Purer than snow,
Subtler than the ether,
Is the Self, the Spirit in my heart.
I am that Self. That Self am I.

Mantram of the Avatar on the White Horse

I stand within the Radiant Path;
I see the needed approach for the Lotus of Man.
You walk upon the Claiming Way;
Your descent is under the Law of Divine Deliverance.

I came in Light; I came with Enlightened Mind.
I was the Illumined Third, the Rod of Radiation.
I fused substance with attractive Solar Fire.
You heard the challenge: Enter the Stream of Light.

I enfolded Wisdom; I embodied Peace
And the Force of Latent Submission.
I am the Cosmic Touch of Acquiescence.
Your way awaits my first Touch of Love.

The Way is open; the Path of Ascent stands ready;
Five steps, each raises your head.
The Approach of Appropriation must begin—
Unfold your wings: Love and Think and seek to Serve.

I await the time: the energies three are absorbed.
Let them confer appropriation (may you see your divinity).
Let them establish on Earth a station of Light and Power.
Let them bring about a New World Order.

Let the Lotus and the Dragon and the Star activate integration.

Service Mantram

O Lord Maitreya, the Christ,
We dedicate ourselves
To be a channel of Thy healing Love,
An instrument of Thy dynamic Peace,
An exponent of Thy compassionate Wisdom,
An expression of Thy fiery Will,
A manifestation of Thy redemptive Power.
To that service
We dedicate our life and our being.

The Great Affirmation

We stand in the consciousness of Brightest Light,
Allowing it to radiate through us
To all kingdoms of the Earth.

We feel the consciousness of Purest Love,
Allowing it to pulse through our Heart,
Opening our Eyes to see Christ in all.

We move in the consciousness of Divine Purpose,
Following the Path traveled by our Teachers,
And knowing the Plan to be the same.

We share in the consciousness of True Brotherhood,
Where creativity and joy are understood,
As we build the New World Order together.

In the Master's consciousness
We serve the Light and the Love—
Empowering all on Earth.

The Great Invocation

From the point of Light within the Mind of God
Let light stream forth into the minds of all people.
Let Light descend on Earth.

From the point of Love within the Heart of God
Let love stream forth into the hearts of all people.
May Christ return to Earth.

From the center where the Will of God is known
Let purpose guide the little wills of all people—
The purpose which the Masters know and serve.

From the center which we call the race of humanity
Let the Plan of Love and Light work out
And may it seal the door where evil dwells.

Let Light and Love and Power restore the Plan on Earth

The Great Invocation
A Mantram for the New Age and for all Humanity

From the point of Light within the Mind of God
Let light stream forth into the minds of men.
Let Light descend on Earth.

From the point of Love within the Heart of God
Let love stream forth into the hearts of men.
May Christ return to Earth.

From the centre where the Will of God is known
Let purpose guide the little wills of men—
The purpose which the Masters know and serve.

From the centre which we call the race of men
Let the Plan of Love and Light work out
And may it seal the door where evil dwells.

Let Light and Love and Power restore the Plan on Earth.

Many religions believe in a World Teacher or Savior, knowing him under such names as the Christ, the Lord Maitreya, the Imam Mahdi, the Bodhisattva, and the Messiah, and these terms are used in some of the Christian, Hindu, Muslim, Buddhist and Jewish versions of the Great Invocation.

Men and women of goodwill throughout the world are using this Invocation in their own language. Will you join them in using the Invocation every day—with thought and dedication?

By using the Invocation and encouraging others to use it, no particular group or organization is sponsored. It belongs to all humanity.

From the website http://www.lucistrust.org/invocation/

16.

USEFUL ADDRESSES

Godshaer Herbal Healing Clinic
The Old Stables, Ducking Stool Lane,
Christchurch, Dorset BH23 1DS, U.K.
e-mail: alanhopking@godshaer.co.uk – www.godshaer.co.uk
    This is the clinic run by Alan Hopking. Healing and herbal medicine. It is open for consultation by appointment.

International Network of Esoteric Healing
(Reg. Charity No. 1032492)
Registered Office: The Hayloft, Palmers Road, Emsworth, Hampshire
P0107DL, U.K.
e-mail: info@ineh.org
www.ineh.org or the following branches of INEH:
USA: www.esoterichealing.com; Canada: www.guerisonesoterique.com;
Germany: www.mit-liebe-heilen.de;
Czech Republic: www.esoternileceni.cz;
Greece: www.global-education.org
    For details of the Network in over 20 countries, please write to the INEH Secretary.

University of the Seven Rays (Faculty of Healing)
128 Manhattan Ave., Jersey City Heights, NJ 07307, USA
www.sevenray.com
    Degree courses (MSE) on many different esoteric subjects including a three-year intensive in Esoteric Healing, pioneered and co-taught by Alan Hopking in USA and UK. The USR also has a high quality journal: The Journal of Esoteric Psychology.

Global Academy of Esoteric Healing

Principal: Alan Hopking – www.godshaer.co.uk/GAEH.php

Now working entirely within the internet, GAEH endeavors to supply assistance to all esoteric healers, answering all questions.

Lucis Trust/Arcane School

UK: Suite 54, 3 Whitehall Court, London SW1A 2EF
USA: 120 Wall Street, 24th Floor, New York, NY 10005
www.lucistrust.org

The most balanced and esoteric training in meditation and service so far available on our planet. Excellent journal, publications and leaflets.

The Esoteric Healer

(Journal of the International Network of Esoteric Healing)
The Editors, 27 South Road, Chorleywood, Herts WD3 5AS, England

The first esoteric healing research journal on our planet. Published biannually since 1985. Covers all aspects of esoteric healing including articles and news of esoteric healing around the world. Articles, research information, letters, information about esoteric healing welcome. Editors: Alan Hopking and Helen Frankland. Sample articles on the web: ww.ineh. org or information about the *Journal,* e-mail info@ineh.org

Institute of Planetary Synthesis

PO Box 128, CH-1211 Geneva 20, Switzerland – www.ipsgeneva.com

Working to make known the Ten Seed Groups as a possible basis for the future world civilization; to help establish a University for Planetary Synthesis for the practice of the science of man; to promote cooperation on a global scale among farsighted individuals, groups and organizations. Many pamphlets and publications. Highly recommended.

Meditation Mount

PO Box 566, Ojai, CA 93023, USA – www.meditation.com

An excellent programme of meditation and study for all stages and ages. Highly recommended.

Sundial House

PO Box 181, Tunbridge Wells, Kent, TN3 9ZA England, UK
www.sundialhouse.4t.com

A well-established meditation program by correspondence. Many excellent books and booklets. Highly recommended.

World Service Intergroup
www.synthesis.tc

The WSI is an international network of Ageless Wisdom groups committed to developing intergroup contact, cooperation and synthetic, subjective work. The purpose of the WSI is to generate a focused, conscious and deliberate intergroup effort to specifically assist the Externalization of the Hierarchy and the Reappearance of the Christ.

GandhiServe Foundation
Rathausstrasse 51a, 12105 Berlin, Germany
www.gandhiserve.org

GandhiServe, a charitable foundation, aims to spread the ethics of nonviolence by disseminating information about and popularizing Mahatma Gandhi's life and works.

Pathways To Peace
PO Box 1057, Larkspur, CA 94977, USA
www.pathwaystopeace.org

Pathways To Peace, a pioneer not-for-profit, non-partisan, local/global Peacebuilding, consulting (UN Consultative II Status, ECOSOC) and educational organization.

World University
Desert Sanctuary Campus
P.O. Box 2470, Benson, Arizona 85602, USA
www.worlduniversity.org

The purpose of the World University is to inspire the world's peoples of goodwill to place their humanity above their nationality, to elevate their faith above their creed, and to reconcile the many diverse cultural and ideological beliefs into a synthesis of understanding.

Artists Helping Artists
PO Box 2529, Aptos, CA 95001-2529, USA
http://www.artistshelpingartists.org

When artists, visionaries and humanitarians gather in proximity and share creative works and missions, *anything becomes possible.* Beauty is increased ... and civilization itself is healed and transformed.

Appendix B:
PHOTOS DEMONSTRATING THE TRIANGLE CIRCUITS
OF ESOTERIC HEALING

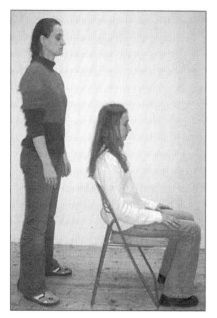

1. The position of patient and healer at the beginning of the treatment. The position for doing Alignment and Attunement, the Higher Triangles to the opening of the healing triangle (pp. 146–154).

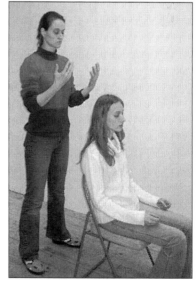

2. Triangle of transfer (see p. 154).

3. *Diagnosis (see p. 155).*
Note the position of the
right hand as it holds the
five centers in the Ajna
(p. 156–7).

4. *Vitalization of*
the bodies of the
patient (see pp.
158–163).
Note: the healer
sits to give this
treatment.

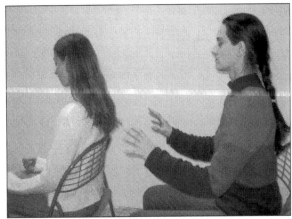

5. *Esoteric healing*
treatment (here doing
the Synchronizing
Triangle, see p. 163).

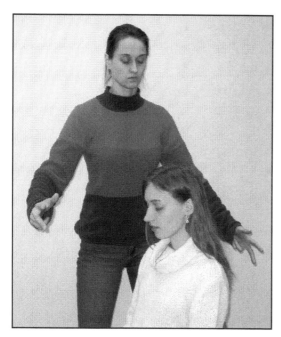

6. The two Triangles of Force (p. 186). Note the use of the three fingers of both hands as they connect with these two triangles.

7. The Head Triangle (p. 213). Note: The ajna is holding the crown center, the right hand holds the ajna, and the left hand holds the alta major center. Note also the hands are held well away from the patient's head.

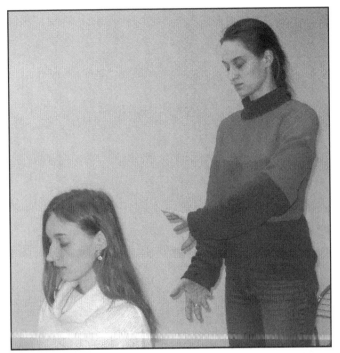

8. Triangle
of Being
(p. 215).

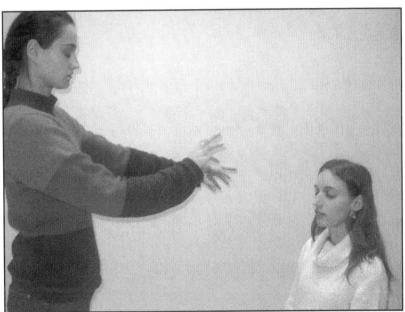

9. Eye Triangles (p. 222). Note: Healer stands in front of the patient
and the hands are well away from the patient's head.

10. Part of the closing procedure (see p. 243), surrounding the patient with protective energy.

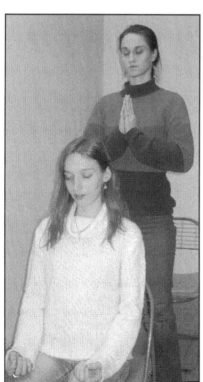

11. Sealing the esoteric healing triangle (see p. 243).

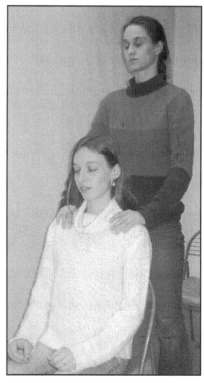

12. Ending the healing treatment (see p. 244).

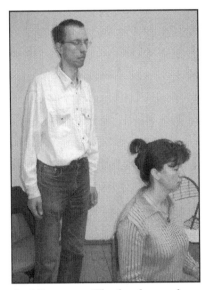

A. Alignment. The healer at the start of the healing treatment making his spiritual alignment and attunement (see pp. 147ff).

B. Esoteric healing: general positioning. The healer usually stands (or sits) at the back of the patient (who usually sits). Note the distance the healer is from the patient and the distance of his hands from the body of the patient.

C. A general view of an esoteric healing treatment being given.

NOTES

Wherever possible I have tried to be accountable for the quotes I have used, but a lot of my sources over the years have, unfortunately, gone to the wind. Some sources come from my association with colleagues and teachers in the International Network of Esoteric Healing.

PREFACE

1. Another word for centers is chakras.

2. Reference to the University of the Seven Rays course on esoteric healing and the Global Academy of Esoteric Healing courses and seminars. See Chapter 16.

CHAPTER 1

1. The author is well aware of the problem of writing in masculine and feminine singular. The flow is disrupted with forms such as his/her, and he/she or s/he. So, where *the singular must be chosen,* he prefers to choose one or other of the personal pronouns in order to keep the flow in the written word. The author writes to inform not offend.

2. The soul is the spirit of the true self which expresses itself as the personality and through it. Where this expression is inhibited, illness arises.

3. The etheric body is the energy-giving life of the physical body.

4. See also Chapter 8, "Treating the Three Inherited Planetary Influences."

5. The astral body is the body of emotions and feelings.

6. Karma is good and bad sowing and reaping as the result of past actions, in this life or in the past.

7. For a full explanation of disease, see "Appendix A: Our Cosmic Purpose."

8. I recommend as an excellent training for meditation: The Arcane School, London, New York, Geneva. Two other schools which have an excellent sequence of training in meditation are the Sundial House training (Tunbridge Wells, England) and the Meditation Mount training in Ojai, California (addresses in Chapter 16).

CHAPTER 2

1. a. Symptoms of Suffering are birth, old age, death, sorrow, pain, grief, despair, the five aggregates of clinging (to material form, feeling, perception, mental forms, consciousness).

b. Origin of Suffering is craving (for the sensual, for eternal existence, for non-existence).

c. Cessation of Suffering is the fading away of craving and its extinction.

d. Path leading to the Cessation of Suffering consists of right understanding, right thought, right speech, right action, right livelihood, right effort, right mindfulness, right concentration.

2. For a full account of the Christ's present influence and what his second coming will do worldwide, see *The Emergence of the Planetary Heart* (Hopking, 1994).

3. For a full account of the etheric body compiled from *Esoteric Healing* by Alice Bailey, see *The Esoteric Healing Handbook* (1988), "The Etheric Body" by Alan Hopking.

4. The personal pronouns of the original text have been edited out in order to bring the material into an acceptable modern idiom, as have exclusive references to the masculine.

5. Of the three equivalent and irreducible aspects—matter, motion, and consciousness—the primordial atoms or monads are the smallest possible parts of primordial matter and the smallest firm points for an individual consciousness as it exists in this Cosmic Being's dimension while it is effecting the healing or repairing what is called in esotericism, the Grand Plan. (*See also* Laurency (1995), p. 27.)

CHAPTER 3

1. Animals are un-self-conscious lives as yet, although domestic animals, dolphins and even some birds are close to the individualization initiation. The animal soul is the fusion of the many (the group, or herd) as one.

2. For further amplification of this anatomy please consult other books, e.g. *The Egoic Lotus* by Douglas Baker, *The Causal Body* by A.E. Powell along with his other compilations, *Advancing in Esoteric Healing* by Alan Hopking, *A Treatise on Cosmic Fire* by Alice A. Bailey, *Rainbow Bridge* by Two Disciples, *Radionics and the Subtle Anatomy of Man* by D V Tansley.

Chapter 5

1. Earlier I mentioned that there were only five pranic energies. This depends on where you stand on the spiritual Path. The higher you go or the more spiritually aware you become, the more pranic energies become available for your use. For instance, mineral beings, the so-called gnomes of the earth, utilize only one energy; plant beings wield two to three energies; animals use four and most humans weave with five. But the more advanced humans, rare in number, can work with seven pranic energies, coming from the highest planes of consciousness.

2. Antahkarana is the esoteric bridge linking the personality to the soul and spiritual triad.

Chapter 6

1. Some of the most beautiful esoteric connections involve the five-pointed star. It can be recognized in the human form, which has five appendages from the body (four limbs and a head), five fingers on each hand, and five toes on each foot. There are five lobes to the lungs; there are five senses. There are five centers which control perfected man: the two head centers, heart center, throat center and base center. There are five pranas. The nadis have a fivefold sheath. There are five ventricles in the brain. There are five Commandments and five Rules (Bailey, 1950a, pp. 184, 188). The Lord of the World, the Buddha, the Christ, the Manu and the Mahachohan "create the five-pointed star of Humanity at this time" (Bailey, 1951–70, v. 5, p. 90). There are five signs related to the unfoldment, in time and space, of the human hierarchy: Cancer, Leo, Scorpio, Capricorn and Pisces. We are in the fifth great Root Race (called in ancient texts, the Aryan, long before the German Nazis in this century perverted the name). This race's evolution has resulted in the five continents: Europe, Africa, Asia, Australia and America. There are five energies (there are usually five dominant ray energies at any time) active during this period: Ray VI (passing out), Ray VII (emerging), Ray II and Ray III (expressing the ray type of the bulk of humanity at this time), and Ray I (which has been evoked at this time because of humanity's desperate need).

2. The correspondences in parenthesis are mine.

3. See more about breath and healing in Chapter 5, Spleen Center; also Chapter 6, p. 122, and Chapter 8, regarding freeing ourselves from inherited taints.

4. The reader is asked to recall that a center or chakra is the crossing point of a number of energy lines (meridians and nadis). On entry the energy discharged, transformed and recharged according to the constant and multiple input; the energy is then passed out (output) of the center to the etheric body and physical body according to the particular magnetism of the energy released, taking with it its effect on tissue and cells, organs and systems—hence the recommended

position behind the patient to hold the center in the etheric spine. Inflow and outflow to and from the center occurs all the time and all round the chakra. There is really no one entry or exit point.

5. To find out if there is an esoteric healing clinic near you, wherever you live in the world, you can write to International Network of Esoteric Healing. See the address at the back of the book. www.ineh.org or for USA, www. esoterichealing.com

6. Telepathy is related to Rule 1, see Chapter 2. For more information on telepathy, see *Esoteric Healing* pages 525 and 550, and *Telepathy and the Etheric Vehicle* pp. 27-8, both by Alice Bailey, and *The Emergence of the Planetary Heart* by Alan Hopking.

7. For example, *Soul Centered Astrology* by Alan Oken or *Best of the Best* by Cheryl Parsell.

CHAPTER 7

1. Esoteric healing is healing by groups, but DK indicates that "it is not always necessary or possible to meet and work together in group formation. This work can be carried forward efficiently and potently, if the members work as a *subjective group*; each should then follow the instructions each day and as if he were working in his group in tangible form. This real linking is brought about by imagining oneself as in the presence of 'brothers' ... a group on the physical plane (would find) it hard to prevent the dissipation of force through discussion, through the ordinary pleasantries of meeting, and through the physical interplay between personalities. It would be inevitable that there would be too much conversation, and the work done would not be adequately effective. From the physical standpoint they work alone; from the true inner standpoint, they work in the closest cooperation" (Bailey, 1951–70, v. 4, p. 102–3). Personally, at my clinic, I heal both alone and with other healers on the physical plane. We do not talk, so the energy is potent. It is, in our group healing experience, a great advantage if you can heal together with others. You are still alone and are responsible, from the soul point of view, and linked on the subjective level with other healers not present, but you are working through the etheric together. As DK says at the beginning of this quote, if it is "possible" and "dissipation" can be prevented, group healing on the physical level is preferable. Another notable statement in *Esoteric Healing* in this connection speaks about our outer aloneness and our inner cooperation: "From the physical standpoint you work alone, from the true inner standpoint you work in the closest cooperation" (p. 103).

2. The description, function, influence and interaction of the rays goes beyond the scope of this book. For the study of this subject I recommend, *A Treatise on the Seven Rays* (1951–70, in five volumes) by Alice A. Bailey and *Tapestry of the Gods* (1988, 1996, in two volumes) by Michael D. Robbins.

3. It is interesting to compare how this Directing Triangle differs from the Triangle for Dissipating Glamor, for although they use the same points, the circulation of energy is different. When all the powers of the body and the directed attention of the healer are centered in the head, and when the astral body is quiescent and the mind is active as a transmitter of soul energy to the three head centers, you then have an established radiance, or energy emanation which is a potent force in healing. This radiation is intense, emanating rays of active energy which can reach the patient and energize the needed centers.

4. "The aura is in reality indicative of the subject's centers. From the study of this aura certain things can be ascertained:

   a. whether the development is above or below the diaphragm.

   b. whether the centers are undeveloped or developed.

   c. whether the nature of the controlling rays is adequately clear.

   d. whether the point at the center and the petals of the lotus are controlled, or whether a balance is being achieved.

   e. whether the personality is outgoing, and is therefore in a state of livingness, or whether a withdrawing is taking place due to introspection and self-centeredness, or to the slow oncoming of the death process.

   f. whether the personality of the soul is in control, and whether, therefore, a struggle between the two is going on.

You can see, therefore how revealing the aura can be to the individual who has the ability to read it with accuracy, and how thankful you should be that such a capacity is relative rare, or is in the possession of an Initiate or of a Master Whose nature is love" (Hopking, 1990, pp. 89–90).

5. For a full description of insanity, see *Esoteric Psychology* (Bailey, 1951–70, v. 2), pp. 457–59.

6. These five pranas are described on page 328 in the book *The Light of the Soul* (1988) by Alice Bailey.

7. This triangle is well worth linking with the triangle which concerns egoic memory and intellectual pride involving the throat center, the ajna and the head center, and connecting with the knowledge petals of the egoic lotus, called the Triangle of the First Thread. This is the first triangle a meditator builds in the etheric matter of the chitta or "mind stuff" on their way to the fifth kingdom. And just as the process of building the antahkarana is threefold involving concentration, meditation and finally contemplation, so is this the stage where the triangle is built by concentration. The healer works with this triangle when it appears the patient has become caught up in intellectual pursuits at the expense of love and reason. This is its connection with illusion. These threads triangles form part of the building process within the creative thread itself (see *Education in the New Age* by Alice Bailey, pp. 33, 147).

8. *Esoteric Psychology I* (1951–70) by Alice Bailey, p. 420.

9. 6th Sense [Mind]—Akasha.

10. 6th Sense -Ether [Physical].

11. This tabulation is derived from the books by Alice Bailey, *The Secret Doctrine* by H.P Blavatsky, and *Spiritual Astrology* by K.E. Krishnamacharya (a close student of HPB and AAB).

12. This tabulation is distilled from many books, especially *Esoteric Healing, Esoteric Psychology*, and *Cosmic Fire*.

13. Key to Vagus Nerve Center = aspiration towards soul control.

14. The will-to-good balancing with goodwill.

15. Soul purpose and personality ambition.

16. High aspiration and lower personality desires.

CHAPTER 8

1. Synonymous with the Triangle of Transmutation.

2. Bailey, 1951–70, v. 4, cf. p. 316.

3. For a detailed account of this, Christ's Sixth Initiation, see the author's book *The Emergence of the Planetary Heart* (1994).

4. This is elaborated in Part II. This "thought" came as a flash of insight which is also captured as Poems I, II, and III and can be found on my WebPage: http://members.aol.com/godshaer/Index.htm

5. Originally given as a talk at a conference in Christchurch, New Zealand, October 1997.

6. A quote from the translation given by DK in Bailey (1951–70, v. 2).

7. H.P. Blavatsky (1977, p. 390) quoting M. Maury in *Revue Archeologique*.

8. This will be explained later.

9. Actually "Our," as a whole Cosmic Universe.

10. "The earliest signs of life on earth are present 3.45 billion years ago, 300 million years after the crust cooled sufficiently to support liquid water, well formed, or what the experts believe are cells are present in the archaic rocks from that period, e.g., coccoid cyanobacteria from 2.15 billions years.... So it was I think in the Cambrian, when multicellular life first tested out its possible modes of being. The particular branchings of life, where the tape played again, might differ, but the patterns of the branching, dramatic at first, then dwindling to twiddling with details later, are likely to be lawful" (Kauffman, 1995, p. 14).

11. For the three poems culminating in this quotation, see www.godshaer.co.uk/GAEH.php

12. PASE should be practiced and strengthened with PETA. That is, Physical (actions and positions) awareness, Emotional (moods and feelings) awareness; and Thoughts (ideas and hopes) Awareness

BIBLIOGRAPHY

Bailey, A. (no date). Unpublished letters.

Bailey, A. (1930). *The soul and its mechanism: The problem of psychology.* New York: Lucis Publishing Co.

Bailey, A. (1944). *Discipleship in the new age, Vols. I and II.* New York: Lucis Publishing Co.

Bailey, A. (1950a). *Letters on occult meditation.* New York: Lucis Publishing Co.

Bailey, A. (1950b). *Telepathy and the etheric vehicle.* New York: Lucis Publishing Co.

Bailey, A. (1951–1970). *A treatise on the seven rays. v. 1 (Esoteric psychology), v. 2 (Esoteric psychology), v. 3 (Esoteric astrology), v. 4 (Esoteric healing), v. 5 (The Rays and initiations).* London & New York: Lucis Publishing Co.

Bailey, A. (1954). *Education in the new age.* New York: Lucis Publishing Co.

Bailey, A. (1957). *The externalisation of the hierarchy.* New York: Lucis Publishing Co.

Bailey, A. (1962). *A treatise on cosmic fire.* New York: Lucis Publishing Co.

Bailey, A. (1973). *Glamor: A world problem.* London & New York: Lucis Publishing Co.

Bailey, A. (1979). *A treatise on white magic, or, the way of the disciple.* London & New York: Lucis Publishing Co.

Bailey, A. (1988). *The light of the soul, its science and effect: A paraphrase of the Yoga sutras of Pantanjali with commentary by Alice A. Bailey.* New York: Lucis Publishing Co.

Baker, D. (1997). *The egoic lotus.* Baker Publications.

Bhagavadgita (Swami Prabhavandanda & C. Isherwood, transl.)

Blavatsky, H.P. (1977). *The secret doctrine, vol I and II.* California: Theosophical Publ. House.

Goethe, J.W. (1780). *Wanderers Nachtlied.*

Hawking, S. (2001). *The Universe in a Nutshell,* New York: Bantam Books.

Hopking, A. (1988). *The esoteric healing handbook.* Christchurch: Godshaer Publishing Co.

Hopking, A. (1990). *Advancing in esoteric healing.* Christchurch: White Ways Publishing Co.

Hopking, A. (1991). *Practical guide to estoric healing.* Christchurch: White Ways Publishing Co.

Hopking, A. (1994). *The emergence of the planetary heart.* Christchurch: Godshaer Publishing Co.

Johnston, B. (1983). *New age healing.* England: Private printing, England.

Kaptchuk, T.J. (1987). *Chinese medicine.* London: Rider & Co.

Kauffman, S. (1995). *At home in the universe: The search for laws of self-organization and complexity.* New York: Oxford University Press.

Krishnamacharya, K.E. (1983). *Spiritual astrology.* India: WTT.

Lansdowne, Z.F. (1987). *The chakras and esoteric healing.* Maine: Samuel Weiser.

Laurency, H.T. (1979). *The philosopher's stone.* Lawrence Publishing Foundation.

Laurency, H.T. (1995). Pamphlet on the Secret of the Sphinx. Lawrence Publishing Foundation.

Leadbeater, C.W. (1925). *Masters and the path.* Chicago: Theosophical Press.

Leadbeater, C.W. (1997). *Monad.* Kessinger Publishing Co..

McMillan, J. Private paper.

Nga-kpa Chögyam (1988). *Journey into vastness: A handbook of Tibetan meditation techniques.* Longmead, Shaftesbury, Dorset: Element Books.

Oken, A. (1990). *Soul-centered astrology.* Bantam Books.

Powell, A.E. (1978). *The causal body and the ego.* London: Theosophical Publ. House.

Robbins, M.D. (1988, 1996). *Tapestry of the Gods, Vol I & II.* New Jersey: Seven Rays Publishing.

Roerich, H. (1971). *Foundations of Buddhism.* New York: Agni Yoga Society.

Steiner, R. (1963). *Path to initiation into the lesser mysteries.* Rudolf Steiner Press.

Steiner, R. (1975). *Spiritual science and medicine.* Rudolf Steiner Press.

Steiner, R. (1985). *Theosophy: An introduction to the supersensible knowledge of the world and the destination of man.* New York: Anthroposophic Press.

Taber's Cyclopedic Medical Dictionary (1977).

Tansley, D. (1972). *Radionics and the subtle anatomy of man.* England: Health Science Press.

Tennyson, A. (1942). *The lotus eaters.*

Thera, N. (1983). *Heart of Buddhist meditation.* London: Rider Books.

Two Disciples (1982). *The rainbow bridge.* California: The Triune Foundation.

Two Students (1985). *Death: The great adventure.* New York: Lucis Publishing Co.

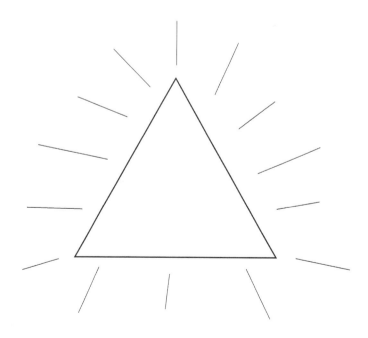

SELECTED READING

Agni Yoga Society
    Agni Yoga (Agni Yoga Series, 1954).
    AUM (1929).
    Brotherhood (1952).
    Fiery World (1976).
    Heart (1934).
    Hierarchy (1977).
    Infinity I & II (1957).
    Leaves off Morya's Garden I & II (1952, 1953).

Assagioli, R. (1975). *Psychosynthesis.* London: Turnstone Books
Assagioli, R. (1973). *The act of will.* New York: Viking Press.
Bailey, A. (1949). *The destiny of the nations.* New York: Lucis Publishing Co.
Bailey, A. (1951). *Initiation, human and solar.* New York: Lucis Publishing Co.
Bailey, A. (1961). *Consciousness of the atom.* New York: Lucis Publishing Co.
Bailey, A. (1976). *The reappearance of the Christ.* New York: Lucis Publishing Co.
Bailey, F. (1979). *The spirit of masonry.* London: Lucis Press Ltd.
Bailey, M. (1990). *A learning experience.* London: Lucis Press Ltd.
Baker, D. (1977). *The seven rays: Keys to the mysteries.* Wellingborough: Aquarian Press
Baker, D. (1974). *The jewel in the lotus.* Essendon, Herts., England: D. Baker "Little Elephant,"

Beesly, R.P. (1969). *The robe of many colours.* England: College of Psycho-therapeutics.

Besant, A. (1908). *The ancient wisdom.* Theosophical Publ. Soc.

Bohm, D. (1981). *The implicate order.* London: RKP.

Brennan, B. (1988). *Hands of light.* Bantam Books.

Burr, H.S. (1972). *The fields of life: Our links with the universe.* New York: Ballantine Books.

Capra, F. (1976). *The Tao of physics.* England: Fontana.

Davidson, J. (1988). *The web of life.* Essex: C.W. Daniel, Essex.

Dethlefsen, T. & Dahlke, R. (1990). *The healing power of illness.* England: Element Books.

Eastcott, M.J. (1984). *Meditation and the rhythm of the year.* Kent: Sundial House.

"The Esoteric Healer," *Journal of the International Network of Esoteric Healing.* England: WhiteWays Publishing Co.

Gerber, R. (1988). *Vibrational medicine.* Santa Fe, NM: Bear and Co.

Gordon, R. (1984). *Your healing hands.* Berkeley, CA: Wingbow Press.

Hall, R. et al. (1980). *Fundamentals of clinical endocrinology.* Pitman Medical.

Hastings, A.C. (ed.) (1981). *Health for the whole person.* New York: Bantam Books.

Jayasuriya, W.F. (1976). *The psychology and philosophy of Buddhism.* Malaysia: BMS.

Jurriaanse, A. (1978). *Bridges.* South Africa: Bridge Trust.

Jurriaanse, A. (1988). *All is relative.* South Africa: Inner Space Publishers.

Karagulla, S. (1967). *Breakthrough to creativity.* De Vorss.

Karagulla, S. (1989). *The chakras and the human energy fields.* Quest Books.

Krishnamacharya, K.E. (1976). *Yoga of Patanjali.* India: WTT.

Laurence, D.R. & Black, J.W. (1978). *The medicine you take.* UK: Fontana.

Laurency, H.T. (1979). *The knowledge of reality.* Sweden: HTL Publ Foundation.

Laurency, H.T. (1979). *The philosopher's stone.* Lawrence Publishing Foundation.

Leadbeater, C.W. (1997). *Monad.* Kessinger Publishing Co.

Le Shan, L. (1984). *You can fight for your life.* Thorsons, Northants.

Medical Group Theosophical Research Centre London (1958). *The mystery of healing.* UK: TPH.

Morrish, F. (1952). *Outline of astro-psychology.* London: Rider & Co.

Pagels, H.R. (1982). *The cosmic code.* Bantam New Age Books.

Parsell, C. (2003). *The best of the best.* Nevada City, CA: Blue Dolphin Publishing.

Powell, A.E. (1979). *The etheric double.* London: Theosophical Publ. House.

Schmidt, G. (1980). *The dynamics of nutrition.* Bio-Dynamic Lit.

Spangler, D. (1977). *Towards a planetary vision.* Findhorn Foundation.

Steiner, R. (1963). *Path to initiation into the lesser mysteries.* Rudolf Steiner Press.

Steiner, R. (1975). *Spiritual science and medicine.* London: Rudolf Steiner Press.

Steiner, R. (1985). *Theosophy: An introduction to the supersensible knowledge of the world and the destination of man.* New York: Anthroposophic Press.

Stone, R. (1985). *Health building.* CRCS Publications.

Tansley, D. (1984). *The raiment of light.* England: RKP.

Thera, N. (1986). *The vision of Dhamma.* London: Rider & Co.

Thera, S. (1981). *The way of mindfulness.* Buddhist Publ. Soc.

Walker, B. (1977). *Encyclopedia of esoteric man.* London: RKP.

INDEX

347

ABOUT
THE AUTHOR

Alan Hopking was born in the cop-
per-mining town of Mufulira, Zambia, on May 12, 1950. At twenty,
while working in Cape Town, he was initiated into Transcendental
Meditation (TM). On his first meditation under his initiator he was told
he had experienced Satchitananda (bliss consciousness). He went to
England and joined the monastery of St. John in Oxford. After three
years he left and attended Shalesbrook Seminary, to train as a priest for
the Christian Community founded by Rudolf Steiner. After two years he
was sent out to test his vocation, first in San Francisco for a year, then to
Coburg in Germany for a year. Here his interest in the teachings of Alice
A Bailey was sparked again. While reading her book *Esoteric Healing,*
he decided he wanted to train in medicine and healing. At twenty-eight,
Alan returned to England and enrolled as a full-time student of the College of Phytotherapy. He graduated in 1981 as a herbal practitioner. In
1982 he founded the WhiteWays Group to study, meditate and practice
group healing. This group continued for fifteen years. In 1984 he trained
as an esoteric healing practitioner under the tutelage of Brenda Johnston,
founder of the International Network of Esoteric Healing. He graduated
in 1985. Soon afterwards he began to teach for INEH. This started and
continues Alan's international teaching career of esoteric healing taking him all over the world. He served on the INEH committee for over
15 years and became vice-president and remains an active consultative
member (as a Fellow); he co-edits the biannual journal, *The Esoteric
Healer.* In 1988 his first book on esoteric healing was published. In 1991,

after three years writing, he published his *Practical Guide to Esoteric Healing.*

He was the first director of the Faculty of Healing in the University of the Seven Rays, co-teaching an advanced degree-level curriculum of esoteric healing in California and in England. In 1994 he published the *Emergence of the Planetary Heart.* In 1998 he founded the Global Academy of Esoteric Healing under which he still teaches today. In 2004 he graduated with a master's degree (MA) in philosophy. Alan is married with two sons. He lives in Christchurch, England. He is still in practice at his busy clinic of herbal medicine in the town center. To contact him go to www.godshaer.co.uk

Made in the USA
Columbia, SC
19 December 2022

74562727R00211